WOMEN WORLD LEADERS PRESENTS

Hope Alive

DEBILITATED TO EXHILARATED WITH GOD

VISIONARY AUTHORS
CONNIE A. VANHORN & KIMBERLY ANN HOBBS

Hope Alive: Debilitated to Exhilarated with God
Copyright ©2024 Women World Leaders

Published by World Publishing and Productions
PO Box 8722, Jupiter, FL 33468
worldpublishingandproductions.com

ISBN: 978-1-957111-26-1

Library of Congress Control Number: 2024905696

Scripture quotations marked ESV® Bible are taken from *(The Holy Bible, English Standard Version®)*, Copyright © 2001 by Crossway, a publishing ministry of Good News Publishers. Used by permission. All rights reserved.

Scripture quotations marked KJV are taken from the King James Version. Public Domain.

Scripture quotations marked MSG are taken from *THE MESSAGE,* copyright © 1993, 2002, 2018 by Eugene H. Peterson. Used by permission of NavPress. All rights reserved. Represented by Tyndale House Publishers, Inc

Scripture quotations marked NASB are taken from the New American Standard Bible®, Copyright ©1960, 1962, 1963, 1968, 1971, 1972, 1973, 1975, 1977, 1995 by the Lockman Foundation. Used by permission.

Scripture quotations marked NIV are taken from THE HOLY BIBLE, NEW INTERNATIONAL VERSION®, NIV® Copyright © 1973, 1978, 1984, 2011 by Biblica, Inc.® Used by permission. All rights reserved worldwide.

Scripture quotations marked NKJV are taken from the New King James Version®. Copyright © 1982 by Thomas Nelson. Used by permission. All rights reserved.

Scripture quotations marked NLT are taken from the *Holy Bible,* New Living Translation, copyright © 1996, 2004, 2015 by Tyndale House Foundation. Used by permission of Tyndale House Publishers, Inc., Carol Stream, Illinois 60188. All rights reserved.

Scripture quotations marked RSV are from the Revised Standard Version of the Bible, copyright © 1946, 1952, and 1971 national Council of the Churches of Christ in the United States of America. Used by permission. All rights reserved.

Scripture quotations marked TPT are from The Passion Translation®. Copyright © 2017, 2018, 2020 by Passion & Fire Ministries, Inc. Used by permission. All rights reserved. ThePassionTranslation.com.

Hope

In the deepest parts of despair,

In the shadows of night,

Hope shines like a star, a guiding light.

It can look different to each and every soul,

But it's what keeps us going, helps us reach our goal.

Hope can be a whisper, a gentle breeze,

Or a raging fire, burning with ease.

It can be found in the darkest of places,

In the midst of sorrow, in the saddest of faces.

We can mend hope that's been shattered, broken, and torn.

We can search for it, even when it's just too worn.

Hope is a gift, a precious treasure,

It's what gives us strength and courage

To endure the length of this race.

Our hope in God is unbreakable, unshakable;

Like a mighty warrior, our faith stands firm,

Guiding us through any storm, making us capable, and keeping us warm.

In the darkest of nights, we find hope in prayer,

Knowing that God's love will always be there.

His presence surrounds us,

His peace fills our soul,

With unwavering hope, we are made whole.

So let us hold on to this hope, this truth so bold,

Where nothing can shake us or keep us in a hold.

For in God's promises, our hearts will hold;

With faith as our anchor, we persevere,

For in Him, our hope is eternal, crystal clear.

And in the end, when all is said and done,

Hope is Alive, shining bright as the sun.

For God is our Hope, our eternal guide;

In His love and light, we will always abide.

Contents

Introduction

What is this hope we speak of? Hope is so much more than wishful thoughts of something you want to happen. Hope is an assurance, a steadfast and most certain anchor in your soul that solidifies the reality that God is your refuge.

In the writing of this book, we have come together as authors to share our stories, depicting that HOPE is very much ALIVE even through the heavy situations we all encounter along life's journey. As you read, you will see how hope became a word of action and a prominent source of strength when we fled to God as our refuge.

> This hope is a strong and trustworthy anchor for our souls. It leads us through the curtain into God's inner sanctuary (Hebrews 6:19 NLT).

Despite all the adversities we face throughout our lives, God is the source of our hope, and He gives us reason to go on. Through reading the pages of this book, you will learn how God brings hope alive to every person who is yearning for a reason to go on.

> "For there is hope for a tree, If it is cut down, that it will sprout again, and that its tender shoots will not cease" (Job 14:7 NKJV).

If there is hope through the Word of God for a tree, can you understand how much more precious you are to God than a tree? You are God's masterpiece creation (Ephesians 2:10), and He has a plan for your life; it is not over. God will lead you to His perfect place and bring prosperity to your life. You, too, can keep hope alive no matter what the circumstances in front of you may look like.

As you read, may you offer a confession of hope to God, the faithful One. His Word instructs us by saying, *Let us hold fast the confession of our hope without wavering, for He who promised is faithful* (Hebrews 10:23 NKJV).

God will not let you go. Through relating to stories in the chapters of *Hope Alive,* we trust you will find that God wants to take hold of your heart and guide you from a state of being down, discouraged, or even debilitated and elevate you to a place of exhilaration with Him. All the writers in this book have prayed for you. We have prayed specifically over the stories you are living out right now, understanding you may need a glimmer of hope to cling to. We all experience varying degrees of hardships, which can shake us to our core and diminish our hope. We have all been there, BUT GOD! With transparency, each writer speaks of the powerful confidence that grew as she placed her hope in God and His promises. Our certainty comes from scriptures that testify how hope can come alive when it's renewed in God, even through the grimmest times imaginable. God is the One who gives us reason to persevere.

> *As for me, I will always have hope; I will praise you more and more. My mouth will tell of your righteous deeds, of your saving acts all day long—though I know not how to relate them all. I will come and proclaim your mighty acts, Sovereign Lord; I will proclaim your righteous deeds, yours alone* (Psalm 71:14-16 NIV).

We believe there is hope for all of us. Through testimonies of suffering and confusion, we share the reality of God's mighty works and His glorious light that permeated our dark situations. We are excited for hope to come alive in you or someone you love whom God is calling you to share this book with!

God spoke of the broken tree that sprouts branches and brings hope. You or someone close to you may feel broken or even buried in a dark place of no return, but when you view that dark situation from God's perspective and trust in Him, you may begin to realize it is a place full of promise and growth. Like a broken tree in a dark place is primed for new growth, God can use the rich soil of your dark place to prepare new life to sprout in you. You have just been planted!

As you trust in God, you become a sprout of hope.

As you learn and grow with Him through tough situations in your life, you will press through the dirt!

As you cling to Him and His promises, you will emerge through the darkness covering you, seeing the Sonshine of light beckoning as you burst from the same soil that once gripped you.

Get excited because as you are watered with stories and given food from scripture throughout *Hope Alive,* you will be strengthened and equipped to survive. We are confident God will speak to your heart and sprout it with hope that will keep you alive in Him.

Connie A. VanHorn

Connie A. VanHorn has a heart for encouraging others to find their God-given purpose. She serves on the Women World Leaders' Leadership Team as an ambassador, is a best-selling author, and writes for *Voice of Truth* magazine. Hoping her story will help someone else, Connie passionately shares how her amazing and loving God spared her, an ordinary woman, and gave her new life.

Connie resides in Winston-Salem, North Carolina, where she has participated in several discipleship classes and taught Sunday school to international students. She has also attended Bible classes at Vintage Bible College.

Being a mother is by far Connie's greatest accomplishment and her first, best ministry. She dreams of changing the world by sharing Jesus and raising world-changers who have a kingdom perspective.

She enjoys being active in her community, making bracelets, journaling, and spending most of her time with her family. Connie wants her readers to know that it's ok to be broken—it's in our broken place that we find God. See past messy, see past broken, and you might just see a miracle.

Just One More Breath

By Connie A. VanHorn

> *The fact that our heart yearns for something Earth can't supply is proof that Heaven must be our home.* - C.S. Lewis

Hope is the desire for something good in the future. Our hope has two sides: In the here and now, we hope for blessings for our earthly life, but our greater hope is a built-in longing for eternity. What significance does this life hold without the hope of what comes next? Life is fragile, and any moment could be our final breath. But what if, by some grace, we were granted one more breath after this life were through? Where would we place our hope then?

Hope. It's such a simple word with immense meaning for those facing hard things. Hope can be a light that guides us through dark times, as it has been for me. Hope can be the strength that keeps us going when all seems lost. I've learned that despite what occurs in my life, my greatest hope is in heaven because the things of this world, including life, are never guaranteed.

Regardless of what you hope for daily, there will come a time when you will take your final breath. I'd like you to consider where your hope will lie in that moment.

Throughout my life, I have always held onto hope. Like others, I have found myself hoping for and daydreaming about various things. Daydreaming with my eyes open when I was a little girl, holding onto the hope of something new, rescued me in many ways. But what exactly is this elusive concept of hope we all hold on to? The best hope is greater than a yearning for a physical object; it is a yearning for an eternal destination. The object of the hope we chase will determine where we will take that next breath after we leave our earthly bodies. My hope is to one day touch heaven.

My childhood was clouded with trauma that lingered into my teenage and adult years. Each of us handles trauma in our own way; I buried it deep down and pretended it wasn't there, that it didn't exist. I also pretended that the hurt part of me didn't exist. We all know that kind of coping mechanism doesn't really work and will eventually find its way back out. But even as I buried those hurt places, I clung to hope.

In my early life, I craved love and acceptance more than anything else. I constantly shaped myself to fit what I believed the world expected of me. I tried to fit; I hid myself so well, thinking I was protecting myself from being hurt—again! I was probably headed straight into self-destruction.

As a teenager, I moved to Los Angeles, California, chasing all the wrong things. Then, one day, my life shifted. It shifted in a way that made me feel the ground move underneath me. At 19, I found myself pregnant. I was alone and scared. Little did I know the beauty that would come from ashes. The mess I was making of my life was about to turn into something beautiful.

I was pregnant with a little girl who would need me to step into the role of a mother. I had no idea how to navigate adulthood, let alone motherhood, but my daughter and I had no choice but to figure it out together. For the first time, someone loved me unconditionally. With her, I didn't have to pretend. Despite the hard things we faced together, she loved me. She loved me even underneath my messiness. However, this newfound love I yearned for created an unhealthy, strong emotional attachment to my child. I was afraid to let her experience pain or learn resilience, constantly sheltering her from every hurt and placing the band-aid on every inner and outer wound.

When my daughter was in middle school, I gave my whole heart to Jesus. This was a miracle, and it was life-changing. I was finally becoming the woman that God had intended me to be. I was also learning to trust Him. I started entrusting various aspects of my life to God, even though I was still struggling with trust in other areas. But releasing the trauma-induced attachment with my daughter wasn't part of the arrangement. I believed I had to be her shield. This new work that God was doing in me and through me had boundaries within my own inner walls that I had set for myself. That's not the way it's supposed to be.

When God comes into your life, He transforms you into a new creation. The past no longer burdens you, and the future holds new possibilities. You no longer need to carry the weight of your past hurts, as God lovingly offers to bear your pain and heal your heart. He invited me to tear down the walls I had built and experience true freedom and hope in His presence.

> *Therefore, if anyone is in Christ, the new creation has come: The old has gone, the new is here!* (2 Corinthians 5:17 NIV).

As my daughter, Annalise, entered her late teens and early adulthood, she began to pull away while I held on tightly out of fear and worry for her well-being. Despite God's reassurance that He had her in His care, I was reluctant to relinquish control. My reluctance to let go hindered her ability to find her own path and spread her wings. God and I engaged in a tug of war until He finally intervened to reveal something significant to both of us.

See, I am doing a new thing! Now it springs up; do you not perceive it? I am making a way in the wilderness and streams in the wasteland (Isaiah 43:19 NIV).

On the morning of January 2nd, 2023, a sheriff showed up at my front door. That is a knock you hope and pray you never receive. He informed me my daughter had been in a car accident; she had been ejected from the vehicle. At that moment, I felt numb and scared to death. I had my four younger children home with me, and I tried to stay calm in front of them. It takes a lot to rattle me, but this hit my core like a bullet. As I drove to the hospital, all I could do was cry and pray. I begged God not to take her. I begged Him to give her more time. I was imagining her lying in the hospital bed in the most unimaginable condition. I was scared to see her that way.

On that particular morning, while Annalise was driving to work in foggy conditions, my daughter found herself in a horrible car accident that tested her resilience and my faith. As her car swerved onto the shoulder and spun out of control, the unimaginable happened: her vehicle flipped four times, and on the final rotation, Annalise was ejected from the passenger window, going through glass, landing on the unforgiving cement of a major highway.

Despite sustaining numerous injuries and fractures, including multiple open wounds and a traumatic brain injury, Annalise emerged from the wreckage as a living testament to the power of God's intervention. An unexpected guardian angel in the form of a homeless man stood by her side, offering prayers and comfort until help arrived. The officer on the scene shared that he knew this man very well and that he was likely praying for her. The homeless man told the officer what he had witnessed that morning. His words echoed a profound truth: "It was like someone lifted her from the vehicle and placed her on the ground." Annalise received immediate medical attention from an off-duty EMS worker who happened to be passing by. By all accounts, she shouldn't have made it out of this.

When I arrived at the hospital, a lady greeted me in the emergency department and walked me back to the ICU Emergency unit. Another officer was waiting outside of her room. The first thing this gentleman said to me was, "Your daughter is very lucky to be alive." I stood there frozen. I still didn't know what to expect or what condition she was in. The officer proceeded to ask me a few questions, and then he pulled the curtain to her room.

I found myself in a state of confusion as I gazed at my child lying in the hospital bed, seemingly unscathed, despite the report of her body crashing through a glass window. How could this be possible? She barely had a mark on the front side of her body. She was awake and speaking to the nurses. Her hair was matted with blood, her shirt stained, and a blanket was draped over her lower body. Without hesitation, I rushed to her side, wrapping her in a tight embrace. As she cried, a surge of that BUILT-IN COURAGE, accumulated over a lifetime, coursed through my veins. In that moment, I felt an overwhelming strength as I held her close, assuring her that everything would be all right.

I sensed God's presence in the room. It was clear He had a significant lesson for us to learn through her car accident. We both became aware of His greater purpose He had used Annalise's accident to reveal. Against all odds, she defied the grim predictions and proved to everyone, especially me, that miracles are still possible.

We witnessed so many miracles that day: There was bleeding and swelling on her brain, but no surgery was needed. Her untouched face and arms left witnesses in awe of the miraculous protection she had received. Angels showed up to clean her blood-stained skin. And the nurses loved on us both. But the biggest miracle was the soft whisper I heard from God that said, "Keep going!"

God's hand was unmistakable in the wake of all this. Through this experience, a sense of purpose began to emerge. This was a miracle God intended to use. As Annalise navigated the days and months after the accident, this beautiful message of faith and perseverance shined so brightly. *Keep going!* The butterfly bracelet she wore that day, untouched by the accident, symbolized the protection and grace that surrounded her. HOPE!

As the days passed and Annalise returned to work, she felt stronger than ever, and it became clear that this experience was not just a trial but a testimony. The journey of recovery was a testament to the power of FAITH and the enduring HOPE that sustains us in the hardest of moments.

> *"For I know the plans I have for you," declares the Lord, "plans to prosper you and not to harm you, plans to give you hope and a future"* (Jeremiah 29:11 NIV).

Despite what we go through, we can always hold onto the truth that God is still good. He is designing a greater purpose through all the trials we face. Though His ways may sometimes be beyond our comprehension, we can place our trust in Him. I knew, without a doubt, that He would use the accident to work through my daughter for His kingdom's purposes, ensuring her protection throughout her life. I finally understood that He would always protect her!

During times of shifting and transformation, things may appear scary and uncertain before revealing their true color. But sometimes, when God is shifting and moving things, it can get messy before it gets beautiful. We can rest assured that our situation is not messy to God or because of God...He's perfect! What we see as messy is often a miracle in the process. We don't have to walk this life in fear. God will lift us and carry us through the accidents of life—just like He did for Annalise. What seems messy to us can actually be a miraculous process unfolding. God, in His perfection, continues to work miraculously in both my life and Annalise's. We don't have to navigate this journey in fear, for God will uplift and carry us through life's unexpected events, just as He did for Annalise in the accident.

Sometimes, God guides us all the way home to Him, while other times, He provides just enough protection to see us through. Annalise's experience—from being thrown into the passenger seat and through shattered glass to awakening in the ambulance—underscores God's hand of protection. The last thing she remembered about that day was losing control of her vehicle and being tossed into the passenger seat in a fetal position. That's it. She felt no pain at that moment. God protected her in that moment, which could have been her last on this earth. Whether that moment would have been her last breath or the gift of her first breath in heaven, both are miracles. But I'm grateful that He gave us more time with her.

Life is a gift.

Heaven is a greater gift.

I want to be ready for both.

You, too, can be ready for both.

True strength and perseverance and a little built-in courage are beautiful. It's those hard things in life—the arrows that really hurt—that build something in us, strengthen something in us, and prepare something for us—making us strong enough to endure all things. This accident dropped a little of that built-in courage in Annalise. It's the kind of courage she will use later in life when a storm hits. God prepares us for the hard things in this life and sends help when we need it most.

> Have I not commanded you? Be strong and courageous. Do not be afraid; do not be discouraged, for the Lord your God will be with you wherever you go (Joshua 1:9 NIV).

Through the experience of her accident, I was freed from the strong, unhealthy emotional bond I had with Annalise. Although we remain close and share a beautiful connection, we now have a healthy bond. I understand she belongs to God first, and I trust in His protection. It is truly remarkable how peaceful and calm I feel entrusting her to Him. She is now free to spread her wings and fly. We are all a beautiful work in progress, and we can take what we learn from the trials and hard things and apply them where it counts. Now, I am also able to use this experience to help me better parent my four younger children and be ready for whatever comes our way. I am thankful for the ongoing work God is doing within me, as I want to be ready for my next breath, whether it be here on earth or my first breath in eternity.

Annalise has made a miraculous full recovery. Through her accident, she went from debilitated to exhilarated; it's been one of the greatest blessings of my life to watch her progress and become the woman that God created her to be. Her scars tell of a greater story unfolding. There is no timer on how fast or slow we progress. God looks at the heart of a person; it's the heart of a person that matters most to Him. Annalise learned the most powerful lesson from her accident: God has gifted her with power and strength. She needed to go through the accident to see herself through His eyes, to see her true strength.

Annalise's story serves as a reminder that every breath we take is a precious gift, a reminder of God's love and protection. Through the pain, the promise of a greater purpose guiding our steps becomes evident. God is making all things new. *Just breathe and trust God!*

> He who was seated on the throne said, "I am making everything new!" Then he said, "Write this down, for these words are trustworthy and true" (Revelation 21:5 NIV).

I hope our story inspires you to embrace life with courage and faith, knowing that God's plan is beyond our understanding but always filled with grace and purpose. Even though we go through hard things in this life, we find strength in knowing that God is with us, guiding us every step of the way. God will protect us always and in every situation, no matter the outcome. Annalise's scars are a constant reminder of the day that God released us both from the need for control that was holding us with a tight grip. We are both free!

The greatest lesson I pray you will take from this is that God is our protector; we have Hope Alive in Him. The hope we have in Him is more than enough to get us through this life and on into the next. Belief in the promise of heaven offers a different perspective on hope. While we may hope for blessings in this earthly life, the hope of heaven adds a deeper space to our existence. Without the hope of something greater beyond this world, there would be no light.

Each day is uncertain, and we never know when our time on this earth may come to an end. If you were granted just one more breath, where would you place your hope? Our hope for eternity with God in heaven can only be fulfilled by giving our lives to Jesus Christ and trusting Him with all we do. Don't wait for your last breath on earth to give it all to Him. Whenever you make that choice, your *next breath* will be your *first breath* of a spectacular eternity with God by and on your side.

We are given the gift of each new breath. It is up to us to choose what we do with it. No matter how long it takes you to reach the end of your progress, by choosing Jesus, you are choosing to make heaven your true and forever home.

Keep going!

> *But our citizenship is in heaven. And we eagerly await a Savior from there, the Lord Jesus Christ, who, by the power that enables him to bring everything under his control, will transform our lowly bodies so that they will be like his glorious body* (Philippians 3:20-21 NIV).

Hope in Heaven

By Connie A. VanHorn

May the God of hope fill you with all joy and peace as you trust in him, so that you may overflow with hope by the power of the Holy Spirit (Romans 15:13 NIV).

It is natural to seek hope and comfort in the things of this world. We seek hope in people, things, money—almost everything. And when we find what we think works, we may begin to rely on our good health, good relationships, money, and power—hoping those things will ultimately bring us a better life.

But hope found in things of this world can never fully satisfy us. One reason is that the world will always lack promise and certainty. The only hope we can trust does not come from this earth. Our only true hope is in God. And our ultimate hope is to spend eternity by His side in heaven.

My personal journey of seeking the hope of heaven has been marked by the presence of butterflies. I enjoy sharing this part of my journey. I like to call it "Chasing Butterflies into Heaven." When God first revealed Himself to me, He was so clever that He used butterflies to get my attention. Now, each time I see a butterfly, I am reminded of God's love for me. These delicate creatures have become a symbol of God's promise of transformation and renewal in my life. Through the beauty and grace of butterflies, I am reminded of God's constant presence and the hope of all that will come in my life on earth and in heaven.

Just like the transformation of a caterpillar into a butterfly, we, too, are being transformed by God. As I chase my butterflies, He reminds me to keep my eyes fixed on heaven, where true hope and joy are found. God wants us to hold on to the hope of heaven. The best promise ever is that in heaven, those whom God calls His children will walk eternally with Him. But we don't have to wait for heaven to experience His presence. If you have given your life to Jesus Christ, you can trust that God will guide you daily through this life; He is with you in every challenging and joyful thing you face as you make your way toward heaven.

Heaven is described in the Bible as a place of eternal joy, peace, and perfect community with God. Revelation 21:4 paints a beautiful picture of heaven, stating, *He will wipe away every tear from their eyes, and death shall be no more, neither shall there be mourning, nor crying, nor pain anymore, for the former things have passed away* (ESV).

As we run our race, let us hold fast to the hope and assurance that heaven is our true eternal home. This world is temporary, but the promises of God regarding our eternal home and final destination are sure and constant.

As you walk with God on this earth, He will give you signs and wonders that He has created to remind you that you are in His presence. Keep your eyes open. Look for the wonder He provides. Maybe for you, like me, butterflies will be a reminder that God is with you, guiding you through life's ups and downs. Perhaps those beautiful, intricate creations will present a picture of how you will emerge from your struggles stronger than before, knowing that your true home and HOPE is in heaven. In whatever way God speaks to you, being aware that He is working all around you, presenting Himself and His glory to you in this world, can help you keep going through the ups and downs, the joys and trials. Always keep the hope of heaven before you—it will never disappoint you!

> *So we fix our eyes not on what is seen, but on what is unseen, since what is seen is temporary, but what is unseen is eternal* (2 Corinthians 4:18 NIV).

Kimberly Ann Hobbs

As the Founder and co-CEO of Women World Leaders, a worldwide ministry empowering women to find their God-given purpose, Kimberly Ann Hobbs oversees all elements of the ministry, including *Voice of Truth* magazine. Kimberly is also the co-CEO of World Publishing and Productions and an international best-selling author, speaker, motivational leader, and life coach.

As part of *Women World Leaders' Podcast,* Kimberly interviews beautiful women from around the world. She also shares daily devotions on the WWL Facebook group and website, womenworldleaders.com.

Kimberly has been a guest speaker on Moody Bible Radio Stations and made appearances on Daystar Television, sharing her passion for bringing women to a closer walk with Jesus through encouragement. She is an artist, with much of her work reaching worldwide, and sits on Kerus Global Education advisory board, helping raise support for South Africa's orphaned children.

Kimberly supports her husband, Ken, in his ministry: United Men of Honor — unitedmenofhonor.com. Together, they serve in missions and ministry and run their own financial coaching business. They have children and grandchildren whom they love very much.

Life in Living Water

By Kimberly Ann Hobbs

> *Show me your ways, LORD, teach me your paths. Guide me in your truth and teach me, for you are God my Savior, and my hope is in you all day long* (Psalm 25:4-5 NIV).

What can a story teach us about hope? Stories with biblical perspectives placed side by side allow us to glean examples of hope and, consequently, faith. I pray that what I am about to share with you, asserted by God, will show how someone can find their hope in Him alone. Hope is God, our security and strength.

My story happened during the drafting of this book. The very content I was pouring into other authors about sharing hope came alive in my life. I waited on God and His perfect timing to illuminate what my chapter in *Hope Alive* would be, and wow, it came to me full force halfway through the journey of preparing this book.

Cutting right to the chase—there I was, in the throes of ministry. Women World Leaders was operating and growing superbly with God. My husband Kenny and I were living in our beautiful South Florida home, happy and content. Our business was going great, and we loved our friends and family in Florida around us. I was pouring into and empowering others when God brought about a change in my life—A BIG CHANGE for me and my husband.

We had been thinking about making a major move to Ohio for two years. My husband and I both had family there who needed us. When we visited, we would look at homes and wonder if we could ever leave Florida. We had specific requirements to make such a change and felt everything would have to line up perfectly to make it a reality. We had a gorgeous home we loved in South Florida, so for us to go through such a significant move, the new place would need to be extraordinary.

We prayed each time we traveled to Ohio, but no doors opened. Every place we looked at had something "off" about it; we only saw dead ends. It was just not God's timing. Two years passed. Then, a glimmer of hope came on a night I will never forget. We were in Ohio visiting family and staying at my mom and papa's house. The night before returning to Florida, I was in bed working on my computer while everyone was asleep. Feeling sad about leaving in the morning, I finished my work and rested my head on the pillow to pray. I asked God if we would ever find that perfect home up North, knowing that locating what we wanted was a one-in-a-million shot. One in ten million!

> *Delight thyself also in the LORD; and he shall give thee the desires of thine heart* (Psalm 37:4 KJV).

After my conversation with God, I felt nudged to sit up again. I opened my computer, typed in house specifications, and BAM! Within moments, it appeared in front of my eyes. A log cabin nestled in acreage with water in proximity (my ultimate prayer.) I always wanted a creek or some kind of moving water around me. I was excited, but then I saw the price. I gasped. It met my whole checklist, but I knew it was far more than my husband would spend. I closed my computer and tucked the cabin in my prayer heart.

In the morning, we said our tearful goodbyes to Mama and Papa. Pulling away with our car loaded, I wondered if that would be the last time I waved goodbye to them. Filled with emotion, we left to return to Florida. Approaching the highway 40 minutes into our drive, we saw a fatal accident. Cars collided, and smoke and tires went flying. At 70 mph, we could not stop, so we prayed. God reminded me how short life is, and, in that moment, I spoke up.

"Babe, that accident was so close, it could have been us! I saw life flash before our eyes!" We both agreed. But God!

I proceeded to tell him about how I was giving up hope of finding the rare gem of a house I wanted, one that would prompt me to leave Florida. Then, I described the log cabin home I had seen. Ken knew how rare cabins were and how long we had searched. I told him this one looked perfect—like a dream come true, but I had been afraid to tell him. He knew why, and of course, the first thing he asked was, "How much is it?"

I knew that dreaded question was coming. I shrunk in my seat and whispered the price.

"What? No way, Babe. Are you kidding me? That is beyond the range we talked about," he said.

I sat silently praying, *God, this would have to be You if there is any hope.* I waited.

My husband's next sentence was, "Where is it?"

I quickly answered, "We are driving right toward it!"

He said, "Go ahead, check the GPS."

I screamed. It was only five minutes away.

We detoured off the highway down a curvy hill, past beautiful, lush scenery, and over a one-lane bridge. I was gleaming! Immediately over the sweet bridge was the driveway! Are you kidding me? In awe, we gazed at it. It was everything I had prayed for, down to the last detail: the most beautiful cabin, nestled in pine trees, with no neighbors. It was on a hilly piece of property with a river running right through it, encircling the home like a horseshoe! The most God artistic view I could ever imagine, His splendid creation.

Miracle after miracle happened like popcorn as we pulled into the driveway and over the next few days. In fact, we drove all the way to North Carolina, turned around, and then drove back because we could not stop thinking about it! We decided to place an offer, understanding only God could make EVERYTHING work perfectly, enabling us to get it. And He did.

The homeowners would have to:

- Accept a lower offer. *Check.*

- Include furniture we wanted, inside and out. *Check.*

- Accept a 3-month contingency so we could sell our Florida house. *Check.*

- Take the house off the market in the waiting. *Check.*

There were more and more and more stipulations. God provided checks to each one. After all the negotiations were accepted, we were on our way to a major move out of Florida.

But we knew God would still have to move mightily on the Florida end. We needed to:

- List our home quickly. *Check.*

- Secure a lender (being self-employed has challenges). *Check.*

- Watch for everything to coordinate in perfect timing for the sale of our Florida house. That took longer, but through it all, we continued to hope.

First came our prayer of faith. "God, please, if this be Your will, can You quickly bring a buyer to our home? God, we know our Florida home is anointed. It is where both of our ministries were born. Souls have been saved here. We have had so many God moments here that are precious to us and You. Is it too much to ask You to please bring a godly couple to this home who love You as much as we love You? It is going to be super difficult to release this home to just anyone. Your presence dwells on every part of this property. Please make this process quick and painless so we will not have to show it over and over or have countless people trample through. We just do not have time. Know that if it does not sell, we are good either way. We trust You. We ask this all in Jesus' name and with a covering. Amen."

Then, we immediately began the work. Our beautiful Christian friends listed our home. We all prayed over it as they released a "coming soon ad." Before the listing was finalized, a realtor called and said their client wanted to see our home over Zoom. By that night, they were preparing an offer. The clients lived out of town but soon arrived at our front door without their realtor. They explained that via Zoom, they had seen pictures with scripture on our walls. Knowing we were believers, they wanted to talk openly with us. They were a lovely couple our age with the same number of children we had, two girls and a boy. They loved Jesus. We talked, we cried, we prayed, and they bought our house that night. It was all God. We arranged for quick closings on both houses to occur just weeks later.

We could hardly believe it! Everything on our prayer list happened exactly how we prayed. God was for us and opened every door—wide open.

We began packing our home. Oddly, the closing for the Ohio house stalled for no legitimate reason despite every requirement being met. The Florida house, however, closed as planned. We were now without a home, though the couple who purchased our home in Florida gave us a grace period to remain, but our moving day was fast approaching.

While all this was happening, a numbness and tingling sensation stemming from a lump on my left back midsection near my spine began to intensify. Months prior, my Christian doctor friend had looked at the lump, which at the time did not hurt, and was adamant that I get it checked out. I was always too busy. Because of her urgency and my unusual sensations, I had Dr. Virginia schedule an MRI. Unfortunately, the only time available was the day my husband was to leave for a Band of Brothers boot camp ministry, so I would need to go on my own. I was not worried.

The morning after the MRI, I received a call while I was packing boxes. The radiologist did not like what he saw and wanted more views. My heart dropped. I was not expecting that. Frightened, I called my husband in tears. Trying to remain calm, the enemy was already putting lies in my brain. I spoke calmly to Ken, and I hid my fear. I knew he would want to come home, and I was right. But he was on an important mission from God, so I told him to stay put. After praying with Kenny, I scheduled the second MRI.

I walked back into the radiology department wearing a positive smile and bringing good news: Women World Leaders LOVE CARDS to pass out in the waiting room. I also brought a couple of Voice of Truth magazines; they were a hit. I figured God would use me as a shining light in a dark time, and He did. I made friends with the woman behind the desk and people in the waiting room—all while trying to maintain my own composure. Even though I went through the MRI feeling quite debilitated, I trusted God, praying, "God help me get through this, please." The same, kind man who had done my first MRI was there to do my second one. I shared my hope of Jesus with him. When he took me out of the machine, he told me he would try to rush the readings to the radiologist so I would not have to wait.

I went home, alone again.

The time on my knees between packing boxes intensified. I blared worship music, put my Bible app on in every room, and packed our house to move. I had questions for God, though! "Why God? I will accept whatever You say, but please help me understand this. Am I going to die? Is this a malignant growth they're so concerned about? You showed Kenny and me our dream home and allowed us to move forward with it. It is now being held up, not closing. Is this part of Your plan to get us to sell our house? Why is this happening, God? Are you taking me home to be with You? Is this why it is playing out this way with our new house not closing?"

Well, at least Kenny will have money to move on, I thought.

The next day was the worst day of my life. I received another call; it was not what I wanted to hear. "Mrs. Hobbs, we need you to come in for a third MRI." I knew this was not good. With my husband still at boot camp, I was crumbling! I was feeling alone, so I called in the troops. This was a matter of urgent prayer. My warring army of women came immediately to my rescue!

The weekend was approaching, so the third MRI was scheduled for Monday. Those three days were like an eternity—but God moved! I packed boxes while praying louder and stronger than ever. I blared my worship music and buried myself in scripture promises as I read my Bible. My Bible app played wherever I was in the house. I packed every special and precious piece I owned into boxes, not knowing if I would ever see them again. Trusting God, I wanted His will to be done. I tried hard to remain strong, asking God to please help me leave this earth as an example of faith. No matter what, I wanted others to know my hope was in eternity with God—even if I were about to die.

The following morning, I went to the market for juice because I had hardly eaten and had no appetite. The ladies of Women World Leaders had called a prayer Zoom to pray over me, so I drove quickly so I could return home and get online. Pulling into the garage, I turned off the car and held the wheel. Before going inside, I went to God with serious warfare prayers. I was thinking about doom and gloom and preparing myself to die. I believed thoughts the enemy had put in my mind that the lump was cancerous and now had spread because I had waited so long. I was convinced I only had weeks to live. I believed the lie. I started asking God to help me be strong through the end of my life. I wanted to be brave for Kenny and my whole family. I also wanted to be an example of strength to the women I was leading. I also prayed that the people who were moving into our house would love it and continue to work for the Lord in it. I prayed Kenny would be wise with the money, go into full-time ministry, and be happy and without stress, serving God for the rest of his life.

I sat in my car in the garage, hands gripping the wheel while crying my thoughts to God. Suddenly, my prayers shifted! In a flash, God shot scripture promises to my heart.

Did God tell me my time on earth was done? NO! Did He tell me why the radiologist needed the third MRI? No! God only told me to TRUST!

Did God tell me why we would not close on the Ohio home yet? No! He said TRUST! Did God say we were moving? Yes! Did He work everything work out perfectly, exactly how He led us? Yes!

Then why was I so convinced I was dying? God did not tell me I was dying. I told me I was dying!

I GOT MAD! Burning with anger at the devil, I shouted at him. I screamed at the top of my lungs, banging on the wheel, "GET BEHIND ME SATAN!!!!! No more!"

> Then they cried to the Lord in their trouble, and he delivered them out of their distresses. And he led them forth by the right way, that they might go to a city of habitation (Psalm 107:6-7 KJV).

"I have heard your prayers; I have seen your tears. I will heal you, and three days from now you will get out of bed and go to the Temple of the Lord" (2 Kings 20:5 NLT).

Heal me, O LORD, and I shall be healed; save me, and I shall be saved, for thou art my praise (Jeremiah 17:14 KJV).

God's scriptures, how I needed His promises! And He delivered! I got so angry at the enemy for taking over my mind. "No more," I said. "God did not tell me He was finished with me here; Satan did, and he tried to stop me again. But it's not happening!" God allowed me to get a grip through His truth and power in His Word.

My child, pay attention to what I say. Listen carefully to my words. Don't lose sight of them. Let them penetrate deep into your heart, for they bring life to those who find them, and healing to their whole body (Proverbs 4: 20-22 NLT).

My hope was coming! Scripture upon scripture came to my mind as I prayed. God did not tell me I was dying. The enemy did. He wanted to stop all God had coming to me. God was preparing the desires of my heart; I only had to walk in obedience and trust Him for them! My hope came from His scriptures! I cried my eyes out to God, releasing my control to Him to silence the enemy. I told Satan I bound him in the name of Jesus, and he must stop attacking me with lies! I knew I had more to give God, and my work on earth was not finished yet. I said, "God, I will praise You and serve You until YOU say it is finished." Finishing with the greatest intensity I had ever prayed with in my life, I walked into the house and got on Zoom. My prayer warring angels prayed over me with faith. It was power-filled.

I finished the day weeping, praying, and praising but exhausted. I had so many calls, texts, and prayers I could barely read them all. I felt loved. Kenny was coming home the next day, and I could not wait, so I went to bed early, unable to pack or pray anymore. I dozed off quickly.

At 1:00 AM, our house alarm went off. Someone was in our home downstairs. I crept down the stairs thinking, *Will I get shot by robbers?* And as soon as I turned the corner, there was Kenny to surprise me, smiling. Surprise me, he did! I was NOT amused. I threw my hands up in the air and went back up to bed. I was at my limit!

Then God.

Kenny felt terrible and came into bed, falling right asleep, leaving me tossing and turning with my heart racing! My husband falling asleep so quickly only intensified my frustration. I prayed, "Please God, I can't take much more. Please help my brain shut off to fall asleep."

I zoned out when God moved! Miraculously, He moved!

I was awakened to a sudden RUSH of water pushing through my insides from my shoulders down to my back and out my pelvic area, a force I will never forget. Like the pressure of Niagara Falls coming from my shoulders out my midsection, it pushed out the weight I carried and whatever was attached to me. I felt as light as a feather in an instant. I sat up straight in bed, asking God, "What was that, God? What just happened to me?" I began to cry because deep inside, I knew. "Did You just heal me, God? Was that the miracle I prayed for?" I shook Kenny. He would not budge; he was exhausted and out cold. I looked beyond him at the clock to document the time. At 2:26 AM on November 12, my hope came alive.

As my body experienced the woosh of cool water, I leaped out of bed in shock, knowing 100% it was God, and I walked to the bathroom. I heard God saying, not once, but twice, "Your faith has made you well."

Standing in the bathroom, gripping my face and looking at the painted cross on our wall, I cried, "God??? You really healed me?" Tears rolled! "You did a miracle, God; You took whatever was in me out with a sweep of gushing water." I felt as light as a feather. The sensations on my back were completely gone.

I opened my phone to an unread text. It was God confirming His words. I read:

> Then Jesus said to her, "Daughter because you dared to believe, your faith has healed you. Go with peace in your heart and be free from your suffering!" (Mark 5:34 TPT).

I read it twice, then three times, crying, "God, You did this for me?" HE DID DO IT! My hope was so ALIVE. I would go to that third MRI on Monday, knowing they would not find anything. God healed me with that gush of water pushing through me like a waterfall. His living water of life propelled me forward.

I went to the third MRI, this time with my husband. While I was inside the tube, my husband was in the waiting room and received a call from the title agency in Ohio. The paperwork was approved and would be ready for us to sign the next morning. I was in the MRI, trusting God. I knew He healed me. I lay there in peace with a smile as the test finished. I came out, got dressed, and Ken told me the news. "We are flying to Cleveland tomorrow morning to sign papers on our new house! It all went through, and it will be ours tomorrow."

I could barely catch my breath. God, it is happening, I thought, *Just like YOU said. From the moment I saw that log cabin and trusted YOU, you were moving!*

We left and prepared to fly the next morning, not even giving a second thought to the still-unknown results of the third MRI.

That night, Ken made arrangements for us to travel. It was another miracle that we could book a flight on such short notice. Eleven hours later, we were on a plane to Ohio to sign papers for our new home. As we pulled into the parking lot of the title agency at 11 AM, my phone rang; it was Doctor Virginia! I did not want to answer. Ken said, "Babe, answer it!" I quickly blurted out that we were so late already and the house would not close unless we got in there before noon. Louder, he said, "ANSWER IT."

And with that, I took a deep breath and answered the call.

"Kimberly, good news! The report came back, and the radiologist said it is a cyst! A CYST! It is not attached to any of your organs, nor is it attached to your spine, and there does not appear to be any abnormalities to it."

My heart burst with relief. I got off the phone quickly, and we ran inside with minutes to spare. It was critical the papers be signed before noon. The seller was leaving the country that same day, and the house possession would have been delayed another month if we had not made it. Another miracle. God went before us! A Christ follower was the title agent. She noticed as we burst through the door. She was in tears as she listened and assured us this was going to happen today, no matter what! She gathered the papers and ran them to her assistant, who ran them on foot across the street to the courthouse! We closed that day!

We drove immediately to our new home. We praised God on the premises and prayed over our new home. We cried.

We called our home by name that day, the name God gave us while walking through the fire:

LIVING WATERS COVE

The Bible clearly tells us that on ridiculously hard days, there is hope for us.

Yes, there is! God is strong! He is stronger than any lies of the enemy. He is stronger than our spiritual foes, stronger than any battles we face, and stronger than our control. The love and grace of God will get us through any forces that revolt against us or try to stop us from doing the good things He has prepared for us.

TRUST IN GOD! TRUST IN GOD! TRUST IN GOD!

> *Whoever believes in me, as Scripture has said, rivers of living water will flow from within them* (John 7:38 NIV).

Living water never runs dry. Living water continues to wash our lives with a newness of hope. This water comes directly from God—the Savior of the world. He is the only Living Water that rescues doubts and disbeliefs, turning them into gushing glories that can only come from Him! TEARS OF JOY! TEARS OF JOY! TEARS OF JOY!

Hope in the Holy Spirit

By Kimberly Ann Hobbs

Is your hope vibrant and alive, or are you barely hanging on to it as it nears the place of extinction? There is good news ahead. God loves His children so much that He provides us with a permanent help and hope for our future. The Holy Spirit is the fulfillment of a promise made by God to always be with us. The Holy Spirit is such an enabling person that He allows us to live victoriously over sin! When He dwells inside the believer who yields himself to God and submits himself to God's Word, then hope alive exudes in that person. God gives us power through the Holy Spirit to do more than we can imagine possible.

> Now all glory to God, who is able, through his mighty power at work within us, to accomplish infinitely more than we might ask or think (Ephesians 3:20 NLT).

As we look within the scriptures, we see the Holy Spirit as a quiet but power-filled force that teaches, guides, comforts, and intercedes for us. If you have surrendered your life to Jesus Christ in obedience to God, the Holy Spirit possesses your inner being. He works inside of you as only God can.

There was a time in my life before my relationship with Christ when I lacked so much, but I never said a word. I held it in silence, covered with shame and riddled with guilt. Even though I was deceived into believing I possessed everything I needed—confidence, self-abilities, strength, happiness—I was void of hope. I was hiding behind a sinful life. I appeared well-suited and extremely happy on the outside, but inside, I was void of God's presence. Something had to change in my life.

If you feel you have nothing left to give or have lost your self-worth, the Holy Spirit's presence will provide you with the creativity you need to conquer anything you set out to do with God. If you are beat up and feel dejected, thinking you cannot go on, the Holy Spirit is longing to work within you to regenerate you and bring new hope. If you are in a place where you feel you have sinned against God to the point you cannot be forgiven, the Holy Spirit will be there, and He will sanctify you.

The Holy Spirit brings conviction to the unbeliever and causes us to see the truth of the gospel is only a prayer of faith away. He gives us the best hope of all—faith in Jesus Christ to receive eternal life and become a new creation. When an unbeliever finally realizes His need for a Savior and accepts Jesus into His heart, the Bible tells us the Holy Spirit comes to live in our mortal bodies. At that point, God calls us His temple because the Holy Spirit comes to dwell in us. Once the Holy Spirit indwells a person who becomes a believer, He is there to stay permanently and will never leave.

> *Don't you realize that together you have become God's inner sanctuary and that the Spirit of God makes his permanent home in you? Now, if someone desecrates God's inner sanctuary, God will desecrate him, for God's inner sanctuary is holy, and that is exactly who you are* (1 Corinthians 3:16-17 TPT).

Wow, God has given us a warning in His Word that once He resides in a believer, no one better mess with that person's temple because it houses a Holy God. Yet even though, as believers, we may do things contrary to God's Word and grieve the Spirit, God gives His word that the Spirit will never leave a true believer. The Holy Spirit comes to protect you, guide you, and seal you with security, but He will also convict you when you do wrong.

And I will ask the Father and he will give you another Savior, the Holy Spirit of Truth, who will be to you a friend just like me—and he will never leave you. The world won't receive him because they can't see him or know him (John 14:16-17 TPT).

When we place our trust in the God of hope and follow Jesus, He fills us with joy, peace, and overflowing hope, all powered by the Holy Spirit.

Will you pray with me?

"Lord, give me the faith to hope in You and not put confidence in things of the world to get me through. Please let me trust that Jesus will forgive me and cleanse me, and the Holy Spirit will dwell in me to guide me. Amen."

If you prayed that to God from your heart, He heard your prayer. He will give you a reason to believe. Trust the God who loves you and created you. Hope is on the way. He wants to reside inside you permanently. But you have to choose to either accept Jesus or reject Him. The choice is yours.

Now may God, the inspiration and fountain of hope, fill you to overflowing with uncontainable joy and perfect peace as you trust in him. And may the power of the Holy Spirit continually surround your life with His super-abundance until you radiate with hope! (Romans 15:13 TPT).

Melissa Gissy Witherspoon

After more than two decades of substance abuse, Melissa Gissy Witherspoon is in long-term sobriety and sharing with the world that recovery from substance use disorder is possible! *With God all things are possible* (Matthew 19:26 NIV).

Originally from a suburb of Atlanta, Georgia, Melissa lives in Winston-Salem, North Carolina, with the youngest of her four children and her husband, Derek, following her calling to love and support those impacted by addiction. Founder and CEO of the nonprofit Sober-Now, Melissa raises proceeds from her best-selling, award-winning book, *I'm Sober... So Now What? A Journey of Hope and Healing,* bringing hope to prison ministries, recovery centers, sober-living housing, human trafficking safe houses, churches, and high schools.

When not working at her church, Melissa advocates for the recovery community, sharing her story of God's love through podcasts, speaking events, recovery walks, supporting accountability courts, and offering inspiration through her social media pages.

Melissa is a Best-selling and Award-winning Author. She is a Contributing Author in International Best-Selling *Miracle Mindset,* 2022 International Book Awards Finalist, 2023 BookFest Award Addiction and Recovery, 2023 BookFest Award Self Help-Inspiration, 2023 Bookfest NY Times Square Billboard Montague.

Stay connected with Melissa at Melissa@Sober-Now.com or https://linktr.ee/sobernow for podcasts and social media.

Prisoner to Purpose in Unity of the Spirit

By Melissa Gissy Witherspoon

As a prisoner for the Lord, then, I urge you to live a life worthy of the calling you have received. Be completely humble and gentle; be patient, bearing with one another in love. Make every effort to keep the unity of the Spirit through the bond of peace (Ephesians 4:1-3 NIV).

In the first three chapters of Ephesians, Paul emphasizes what God has done for us through His son, Jesus—how He has blessed us, how He has saved us, and how He has redeemed us. The entire focus is on the beautiful works of grace and mercy God has bestowed upon us.

In contrast, as Christians, we too often focus on what we do for God. But the absolute foundation of Christianity is not what we do for God, but rather what He has done for us through His only son, Christ Jesus.

In chapter four, Paul's letter shifts to expressing how this great theological truth explained in the first three chapters really matters in our lives—that is, how we should be living every day in light of what God has done for us. The chapter does not focus on the specifics of Christianity; instead, Paul explains Christian principles by deliberately laying the groundwork for living to the glory of God. He doesn't just give us a list of do's and don'ts but beckons us to answer the call from God and live in light of it. Only then can we walk humbly in gratitude for all He has given us and truly serve the Lord.

I wasn't always an author. My connection with you through this chapter is indeed by divine doing. In fact, my calling to write and share my faith story didn't come to me until much later in life. I certainly never thought I would be writing about a God who, for so many years, I had hidden from and turned my back on. But using the gift of writing was exactly what He had planned for me.

God rescued me from my suicide attempt on my basement floor during my rock-bottom experience with drugs and alcohol. He freed me from the bondage of addiction and released me from the depths of hell I had been walking through for twenty-plus years. He delivered the promise that I would never have to feel alone again through unity in recovery if I would only turn my will over to Him, repent, and allow my healing journey to begin. Through divine intervention, God granted me a new lease on life with a calling to share hope with those who are lost and broken.

Desperate, I accepted the grace He granted me. And every day moving forward from that point, I have been determined to go to whatever length to do what He asks of me. Over time, my healing journey has turned into a spiritual awakening and opened up a floodgate of opportunities to know God on a more intimate level. What better way to do this than by studying Scripture, right?

Studying the Bible has always intimidated me. For many years, my dyslexia had me convinced I wasn't intelligent enough to read. When I tried, I would get frustrated for not being able to process words and retain information long enough to digest what I had just read. This made it almost impossible for Bible study to be an interest in my life. But in my spiritual awakening, I noticed the Bible passage I opened this chapter with appearing in front of me at every turn. It became clear to me that the Holy Spirit was asking me to pursue God's truths. In obedience to the loving Father who rescued me from the depths of addiction, I cracked open the Bible and started investigating.

The opening words of this particular passage, "prisoner of the Lord," stumped me from the beginning. I thought to myself in my most obstinate inner voice, *A prisoner for the Lord? What does this even mean? Who wants to be a prisoner of anything or anyone?* When thinking about all the freedoms God had granted me on my path to recovery from substance use disorder (better known as addiction), I couldn't begin to wrap my head around why I had to submit to such a concept.

For so many years, I was a prisoner of mental illness. My body was held captive by active addiction. Even worse, I was held against my will for days by drug dealers who used me at their discretion. This captivity kept my heart and soul imprisoned for decades. I was incarcerated several times by the criminal justice system. I made terrible choices while in active addiction that led me to the inevitable—jails, institutions, and nearly death. I was finally walking a path of freedom— and the last thing I wanted to claim over my life was to be a prisoner of anything.

Before judgment sets in, I ask you to read this chapter with compassion and understanding that my faith hasn't always run as deep as it does today. But as a woman of faith, I challenged God's written Word. I dug deep for answers and meaning within the teachings and trusted the loving guidance from good stewards of the Christian faith. As a result, I have grown in my understanding of Scripture. Questioning, or rather, discerning faith, as it develops, can be quite beautiful and beneficial if done from a place of respect and with a yearning to understand the Bible's teachings. How can we become more intimate with something or someone without asking questions that help us gain understanding, right?

Jesus was fond of the children because He knew their hearts to be pure and humble— not weighed down by the world's burdens. I may have been well into my forties before I dove into studying Scripture, but God's Spirit within me was new. Freshly born into a sober life, my soul was much like the children Jesus speaks of written in Mark 10:14-15, *"Let the little children come to me, and do not hinder them, for the kingdom of God belongs to such as these. Truly I tell you, anyone who will not receive the kingdom of God like a little child will never enter it"* (NIV).

I took comfort in learning that Jesus embraced the children in this way. It helped me trust that I can always ask questions and seek the truth about Christ's teachings as I grow. No matter our age or where we are in life, we can always turn to our Creator to find refuge and guidance.

My initial questioning of being a "prisoner of faith" turned into a search for the truth behind those three simple words. I had to discover why, after having found great freedoms in recovery, I was still to be labeled a prisoner. It didn't take much searching to realize a prisoner of faith was what I was already becoming. Rather than being bound to addiction, I was becoming bound to the Lord.

I was in awe as I discovered that the very meaning of these words aligned with the path I had already begun to walk on my sobriety journey. In my recovery from addiction, prior to fully turning my will over to God, I had worked a twelve-step program through an organization called Alcoholics Anonymous. The program's principles taught me humility, and my self-seeking slowly slipped away. Through the twelve steps, God primed me to receive the written Word in His perfect timing.

Being a prisoner of faith did not mean I was being held in captivity, as I had experienced in the past. It meant my time, talents, and treasures were no longer mine. Walking in God's calling meant that everything I used to consider valuable no longer belonged to me. My identity and character were no longer linked to money, drugs, alcohol, sexual gratification, or anything else that had been driven by self-will and ego for so long. God was now calling me to walk as a faithful servant, to follow His will for me, to share hope with and love others, and to be an instrument of peace in His beautiful design. I was freed from the prison of my past and launched into my purpose.

Following this call did not come easy. To be completely authentic with you, I still struggle some days. Accepting I am of flesh and can easily be misguided when my eyes are not on God allows me the grace to continue growing through life, one day at a time.

Through prayer and meditation, I can stay connected with our Father and work through the distractions from a world so heavily focused on fame, fortune, and instant gratification. It is in this practice of mindfulness through prayer that I have been able to embrace true humility—a humility that replaced the things of this world that no longer serve me with connection, friendships, and unity with all God's people.

One of the most beautiful parts of my recovery journey is the unity I have found along the way. This includes beautiful, authentic friendships built on respect and mutual understanding. I spent so many years of my life longing to feel a part of something. Throughout the years, I always found myself in circles or situations where I didn't quite fit the mold. I was a part of many things but never wholly committed to anything. My protective walls would get in the way of sharing myself completely, which meant I was unable to let people in fully. I sometimes still find myself in these scenarios.

God continually opens doors for me to carry my message of hope to groups where I feel like I don't belong. I speak to doctors and counselors about the disease of addiction even though they have degrees in fields where I do not. I do not carry fancy titles and letters behind my name, but God allows me time and time again to share my perspective as a recovering addict. I sit with court programs and share how what they do daily offers people like me a chance for a better way of life. I am not a judge, attorney, officer, or prosecutor. I am simply a woman in recovery, whom God has allowed to bring a fresh perspective to their programs, encouraging them to keep going because what they are doing is working—I am living proof. I have also spoken to health organizations and non-profits, sharing ideas for spreading awareness and giving insights from my own experiences and successes.

I am not downplaying the important role God has ordained for me in participating in these different programs, nor do I lack gratitude for the opportunity to feel a part of the movement that breaks the stigma of addiction. But I feel the urge to share with you my raw truth that feelings sometimes creep in and play tricks on my mind, telling me I am not worthy and not qualified to partner with the people I am surrounded by. The devil feeds off that feeling of worthlessness. It is one of his greatest tools to distract us from the calling God has placed on our lives. And because of his cunning and baffling trickery, I must always stay connected with my Creator.

Each and every Christian has been called graciously by God's Spirit, transcending us out of spiritual darkness into God's marvelous light. When thoughts begin to creep in that I do not belong, I quickly remind myself that I am exactly where I am supposed to be, doing the work I am called to do in the Spirit of unity for the glory of God.

We all have insecurities and weaknesses. But when we fully share ourselves in unity with the Spirit of God and another person, we find humility. Although this can be uncomfortable, it is truly an exercise of deep awareness of God's great glory and our own frailty and sinfulness. Paul declared this lowliness when he spoke of himself as *less than the least of all saints* (Ephesians 3:8 KJV). It is one of the chief marks of godliness and of Christianity.

By staying connected with God and others, I am protected from the isolation that fueled the devil to ignite my disease of addiction and kept the fires in the furnace of that terrible disease burning.

The opposite of addiction is connection, so it makes sense this tactic would be used by the accuser. But the unity of the Spirit is the gift God has granted that offers a bond of peace, connecting us all as one. With this, I am encouraged that we are never alone. Instead, we are loved, and we belong.

Hope is truly alive through so many avenues if only we seek the light and walk in it. Hope is alive in the written Word of God. Hope is alive in the calling He has placed in our lives. Hope is alive in the unity built through the Holy Spirit, connecting His people in ways we could never imagine. Hope is alive in the everyday graces God grants us, and hope is alive in YOU!

My prayer for us all is that we can walk together in unity on this earth, loving one another and creating a bond of peace within our hearts so we may fulfill our purpose here on earth with the belief that, one day, we will unite fully in the kingdom of heaven. Until we meet again, may God grant you the bond of peace through the unity of the Spirit and the grace to keep hope alive in your hearts, one day at a time.

May the God of hope fill you with all joy and peace as you trust in him, so that you may overflow with hope by the power of the Holy Spirit (Romans 15:13 NIV).

Hope in Brokenness

By Connie A. VanHorn

In our brokenness, we have an extraordinary opportunity to draw closer to God and experience His love more deeply. In our brokenness, we can see God's grace and mercy at work.

Just as a potter molds and shapes clay into a beautiful vessel, God can take our brokenness and create something new and beautiful out of it. We can learn to rely on God's strength and find peace in His presence, no matter what circumstances surround us.

In June of 2022, I lost my younger sister to an accidental drug overdose. Although Amanda struggled with addiction, she was a believer in Jesus Christ. She loved God, and she begged Him to remove her addiction and her brokenness. I prayed for this with her on the phone countless times. Amanda wanted to be sober so she could tell the world how God saved her. She wanted to be used as a broken vessel. Amanda had hope. Unfortunately, she lost her battle with addiction and never got that chance, or so she thought.

I was asked to share a message at Amanda's funeral. As I prepared, the pastor and I decided to use Amanda's service to celebrate Jesus' love. On the day of the funeral, I stood in front of everyone and shared about Amanda, but I also shared about God's love and the hope we have in Jesus. We invited others to experience this amazing love, praying that if anyone needed to surrender or be saved, that would be the day. We had hope that someone might be encouraged to make a change for themselves. Everyone there that day witnessed many miracles—several people surrendered their burdens at the altar, and at least one life was saved. Amanda was a broken vessel—but

God used her life for His glory. Never count yourself out or think that you are too broken. God can shine through the cracks of a broken vessel.

> *But we have this treasure in jars of clay, to show that the surpassing power belongs to God and not to us* (2 Corinthians 4:7 ESV).

At some point in our lives, we will all face moments of brokenness—shattered dreams, lost relationships, deaths, and unexpected challenges can leave us feeling confused and alone. In these moments, we may find ourselves searching for hope. But what if I told you that true hope can be found right in the center of brokenness? What if I told you that God uses broken things and turns them into something beautiful?

God's Word is filled with stories of hurting people who faced bitter odds yet found hope in their brokenness. One of these stories is found in the book of Isaiah, where God promises to bring beauty out of ashes, *to bestow on them a crown of beauty instead of ashes, the oil of joy instead of mourning, and a garment of praise instead of a spirit of despair* (Isaiah 61:3 NIV).

God can transform the broken pieces of our lives; He can take our pain, sorrow, and failures and turn them into something beautiful. He can replace our pain with praise, our tears with joy, and our ashes with a crown of beauty.

> *But he said to me, "My grace is sufficient for you, for my power is made perfect in weakness." Therefore I will boast all the more gladly about my weaknesses, so that Christ's power may rest on me* (2 Corinthians 12:9 NIV).

God's strength is made perfect in our weakness. When we recognize our brokenness and surrender it to Him, He will work in and through us in ways we never thought possible. In God's hands, the broken tapestry of our lives becomes a canvas for His grace and power to be beautifully displayed. We are all scarred by sharp things this life tosses at us. But it's in our broken places that we find hope. It's in our brokenness that we find God shining ever so brightly!

Despite what you go through, your life can become a testimony of God's faithfulness, a story of redemption and restoration that points others to the hope found in Christ. It's okay to be broken. From the shattered pieces of our lives, God will create a masterpiece of hope and healing. Trust in His promise to bring beauty out of ashes, and trust that God is turning your pain into something beautiful.

I hope Amanda's story has shone a light on the significance of every single life, including yours. God can use every broken thing for good. Never lose hope.

Being broken does not render our lives meaningless. When you can't foresee a positive outcome, trust that God is in control; He is greater than any force that can come against you. Choose to focus on God's glory, and He will infuse you with HOPE beyond the world's understanding.

. . . .

Kimberly Ewell

Kimberly Ewell has been walking with the Lord for eleven years. During that time, she learned to walk in faith and obedience, which brought her to where she is today. After years of healing and training, Kimberly founded WildFire International Ministries in Orlando, Florida. She has become a published author sharing her real-life experiences and the love of God that changed her life forever.

Because of Kimberly's personal experiences of childhood trauma, abuse, pain, grief, and loss, Kimberly has been given a powerful testimony of God's love and healing power.

As part of Kimberly's journey, the Lord called her to Colorado Springs, CO to learn ministry work at Focus on the Family. Here, she gained experience of what it's like to be on the battlefield's front lines. The Lord opened Kimberly's eyes to the depths of the brokenness that runs rampant across the world. During her time at Focus on the Family, she ministered, counseled, and poured out the love of Jesus to many people across the nation.

Kimberly firmly believes that every person should be empowered to fulfill their God-given calling and destiny. She desires to see God's people healed and equipped and to live in freedom.

The Prodigals Are Returning!

By Kimberly Ewell

I arrived on a Monday morning to work. I greeted my co-worker, who sat behind me in her cubicle. As I prepared for the day, I thanked the Lord for what He would do for those calling in for prayer. I put on my headset, clicked the start button on the screen, and the phone began ringing.

"Thank you for calling Focus on the Family. How may I help you?"

I heard a sweet voice say, "Hello," and then start sharing her guilt from her mistakes as a mother, which had cost her relationships. It had been over ten years since she had a conversation with or seen her family. She mentioned several grandchildren whom she longed to meet. But even though her heart hurt, she trusted that the God of Hope would reunite her with her family one day.

Hearing her story awakened pain deep within me. It triggered a wound I'd hidden for many years, causing me to remember all I had buried so deep under a concrete slab created to protect myself from what I no longer wanted to feel. But the Lord was using this woman to begin my healing. I had chosen to cover that wound again and again because the pain was too great—until that day.

I hesitate to share the details of my heart with you, but I will. Like the woman who shared her heart and hope with me, I am choosing to surrender to the Lord the pain, guilt, and shame that has been buried underneath the concrete slab for ten years so I can heal, and my hope is you may find healing from the Lord, too.

As I dig deep within, I can feel my heart harden as tears form in my eyes. *No! I can't! Lord, please help me. Please give me the strength to move forward!*

My stomach is sick with the guilt deep inside while the Lord shows me where it all started. I see my child in the distance, standing in the living room as he watches his mother getting her head slammed into the wood floor by his stepfather. At the time, my son was just in first grade.

Weeks passed, the weekend was approaching, and it was time for my son to visit his father in Southern California. We lived in Northern California, and he saw his father during long school breaks. While he was away, I knew my son wouldn't be subjected to the abuse. With a mother's protective stance and knowing our home wasn't a safe place for my boy, I called his father and told him what was happening and that I felt it would be best for our son to remain with him. His father agreed, and Daniel didn't return.

I chose to stay in the marriage, like other abused women who wear rose-tinted glasses. Most abused women believe that if only this or that would happen, the spouse would change. I was one of those women.

Later, we would move to Florida. I believed my relationship was improving and that moving to a new place would make it all right. I wanted my son to come with me, but his father said no. I drove to Ventura, California, to express my goodbyes to Daniel. I visited him for a few hours, and then it was time to go. We climbed into the car and drove off. While looking in the rearview mirror, I saw Daniel running and crying, "Mom, don't leave!" I questioned if I was doing the right thing. I told myself to stop and return, but I knew I was too deep into my commitment to leave California. I also knew I wasn't sure my husband was a changed man and didn't want my son to experience what he had seen just a few months earlier. Daniels's father promised me that he could visit for the summers and holidays.

Unfortunately, I didn't see Daniel until a few years later, over Christmas break. What a wonderful time it was.

I divorced my husband and later moved back to California. I lived only blocks from my son, and we saw each other daily. We regained a mother-and-son relationship. Daniel attended Christian schools where he learned about Jesus, but neither I nor his father took him to church. For us, it was more about him receiving a better education in a private school versus a public school. But God was working. Daniel accepted Christ into his life and became, as he says, "a die-hard Christian." He loved the Lord.

Some years later, things turned around when Daniel was seventeen. Like his older brother Christopher, he started to smoke pot. It became his lifestyle. His father felt it best to send him to a Christian camp in Montana that took troubled boys. I wasn't on board with this idea. I had abandoned my son once, and I didn't want him to feel that way again. We had rebuilt our trust and had a good relationship I didn't want to lose. However, his father sent him to the camp without my signature on the necessary legal papers. My son's father later described to me what happened: several men from the camp arrived at midnight and woke Daniel up from his sleep, taking him against his will. He said our son was crying out to his dad to stop the men from taking him, but he didn't stop them. My heart was beyond crushed, envisioning my son once again crying, "Don't leave me!"

I didn't have any communication with Daniel for three months. During this time, Christopher, his older brother, said it was best for his brother to be where he was to get the help he needed. Christopher had cleaned up his act, stopped smoking pot, and accepted Christ into his life. Just months later, Christopher died in a motorcycle accident. I was devastated! His life ended, and all I could think was I didn't want to lose Daniel, too.

I called the director at the camp and told them about Christopher's death and that I needed to speak to my son. I shared the horrific news with Daniel, and it devastated him. He wanted to leave, so I requested that he return home for the funeral, but his father and the camp directors said it wouldn't be best because it would interrupt my son's progress in the program. In my troubled state of mind, I put on my rose-tinted glasses and hoped this was the best thing to do.

After Christopher's passing, I surrendered my life to Christ, and months later, Daniel turned 18 and left the camp. He was a different person. He appeared to be a new, mature young man. We talked about God and shared scriptures; I enjoyed telling him all the great things the Lord was doing in my life! We did things with his other siblings as a family, and all I could do was rejoice that I had my son back! It was like he had never left, and we picked up where we had been before he left for camp.

Until Mother's Day 2014. The relationship I had with my son ended suddenly without explanation. I called. I texted, and there was silence. I didn't overthink it at first. I even thought I should give him his space because I knew he was working hard at his father's law firm, going to college, and had a new girlfriend. Days, weeks, and months passed. I called, texted, and instant messaged Daniel on Facebook but received silence. I contacted his father several times, who reassured me that our son was busy and doing well and that I should not worry.

> Be anxious for nothing, but in everything by prayer and supplication, with thanksgiving, let your requests be made known to God (Philippians 4:6 NKJV).

A year passed, and my heart was anxious. After months of texting and calling only to get a voicemail, I realized my son was no longer speaking to me, and I didn't know why. Later, I learned that my son wasn't talking to his father anymore and was living at his grandmother's house. At least I knew where he was and that he was safe. I prayed, but now I was praying harder; I presented my request to the Lord and thanked Him for bringing my son home. But still, there were only crickets.

In 2017, after years of prayer, sleepless nights, and crying, I heard within my heart to let go and give my son to the Lord, and I did. This occurred months before the Lord called me to Colorado Springs to work at Focus on the Family, where I would later have a conversation with that sweet lady who began breaking up the concrete over my heart. I never stopped praying for my son, but I stopped begging God, and I started to trust the God of Hope to restore our relationship.

> Jesus said to him, "If you can believe, all things are possible to him who believes" (Mark 9:23 NKJV).

The day I listened to the Lord telling me to let go and give my son to Him, I knew the Lord was doing something; I couldn't see it yet. I had to believe and find hope in Him, the God of Hope, and hang on to that.

In January 2022, I was living in Florida; a friend told me the Lord had a word for me; she said, "If you can believe, all things are possible to him who believes." I didn't understand what she meant; however, I knew in my head that it was true.

In August 2022, I was at a friend's house; we were learning to walk in the prophetic, listen to the Holy Spirit, and agree with His Word. The Holy Spirit instructed the host to write the things He wanted to say on paper, place them in a bag, and then pass the bag around the room. We were all to take one. Once everyone had a paper, we were to say it out loud and then declare that word to come to pass. I was excited to find out what I was going to get.

The bag came to me; I reached in and took the prophetic word the Holy Spirit had for me. I didn't look at my piece of paper. People took turns and read and declared the word they received. It was my turn; I was a bit nervous. I read the word silently to myself, my insides began to heat up like fire, and I heard the Holy Spirit say to me, "DANIEL!"

The words from the paper flew out of my mouth, "The Prodigals are Returning! I declare this in the name of JESUS!" I knew without a doubt my son was coming home!

Shortly after this powerful word from the Lord, I considered attending prophetic training in Simi Valley, California. I prayed and asked the Lord to send me. He made a way for me to purchase my flights, and I arranged to stay at my friend's house in Ventura, California, for five days. A couple of days before leaving for California, I told the Lord, "I'm leaving soon, and you haven't told me to pay for the training class yet. When are we going to do that?" Of course, I said it with urgency because I didn't want to miss this training.

His reply was, "You're not going to the training."

I stepped back and said to Him, "Well then, why am I going?"

He replied, "To see Daniel!"

"But Lord, I don't know where he lives! I don't know what to say; what if he's not there?" I wanted to argue with the Lord and find every reason not to see my son, which was because of FEAR.

Two days later, I was on a flight to California and was rehearsing what I would say when I saw my son. I was unprepared and learned that was the best way to go because I would have gotten in the way of what God wanted to do.

I spent each day with my friend, wondering when I would see my son. I searched the internet to locate him. A few days later, I found him; he was five minutes away from where I was staying.

I asked the Lord when I would be going to his house. He told me to go the next day. I decided to go after 5:00 PM in case he worked regular business hours. But I was instructed to go in the morning.

I woke up the following day nervous and feeling a little sick. I had to remind myself that this was the Lord's doing, which meant He had already made way for this meeting and knew the outcome. God wasn't setting me up to do this alone; He was going with me.

I prayed for His peace as I drove to my son's house, and as I pulled up, I took a deep breath, got out of the car, and walked to the door. My hand shook as I knocked on the door, and my son's aunt answered. After eight years of not seeing me, she initially didn't recognize me. I explained to her I was there to see my son; she wasn't sure if he'd come to the door but said she would let him know. A few moments later, my son was standing in front of me. I desperately wanted to reach out and hold him and tell him how much I had missed and loved him. However, I didn't; I wanted him to take the lead.

I want to say it was a warm greeting, but it wasn't. He said a few choice words out of anger and then asked why I was there. I had no answer other than telling him the Lord sent me. It was pressed on my heart to ask for forgiveness, so I did. My son proceeded to tell me he was angry with me because I signed the papers allowing the men to pick him up that night and take him to the so-called Christian camp. He went on to say that while he was there for almost a year, the people who ran the place would beat him and the other boys and leave them in their underwear out in the cold snow for weeks to die. As I listened to him, I cried, and my heart became angry at his father and the men who hurt my child.

Looking at my son, I explained to him I didn't sign the papers, and I was so sorry for what happened and that I wasn't aware of it. He told me he wanted nothing to do with a God who would allow this to happen. I listened to his heart and saw the brokenness from what had happened all those years ago.

Then something changed. Daniel asked about his youngest sister, Cheyanne, and I told him she wanted to see him and that she missed and loved him so much. He began to cry. We talked more and arranged to spend the following day with his sister. I told my son I loved him and hugged him. He replied while holding me tight, "I love you, MOM."

I left and immediately called Chey and told her what had taken place, and the next day, we all met and had one of the best days ever. We talked, walked the Ventura Harbor, caught up, and took pictures. Then it came time to go. We took Daniel back to his house, which was a hard goodbye. I was leaving the next day to fly back to Florida, and we arranged to see each other again in December 2022.

He heals the brokenhearted And binds up their wounds (Psalm 147:3 NKJV).

The morning of my flight, I was prompted by the Holy Spirit to go to my son's house again to tell him how much I loved him. So I did. It was early, and I woke him up; I quickly thanked him for spending time with us and told him I loved him very much. He hugged me, and we parted ways. I was almost in my car when I heard Daniel say, "Mom!" I turned and saw him looking at me. He said, "Thank you for coming; it means a lot to me. I love you, Mom."

I drove off, thanking the Lord for what He had done and telling Him that I trusted Him, knowing that Daniel was in His hands and that He would heal his brokenness and bring him back to the Lord.

I want to say all went well, and there was a happy ending when I returned to California to see Daniel in December 2022, as I promised. We saw each other the day after I arrived, only for a few hours. We made plans to hang out for the rest of my four-day stay. However, he didn't return my calls or texts after our visit. I continued trying to see him, but there was no answer. I knew he had changed his mind. I left brokenhearted, crying to the Lord, "Why? What did I do wrong? You said he was coming home!"

At that moment, I was reminded of the Prodigal Son, and the Lord said in a still, small voice, "He is returning home to Me."

I haven't seen or heard from my son in this past year. I am still healing and may or may not see Daniel again; however, I'm holding on to the God of Hope and His Word that The Prodigals are Returning home to Him, and God will be glorified!

Hallelujah!

Hope in Restoration

By Kimberly Ann Hobbs

> *Therefore, if anyone is in Christ, the new creation has come. The old has gone, the new is here!* (2 Corinthians 5:17 NIV).

There is some great news in the word restoration. The Bible is full of scriptures that bring us hope despite the hurt that has been inflicted on so many of our hearts.

Have you ever felt robbed of something and in need of restoration? If something has been taken away from you and needs to be replaced or can't be returned as it once was, if you were hurt in a relationship and long for it to be revived, or if someone in your life is "lost" and living a life that requires renewal, there is hope. Whatever your situation may be, God offers the hope of restoration through His Word, the Bible. By focusing on the Bible, our minds can be renewed. God's Word can help you on your way to living a life of restoration.

Do you know that the word "restore" appears over one hundred times in the Bible? We have examples of healing and restoration in both the Old and New Testaments—that's great news! The beauty is in the promise that God's Word gives us: restoration is possible. God offers us hope when all else seems to oppose it.

I have longed for and have been praying for restoration to take place in my own life for over seven years now. Through this time, I have faced many trials that have caused anxious worries beyond my control and given me an urgency of wanting to be rescued from the pain of two wounded relationships. One thing that has truly helped me through is trusting God with the restoration process—learning to trust what His Word tells me. I can tell you clearly that this is a continual process of praying, seeking, and growing an intimate relationship with God as I trust His path of restoration.

The renewal of individual hearts and wounds, turning from sin, and returning to God does not happen overnight. It is a process. I had to learn patience and wait for God to show me things He would reveal through my journey. Our physical bodies continually process and daily re-live pain while our spiritual bodies grow as we walk closer with Jesus. When we allow God into this restoration process, He brings things to light for us to see. Otherwise left to us, we would remain selfish and only look at ourselves and our own wounds, often blind to the situations on the other side. But by reading His scriptures, we are given hope in otherwise bleak situations.

One of the key scriptures God used in my restoration story is Ezekiel 36:26, which talks about God replacing our hearts of stone with hearts of flesh. God continually works to restore marriages, broken families, and even our physical bodies. When my mind opened where the hurt took place, my heart began to soften even more, and I was able to review with God what needed to be restored regarding the brokenness in my life. God removed my own selfish and bitter wounds, filling me with His unconditional love so that I can be ready to receive the restoration He promises will come.

And after you have suffered a little while, the God of all grace, who has called you to his eternal glory in Christ, will himself restore, confirm, strengthen, and establish you (1 Peter 5:10 ESV).

I will give them an heart to know me, that I am the LORD, and they shall be my people, and I will be their God: for they shall return to me with their whole heart (Jeremiah 24:7 KJV).

Therefore I tell you, whatever you ask for in prayer, believe that you have received it, and it will be yours (Mark 11:24 ESV).

I will search for the lost and bring back the strays. I will bind up the injured and strengthen the weak, but the sleek and the strong I will destroy. I will shepherd the flock with justice (Ezekiel 34:16 NIV).

The Lord upholds all who fall and uplifts all who are bowed down (Psalm 145:14 NIV).

He refreshes my soul. He guides me along the right paths for His name's sake (Psalm 23:3 NIV).

When we look to God's Word, He gives us a great hope to follow. For example, when the locusts have devoured a plant, God promises not only to restore that plant to its full beauty but also to make it stronger and better in the process. He restores the full benefits as only He can—because He is the Creator!

As we meditate on God's Word and follow Him, our souls, emotions, and bodies are renewed and restored. The enemy is a roaring lion who seeks to destroy and rob you, but our God is a conqueror—He is victorious and will restore to you what the enemy has stolen. God removes what needs to be discarded from your mind and cleans up the wounds of your soul as the Holy Spirit within you becomes your counselor, strengthener, comforter, helper, and guide, delivering you from the oppression the enemy seeks to rob you with ongoingly.

Please go to God's Word and believe by faith that He can restore whatever has been stolen from you. Then, as you hold onto that faith, believe it, speak it, and act on it. And God will give you the hope you need to claim that full restoration will occur in God's perfect timing.

. . . .

Carol Ann Whipkey

Carol Ann Whipkey is a best-selling published author. She is a Christ follower, and much of her retired time is devoted to serving in the Women World Leaders ministry as a writer and encourager through her uplifting, joyful spirit, guidance, and love for writing.

Carol has enjoyed her career as a beauty consultant and worked in an accounting position at UPS until retirement.

She is an artist trained by the world-renowned wood carver Joe Leanord, whose work is in the New York Museum of Art and Disney in Paris and the USA. As a hobby, Carol spends much of her time carving horses, birds, and other commissioned work that comes her way.

Carol lives in her own park-like setting on 52 acres in Thompson, Ohio, with her husband, Mel. She is the mother of four, which includes her first-born child Kimberly Hobbs of Women World Leaders, and is the grandmother of seven and great-grandmother of eight.

Angel Horse

By Carol Ann Whipkey

God is our source of hope for all things. He is the One who has kept Hope Alive in me for my lifetime. In the story I am about to share, you will see how God first gave me hope and then kept hope alive in and through my heart's desire to receive a horse, which was very important to me.

God has a plan for each of us. He showed me His plan, and although it took years to unfold, He allowed this precious animal to be used in my life. I know God has a plan for your life, too. May my story bring you to awareness of His plan for you.

I have loved horses all my life! When I was a little child, I'd lay in my bed or on the couch and listen to my mom's radio as she would turn on *The Lone Ranger* or *The Gene Autry Show* so I could hear the horses galloping or whinnying. It was my true hope that I could one day, someday, have horses in my life.

I would look at pictures in books and try to draw the beautiful horses I dreamed about. I loved making believe I was a cowgirl riding my beautiful steed. My family knew of my love for horses, and they would let me play as I pretended to be their horse. God knew my heart's desire because my mom taught me to pray for the things I wanted. Oh, how I wanted a horse so badly.

In the book *Tears to Triumph,* the first anthology by Women World Leaders, I shared a very traumatic story about how a horse played such an important part in my life. The horse saved me from a terrible journey with an evil man who would try to do horrible things to me in the woods. I still have pictures in my mind of the beautiful animal that came to my rescue. God has, in fact, used horses to impact my life so many times.

But although my hope as a child was to have a horse to call my own, little did I know there was so much more to hope for in life. Looking back, I am amazed at how our awesome God used this magnificent animal to speak to my heart in many situations.

> So, God has given both his promise and his oath. These two things are unchangeable because it is impossible for God to lie. Therefore, we who have fled to him for refuge can have great confidence as we hold to the hope that lies before us. This hope is a strong and trustworthy anchor for our souls. It leads us through the curtain into God's inner sanctuary (Hebrews 6:18-19 NLT).

I was seven years old when my dad came home with my first horse. I was so excited, but I was too little to ride it. It was so big and not trained very well. Consequently, my dad sold him, and my heart was broken. But my mother always told me to pray when things like that happen. So, I did that. I hoped, and I prayed that I would get another horse someday.

> God will make this happen, for he who calls you is faithful (1 Thessalonians 5:24 NLT).

Although I was little, I had never heard this scripture nor had the belief that God is faithful or that He is the One who makes all things possible. When I was a little older, there was a riding academy not far from our house, so I thought my friend and I could walk to it. Maybe we could get a job mucking stalls and then ride for free. We would walk miles trying to find a place to work, but we could not find anything. My dreams were shot down again, but my heart still hoped for a horse, any kind, just a horse.

A few years went by, and my friend and I found a place we could ride. We went almost every week in the summertime. We both learned to ride without lessons. I continued to hope and pray and draw pictures of horses—thinking that if I could at least have them on paper, that would satisfy my longing. God gave me the ability to draw the most beautiful horses. I still have the pictures I drew as a child.

Although I had some mishaps and made some bad choices along life's way, in many ways, I always felt that someone was watching over me. Through it all, I always kept my hope alive for horses, that one day I would own one myself.

One day, while reading the newspaper, I saw a horse listed for sale. It was a beautiful black stallion! I had never studied horses or knew what a stallion was or why they were called stallions; I just loved horses. They stood so tall and proud, big and beautiful. I talked to my mom about taking me to see the stallion. She agreed. When we arrived at the place, I laid eyes on him, and I wanted to ride him so badly. I rode it down the road, and I turned him around, and suddenly, he took off at full speed, going past his home at about 30 miles an hour. I didn't expect him to turn, but when he did, I kept going straight and arrived right at a fence post, which knocked me out cold. Yes, I could have been killed or paralyzed, but I was still alive. I was learning lessons along the way. Still, I always hoped to have my own place with my own horses one day. But it didn't always go exactly the way I planned in the time frame I desired.

The Lord eventually led me to the man I married, who also loved horses. But he loved racehorses, so we spent a lot of time at the track. I saw horses every time we went there. I talked my husband into letting me buy a horse for my daughter. We didn't have the acreage at our home, so I had to keep it at my mother's place on her property. It was a smaller horse, a little bigger than a pony, but not well broken. I decided to ride it first so the kids wouldn't get hurt. I took it out of the barn and got on his back; immediately, the horse galloped full speed across the field. It propped (in other words, it stopped, put its head down, and threw me in the air over its head). I landed in the hospital with a ruptured kidney. The doctor said I had to lay perfectly still for the next ten days to heal. If I didn't, he said he would have to remove my kidney. I almost died. All that time, I kept asking, "Lord, why do these things happen to me?" But I was not getting any answers to my questions. I didn't really know the Lord back then, but I would pray and talk to God as my mom taught me as a child.

Life with my husband went on, and I managed to get more horses over time. I couldn't keep them in the city limits, where we lived, but at least I had horses. I was thankful.

About 19 years after my husband Mike and I were married, I accepted Jesus into my heart as my Lord and personal Savior. This was a very eye-opening time in my life, and I found a great church and got baptized. My life and my hopes were slowly changing, but I wasn't realizing then what the Lord's plan for my life was. What does this have to do with my love for horses? I had four children and, as life was very busy, my brother took over my horses. Although my love for them was still in my heart, I became more and more interested in serving the Lord. My husband accepted Christ during this time in our lives, praise God, as not long after he did, God called my husband home to be with Him.

Remember that the Lord will give you an inheritance as your reward and that the master you are serving is Christ (Colossians 3:24 NLT).

It seemed like my life was over the moment my husband passed, but God quickly showed me He had an inheritance for me, which became evident as I chose to serve God as my King. Later, I met another man with whom I had a lot in common. We got married and bought a house with lots of land. We joined a church and started our lives together. Although this man knew nothing about horses, he quickly learned that I had a love for them. One day, he bought me a horse, and I turned around and bought one for him. Oh, the fun we had as we were riding the horses on our property together. We bought lots of acres in a beautiful country setting. My dreams were finally becoming reality.

At the church we attended, I met a woman with the same dreams for horses I had. We both loved the Lord and started a riding ministry called Riders For Christ. We did parades and events with our horses, allowing my hope and passion to come alive for Jesus and involve my love of horses. These were memories that would last a lifetime. Eventually, I would have to give up that part of my life due to many other responsibilities.

No longer owning horses, I still had the desire in my heart to do something that involved horses as I served the Lord. My daughter enrolled me in a carving class with a famous person who taught me how to carve carousel horses, birds, and other animals out of wood. My teacher lived close to an Amish community, so I almost always saw horses when I went to the carving classes. I loved driving there, looking at the farm animals, and remembering when I had my own horses.

My husband's family lived in Pennsylvania, and we would go there quite often to visit them. They were wonderful Christian people; Mom Whipkey always sang while Dad Whipkey played his guitar. We would eat, gather for fellowship, and go to church with them. We loved to sing in their church. When we'd return to the house, Mom Whipkey would tell us so many things. I learned so much more about God, faith, and the joy God brought me through her. I grew to love her as my own mom.

Mom Whipkey's birthday was in November, and we often drove from Ohio to Pennsylvania to celebrate with her. One year, after we'd had a wonderful time and were leaving to go home, she prayed over us, saying a special prayer for us to have a safe trip back to Ohio. I didn't think too much of it then because they always prayed for us. We packed our little dog, Peanut, in our beautiful decked-out Caravan and headed for home. It was a quiet evening with crystal clear skies. It was cold outside but not freezing. My husband usually drove, but sometimes we'd switch drivers so he could rest. He was driving; we were listening to Gaither music and some recordings Mom and Dad Whipkey had made of themselves singing and playing the guitar—we were caught up in the beautiful music on our three-hour drive home. There was not a lot of traffic, including no buggies, as we drove through the Amish country. Feeling my husband might be tired, I asked him if he wanted me to drive, but he told me he was fine. So I just sat back, rested, and prayed. Peanut was sleeping on the floor in front of my feet.

Suddenly, my husband started yelling in a frightful voice at the top of his lungs, "NO, NO, NO!"

I sat up straight, and right in front of my eyes, I saw the most beautiful image. It was a horse with beautiful sparkling jewels on his bridle and all along his sides. There appeared to be wings, looking like the Pegasus horse I worked on with my carving teacher. The wings on this horse appeared to be as white as snow and glittering.

Then, "BOOM!" A crash louder than thunder—unlike anything I had ever heard—permeated the interior of our van. The noise went from the front to the back in an instant. Then everything stopped. It was like time stood still. There was no sound anywhere. My husband and I looked at each other and asked, "What just happened?"

We looked around the front window, which was shattered to smithereens and hanging in front of us like a sheet, only inches from our eyes. My husband said we had just hit a horse and buggy! I regained my senses and realized our dog, Peanut, wasn't anywhere on the floor. Both my husband and I panicked as we looked all around, thinking she had been thrown out of the vehicle. Instead, the impact had thrown her all the way to the back of the van. She was shaking and whimpering, but she was not hurt, which was a miracle.

My husband's side of the car was not damaged as badly as my side, which was completely caved in from the front to the back. When we hit the horse, he had flown into our windshield with such intense force that he was catapulted up and over the top of our van, crashed on the roof, and then rolled over it and down the side of the car to the back. Our airbags never deployed. Our beautiful, customized van was demolished, BUT we were ALIVE! We were never touched except for a tiny scratch on my husband's forehead. Truly a miracle of God. He protected us.

We gathered our thoughts and realized the severity of hitting a horse and buggy. My husband immediately got out of the car to assess the situation and see if there were any survivors. By this time, the Highway Patrol was arriving along with many Amish people, some of whom sat by the road, praying. We were told a young man had been driving the buggy which had children in the back. The buggy was smashed, but miraculously, everyone, including the children in the back, only had a few scratches. They were all OK. The buggy had been whirled into the air over to the other side of the highway, but God miraculously held that buggy, bringing it back onto the ground and keeping the children alive and unharmed.

I gathered the strength to ask about the horse but received no answer. Within moments, I heard a gunshot. My heart leaped into my throat, knowing they had to put the horse out of his suffering. All his legs had been broken, and he was crushed. I am sick just thinking about this whole situation again as I write about all that happened.

But the Lord spoke in His gentle way to my heart, "You see, Carol, your hope was not to be put in horses or things to save you, but your hope for all things is alive with me. I Am the ONE who saves."

That message from the Lord and the second chance at life He gave me propelled me to go on and do the work that He would eventually call me to do. God spared my life that night when I should have been killed. And He would be the One to direct me to what would come next.

I had spent most of my life up until that season dreaming and thinking of ways to achieve MY plan. It was God's plan for me to go through all the ups and downs, the good and the bad, so that I could see and understand His plan for me. He is the God of second chances.

> "For I know the plans I have for you," says the Lord. "They are plans for good and not for disaster, to give you a future and a hope" (Jeremiah 29:11 NLT).

As for the Amish boy and his sisters, we visited them and became friends with their parents. My husband offered to drive them places, help them, and show love to their family. We experienced an Amish wedding, which was wonderful and unique. We even had them do some work for us at our home. We eventually purchased a new van because the old one was totaled. God, in His ultimate glory, kept us alive. I realize now God had a plan for my life and for my husband's. Today, I can do God's work in the ministry of Women World Leaders and write stories He has given me for His glory.

When people read these stories, my prayer is that they will know that the Lord is good. He is the Lord over your life if you allow Him entry; He has a plan for your life. He will direct your path as you ask Him to come into your heart, trust Him as your Lord and Savior, and look to Him for guidance.

With all that has happened during my lifetime, I have realized whenever I now see the horse with wings, it is the "Angel Horse." The horse God let me see His protection through. He allowed me to see His hand intervene. I saw

HIS plan for my life.

I have been thinking about drawing this Angel Horse to show others. God sends angels in different forms to help us see things and realize things that happen in our lives. We can fully understand that He is the creator of life and can give life and take life.

All of creation belongs to God, and He is always in our midst.

Hope in Unfailing Love

By Kimberly Ann Hobbs

Yet I still dare to hope when I remember this: The faithful love of the Lord never ends! His mercies never cease. Great is his faithfulness; his mercies begin afresh each morning (Lamentations 3:21-23 NLT).

God's love is constant. He is consistent with His love and steadfast expression to us. Even though we mess up, carry sin in our lives, and sometimes even walk away from God, His great love, which is unconditional, draws us even closer, pulling us back to Him.

Have you ever been wounded by receiving love that is based on conditions? We are human, and many times, we cannot meet the expectations that are placed on us. But God's love is not based on us meeting conditions, especially earthly ones that are constantly changing according to various circumstances. God loves us for who we are and how He created us, despite our shortcomings. His love is stable and never changes.

The Bible is a place where we can go to be reminded and reaffirmed that God's love is unfailing. There is no way we can ever compare God's love to that of any person on this planet who has loved or claimed to love us. God's love never gives up. It is both far-reaching and powerfully present in your life. He loved us so much that even though we were stuck in our sins, He gave us a precious gift. He showed His love to us that while we were yet sinners, He sent His son, Jesus, to die for us.

For God so loved the world that he gave his one and only Son, that whoever believes in him shall not perish but have eternal life (John 3:16 NIV).

The God who created you has tremendous sacrificial love beyond your understanding, proven by the fact that He allows you to confess and believe in His Son and, because you do, gives you an eternal home with Him. Your love for Him will continue throughout eternity because of how He loves you. The magnitude of it all is sometimes beyond our comprehension—that He would demonstrate such love by sending His Son from heaven to come to earth and die for YOU!

The love of Jesus Christ is not based on any conditions. You cannot earn your way into His heart. His love is an active presence, freely available for you to experience. His love presses on despite how you behave or the choices you make. God's love for you will endure forever.

Give thanks to the God of heaven. His faithful love endures forever (Psalm 136:26 NLT).

We are accustomed to seeing love fade away in relationships around us because, here on earth, we often see with our eyes, and that kind of love can dissipate quickly. But our Father, who is in heaven, has a love for us that remains intact through every circumstance. God loves us when life gets tough, strengthening us when we are weak. He guides us with His love when we get wobbly and lose our sense of direction. He never abandons us, even when others who are supposed to love us show a lack of care. God's love is always present in abundance, even in our darkest moments and even when we ask, "Where is God?" He does not run from your questions and will never leave you or forsake you.

"For my thoughts are not your thoughts, neither are your ways my ways," declares the Lord. "As the heavens are higher than the earth, so are my ways higher than your ways and my thoughts than your thoughts" (Isaiah 55:8-9 NIV).

"I promise that I will never leave you helpless or abandon you as orphans—I will come back to you!" (John 14:18 TPT).

God will never leave you without love. His words are true, and His promises within the Bible are to be trusted.

Your unfailing love, O LORD, Is as vast as the heavens; your faithfulness reaches beyond the clouds. Your righteousness is like the mighty mountains, your justice like the ocean depths. You care for people and animals alike, O LORD. How precious is Your unfailing love, O God! (Psalm 36:5-7 NLT).

. . . .

Kelly Williams Hale

Kelly Williams Hale is the Creative Director for Be Brave Design. She helps heart-centered entrepreneurs increase their visibility with stunning visual branding that captures and conveys their unique message.

As a coach and mentor, Kelly also teaches women how to cultivate confidence and find purpose beyond their pain. She's passionate about helping Christian women claim their calling and discover the destiny God has for them.

Kelly is also a sought-after speaker inspiring women to live their best lives. Her talks cover a wide range of topics, including personal growth, relationships, and leadership. Kelly is known for her ability to connect with audiences on a deep and meaningful level and for creating a safe and supportive space for women to share their stories and experiences.

She is happily married (third time's a charm!), a mom of three—all born about a decade apart— delivering her youngest when she was 44 years old. Kelly is living proof that past mistakes don't define future success.

Kelly loves sushi, music, and Taco Tuesdays. She can often be found singing and dancing to anything by the band *For King & Country*.

You're invited to join her free Facebook community: *Sisters Who Shine*.

Finding Freedom in Failure

By Kelly Williams Hale

And the God of all grace, who called you to his eternal glory in Christ, after you have suffered a little while, will himself restore you and make you strong, firm and steadfast (1 Peter 5:10 NIV).

The day began like most Saturdays leading up to hunting season. My husband and I, along with our 18-month-old son, took a leisurely drive through the Georgia woods. As I began to engage my husband in conversation, sharing my thoughts and feelings, he kept shutting me down. He was a master at deflecting and turning how I felt into an attack on him. He often talked down to me and was, in fact, quite dismissive.

I don't recall what I wanted to talk about, but to this day, I can *physically* feel the tightening in my chest and the sensation of suffocating—like my voice was literally being smothered.

Have you ever experienced a moment in your life that changed everything?

I can honestly say I tried to make my marriage work. I was raised in the church and taught that God disapproved of divorce. Yet, ironically, this was my second marriage! And so, I didn't want to get *another* divorce just because we "didn't get along." But that Saturday, at that moment, I knew— deep down in my soul—that something had to change. I wasn't sure what yet, but feeling so helpless, hopeless, and suffocated wasn't right. It wasn't healthy. And it wasn't how I wanted to live. So, I sought counseling.

During our first few sessions, my therapist asked about my childhood. I am the oldest of four kids—the only girl. My dad was a Vietnam vet, drafted at age 19 to serve in the Marines as a combat soldier. He never talked about Vietnam. My dad went to heaven in December 2021; I miss him like crazy. I'm only now understanding the life-long effects of his time in the war and am heartsick imagining what he witnessed. I realize more clearly now why he drank. You see, my dad was an alcoholic. He wasn't a "mean drunk." He was a fun dad when he was drinking, but his short fuse was often lit the next day when he was hungover and had to deal with four young kids and a wife who craved his attention.

My mom did the best she could. She loved my dad dearly, and us, too, of course. But growing up in a home with an absent—at best—daddy and a mom who was trying to survive, I learned my own survival skills. I did what I could to keep the peace and make everyone happy. I was my mom's helper and took that responsibility seriously. I may or may not have been a bit bossy! God began developing my leadership skills back then!

Counseling helped me understand that the survival skills I developed served me well as a child and helped keep me safe. And though they followed me into adulthood, they weren't required anymore.

My coping mechanisms included the need to make everyone happy. As an adult, I found it very difficult to say no. I was a classic people-pleaser. I believed people wouldn't like me if I said no to them. Deep down, I never felt like I was enough. As a teenager, I spent way too much time comparing myself to other girls and coming up woefully short. My insecurities manifested as worry, fear, shame, and unacceptance.

I had no idea who I was.

My counselor helped me understand that I needed boundaries in my relationship. Boundaries? What are those? At 32 years old, I was just becoming aware that I had choices about what I was comfortable with. Wait a minute... do you mean I can actually say no?! For so many years, I felt obligated to meet everyone else's expectations and desires. To move forward in my marriage, I needed boundaries that let my husband know how I wished to be treated.

Let's just say this "new me" was not well received. When a person with narcissistic tendencies is threatened with a change in the status quo, their insecurities are activated, and, for me, it was time to exit the relationship. I share this part of my story because it's where my healing journey began, where I discovered hope.

But those who wait on the LORD
Shall renew their strength;
They shall mount up with wings like eagles,
They shall run and not be weary,
They shall walk and not faint.
(Isaiah 40:31 NKJV)

I became a twice-divorced 33-year-old with two children from two baby daddies. I was a total statistic, but I was free. I literally went from debilitated to exhilarated. There was a renewed hope in my spirit, but it was certainly not smooth sailing afterward. On the contrary, there would be many storms and rough seas. I was a single mom again.

I soon reunited with my first true love—the one who never left me and had been by my side when, as a kid, I would lie awake listening to my mom and dad fighting. The one who said He'd never forsake me (Hebrews 13:5).

Jesus.

I mentioned earlier that I had been raised in the church. Despite this, I didn't really understand the enormity of God's love. What I heard during Sunday sermons was that I would end up in hell if I didn't get baptized. I obediently sang all the classic hymns acapella (without any instrumental music) and believed Jesus died on the cross to forgive my sins—I didn't want to go to hell when I died. I'd like a one-way ticket to heaven, please. So, I got baptized at 11. I knew what was right and wrong, and I was one to follow the rules.

Looking back now, I see my faith was based more on religion than a relationship. In my mind, I had to be a good girl for God to love me. My view of God was shaped by what I was taught and, honestly, how I received it. I know there were well-meaning people in my church, but for a kid growing up in a dysfunctional household, my beliefs about God's love were formed by how I witnessed my world and my day-to-day existence, and it didn't feel safe.

As Christians, we are called to become more like Christ. When we accept Jesus as our Lord and Savior, we are given the "mind of Christ" (1 Corinthians 2:16), yet we still live in a fallen world. We want to follow Jesus, but we have habits and patterns of thinking that can challenge (at best) our pursuit of Him. 2 Corinthians 10:5 says, *We destroy arguments and every lofty opinion raised against the knowledge of God, and take every thought captive to obey Christ* (ESV). We are instructed to take these thoughts prisoner, lock them up, and throw away the key!

After my divorce, I truly began to seek God. I always had a level of faith that I kept on the back burner, meaning when things got hard, the proverbial "rock bottom," I would cry out to the Lord. I always prayed. But when I began to read God's Word, the truth of who God *really* is—and who He says I am—started to seep into my brokenness. I am loved, just as I am. The Bible says we are fearfully and wonderfully made (Psalm 139:14). I began to realize that I had been making choices my whole life in reaction to the behaviors of others. Talk about hope coming alive! You mean that I get to decide what I want?

I began to cry out to the Lord. I couldn't do this on my own anymore. Isn't that what we do? We put God in a little box and pull Him out only when life gets difficult. But thankfully, He meets us right where we are. I'm reminded of the prodigal son we read about in Luke, chapter 15—the son who demanded his inheritance, left his family, and basically went along his merry way. He spent years in the world doing what he wanted, selfishly satisfying his desires, and living the good life. Until the good life wasn't so good anymore.

> *A few days later this younger son packed all his belongings and moved to a distant land, and there he wasted all his money in wild living. About the time his money ran out, a great famine swept over the land, and he began to starve (Luke 15:13-14 NLT).*

When this young man finally came to his senses, he decided to go home.

> *So he returned home to his father. And while he was still a long way off, his father saw him coming. Filled with love and compassion, HE RAN TO HIS SON, EMBRACED HIM, AND KISSED HIM* (Luke 15:20 NLT, emphasis added).

Like the prodigal son's father, God welcomed me with open arms. He was patiently waiting.

As I dug into God's Word, the scriptures spoke to me in a fresh new way, and I truly started to believe what He said: I am chosen. I am enough. I am victorious. I am loved.

That was over 20 years ago. I came to know Jehovah-Rapha, God the Healer. Jesus healed that part of me that felt unworthy. He provided the safety I craved and tried so diligently to control by taking care of everyone else. I had finally surrendered to God's plan for me.

About two years after my second divorce, I wanted to move my little family closer to where I was working as I was commuting almost an hour each way. So, I put my house up for sale. When two buyers were interested but didn't have the resources, I wanted to sell so badly that my first inclination was: *how can I make this happen?*

I had equity in my home that I wanted to use for a down payment, and once I recognized that I was ultimately *forcing* something to happen and rent-to-own or owner-financing was not an option, I had to trust God.

> Trust in the LORD with all your heart and lean not on your own understanding; in all your ways submit to him, and he will make your paths straight (Proverbs 3:5-6 NIV).

And so I began praying, simply trusting God each day. That was revolutionary for me. As someone who spent so much time worrying about tomorrow, letting go of how I thought things should look tested my faith. Each day, I released my expectations and believed that a buyer would show up with cash in hand! In the meantime, I started looking at homes. I created a list of everything I wanted in my new home: a pool, a fireplace, an office, and bedrooms for my daughter and my little boy. I also wanted a driveway that would accommodate many vehicles for when my family and friends came to visit. My prayers were very specific!

Little did I know that God was preparing a home for me that would eventually appear. It took five months. And then I got the call. A fellow was interested in my house, but he needed to sell his first. I asked him where he lived, and when he told me where it was, I said I'd love to come to see it.

To make a long story short, he purchased my home, and I bought his. Six months after I released control of how I thought the sale of my house would look, I moved into my new home consisting of three bedrooms, two baths, a converted garage (my office), a pool, fireplace, super large screened-in back porch and a driveway that fit six cars!

Incredible things happen when we choose to trust God. For me, that looked like letting go of my belief that "If it's meant to be, it's up to me." As I learned how to surrender and truly began to believe His Word, the hope I felt in my spirit continued to grow. Romans 12:2 says, *Don't copy the behavior and customs of this world, but let God transform you into a new person by changing the way you think. Then you will learn to know God's will for you, which is good and pleasing and perfect* (NLT).

The renewing of our minds is not a one-and-done deal. It's a daily practice of transformation. God will use our mishaps, mistakes, and even our momentum to work all things out for our good, according to His purposes (Romans 8:28). He will cultivate confidence in us as we trust Him and walk out our faith. When we fully surrender and confess, *not my will, Lord, but Yours.*

Since that fateful Saturday in the woods, God has proven so faithful. I have come to know—and *truly love*—myself, flaws and all.

I spent so many years feeling unworthy. Not good enough. Wondering how God could use me when I was such a mess. I was haunted by not only my two divorces but also the many mistakes I made as a young woman—particularly the choices I made as a single mom when it was just my daughter and me. I had no idea how to care for myself, much less for me and my baby girl. That's a whole other story!

The reality is we all screw up. But we *can* turn our life around. The first step is to acknowledge that we are nothing without Jesus. His sacrifice cleansed us from all our sin (2 Corinthians 5:21). He was patiently waiting—arms open wide—for me to come running to Him. Secondly, we must understand the role we play in our lives and take 100% ownership of our choices. I humbly asked God to forgive me, and over time, I began to forgive myself. And finally, we must embrace who God says we are: His precious daughters. I had another failed marriage under my belt, but I was still God's girl. And I always will be.

Failing is a gift. Our failures teach us that we need Jesus. The Holy Spirit is our comforter and guide while we're on this side of heaven. He will illuminate what's not working in our lives and empower us with the wisdom to make better choices. Praise God!

One of the scriptures God led me to after my divorce was Jeremiah 29:11 (NIV). *"For I know the plans I have for you," declares the Lord, "plans to prosper you and not to harm you, plans to give you hope and a future."*

What a blessing to know that God has plans for us! He's given each of us unique gifts and talents meant to glorify Him and bless others. I believe He allows us to experience challenges so that when we find ourselves on the other side, we can help someone through a lens of compassion and love. Hope comes alive when we recognize that we were created on purpose for a purpose.

Because of my previous doubts and insecurities, I didn't fully understand God had a purpose for my life. Most of my life was spent wanting to make everyone else feel comfortable. The enemy used fear to keep me from fully accepting that I am fearfully and wonderfully made (Psalm 139:14). God has a path of destiny for each of us that includes all that we deem weird, quirky, or just plain wrong when we look at ourselves through a worldly lens. But when we see ourselves through God's kingdom eyes, we know we are called to be bold and brave.

Assessing our feelings and learning not to react to them is a skill we can cultivate. Daily renewing our minds is a choice. We get to decide. Will we default to our human response, or will we trust? God tells us to trust and obey. He gave us the Holy Spirit to guide and instruct us. Obedience is simply belief.

Ask yourself, *Do I believe what God says? Do I believe I am who God says I am?* When we choose to believe God, we get access to everything He has already supernaturally provided. He has given us all that we need to fulfill His plan for our life here on earth: the provision, the abundance, the hope, and our future.

The pain of my past became the fuel for my purpose. My passion is to guide women on their journey, lead them to a healing place of hope, and help them discover how their mess can become a message for others. Through my own experience, I found that I am a beautiful daughter of the King, and God has a plan for my life despite my own sin. I learned that, through Jesus, I am forgiven and free. Once I became aware of what was missing in my life, I found a peace that surpasses all understanding.

> *Rejoice in the Lord always; again I will say, rejoice. Let your reasonableness be known to everyone. The Lord is at hand; do not be anxious about anything, but in everything by prayer and supplication with thanksgiving let your requests be made known to God. And the peace of God, which surpasses all understanding, will guard your hearts and your minds in Christ Jesus* (Philippians 4:4-7 ESV).

The truth is we were created in the image of the Creator, which means we can co-create with Jesus and design a magnificent life here on earth, not just bide our time until we get to heaven.

God has done incredible things in my life. After a couple of years of living in my new house, I met a man (at 40) who was a direct answer to prayer and married (again!) a year later. We welcomed our son, Austin, when I was 44! God is so good.

My marriage is strong. My children are healthy. I'm an author, a speaker, and a life coach. God has blessed me with the gift of encouragement, and I give Him all the glory as I help other women understand who they are in Christ.

We've all made decisions we are not proud of. And most likely, we have witnesses or evidence of those choices. (Can I just say I'm so glad we didn't have social media when I was in my 20s!) The world may judge us for what we've done in the past, but we are not defined by our mistakes. We are defined by who God says we are.

God has a plan for your life. A good plan. As you transform and intentionally seek God's will for your life, you will see miracles occur. When you renew your mind daily and surrender, God will bless you.

> Now to him who is able to do immeasurably more than all we ask or imagine, according to his power that is at work within us (Ephesians 3:20 NIV).

My faith walk has been filled with potholes, unexpected exits, twists and turns, detours, and the occasional re-routing (well, maybe more than occasional!). My journey has also been filled with joy, love, and grace.

> But he said to me, "My grace is sufficient for you, for my power is made perfect in weakness." Therefore I will boast all the more gladly about my weaknesses, so that Christ's power may rest on me (2 Corinthians 12:9 NIV).

I learned some of the most powerful lessons when I was the weakest. We find Jesus in the fire. He's with us; it's through Him that we receive life. Our life is God's gift to us. What we do with our life is our gift back to Him.

I believe in you.

Hope in Achieving Our Goals for God

By Connie A. VanHorn

In today's world, it's easy to get distracted, lose sight of our purpose, and deviate from achieving our goals and doing God's work. We can get caught up in life's busyness and hit hard with illness, pain, confusion, and overwhelming circumstances that easily keep us from pursuing our goals for God. However, during those hard times, God calls us to have hope and keep going toward our goals.

I recently went through the unimaginable, one of the darkest periods in my life. It would have been easy to abandon God's work and succumb to the circumstances around me. But my commitment to God's work became my hope and kept me spiritually alive. Each day, as I worked toward achieving my goals, I found joy and purpose. Despite the chaos and storm raging around me, I remained focused and determined to keep going.

Achieving our goals for God is an important part of our Christian walk. God wants us to achieve our goals! This takes faith, perseverance, and dedication. It requires a solid belief in God's plan for our lives and a relentless pursuit of His purpose. As we strive toward our spiritual goals, it is so important to anchor ourselves in God's Word. No matter what kind of work God has called you to do, I can bet it keeps you in His Word and His presence. This is powerful—especially when we are going through hard times.

I press on toward the goal to win the prize for which God has called me heavenward in Christ Jesus (Philippians 3:14 NIV).

There are several ways that we can achieve our goals for God!

1. Seek God's Guidance: Start by seeking God's guidance through prayer and meditation. Allow His wisdom to lead you as you pursue your goals.

2. Align Your Goals with God's Will: Make sure your goals are in alignment with God's will and purpose for your life. Seek to glorify Him in all that you do.

3. Stay Focused on Eternal Things: Keep your focus on eternal rewards rather than temporary gains. Remember that your ultimate goal is to serve and honor God.

4. Trust in God's Timing: Trust that God's timing is perfect. Be patient and persistent in pursuing your goals, knowing He will fulfill His promises in His own time.

5. Lean on God's Strength: Rely on God's strength and power to overcome difficult circumstances and struggles along the way. Lean on Him for courage and perseverance.

6. Surround Yourself with a Supportive Community: A supportive community of other believers will encourage and lift you in your journey to achieve your goals.

7. Embrace Growth and Learning: Embrace opportunities for growth and learning as you work toward your goals. Allow God to mold and shape you through the process.

8. Celebrate Small Victories: Celebrate the small victories along the way as you progress toward your goals. Acknowledge God's faithfulness in every step of the journey.

9. Stay Committed and Consistent: Stay committed to taking consistent action toward your goals. Trust that God will honor your efforts and dedication.

10. Rest in God's Peace: Find rest and peace in God's presence as you work toward your goals. Trust Him and know He is with you every step of the way. Never lose hope.

God's plans for us are good and filled with hope and a promising future. He wants us to trust in His guidance as we pursue our goals. No matter what is happening around us, God gives us the power to stay focused and hopeful in our pursuit of His purpose for our lives. By anchoring ourselves in faith and seeking His guidance through prayer and scripture, we can keep going, trusting we can overcome anything and fulfill the goals God has set before us. Keep going!

> *"For I know the plans I have for you," declares the Lord, "plans to prosper you and not to harm you, plans to give you hope and a future"* (Jeremiah 29:11 NIV).

. . . .

Arlene Salas

Arlene Salas is an author in two best-selling books: *Victories: Claiming Freedom in Christ* and *Surrendered: Yielded with Purpose.* She is also a breast cancer survivor, a Christ-follower who loves Him with her whole heart, and a greeter at her church. Arlene is a devoted wife to her high school sweetheart Angel, whom she has known for over 39 years. They have two amazing children, Valerie and Fabian, and two precious granddaughters.

Arlene has worked in the medical field for over 28 years, currently in Account Receivables for a hospital. She is also a District Leader for her own financial services business. She loves helping people, which fits with the God-given purpose He has placed in her heart—serving others.

Arlene was born and raised in New Jersey and is Puerto Rican by blood. She later moved to South Florida and still resides there. She loves spending time with her family and beautiful granddaughters and reading the Bible and other books that inspire her to improve herself.

Arlene is a leader in Women World Leaders ministry, which was the catalyst for her opening her own purpose.

Hope in the Darkest of Times

By Arlene Salas

As On a typical fall day in September 2022, I found myself on a path I hadn't expected. My routine mammogram returned with unexpected news— Ductal Carcinoma In Situ (DCIS), stage zero. In lay terms, I was in the earliest stage of breast cancer. The disease hadn't invaded the surrounding tissue and was highly treatable, yet that reality didn't make the news easier to swallow.

Hearing the words "Ductal Carcinoma In Situ" shattered my world. I was sitting at my desk at work when I got the call and immediately rushed out, crying uncontrollably. I learned I needed to see an oncologist and a surgeon to determine the next steps. Everything happened so fast that I didn't have time to digest one appointment before I had to go to the next.

The world as I knew it seemed to topple. I recall the raw pain, disbelief, and shock interspersed with uncontrollable tears. I took a few days off work to let the new and temporary reality sink in and to figure out my next steps. The doctor's proposed lumpectomy and radiation plan didn't resonate with me. Trusting my intuition, I opted for a bilateral mastectomy. The thought of extensive surgery was overwhelming, but the peace of mind it promised was a beacon of hope. Cancer. A word I never thought I'd have to hear or worry about, a term that carries so many punches to the gut, had already affected nearly every aspect of my life.

My husband was diagnosed with a tumor in his kidney back in 2017. Doctors didn't know if it was cancerous or benign, but it had to come out no matter what. Once removed, we found it harmless, but the surgery and the trauma to his body were too much. He had developed arthritis over the years, and this added pain and discomfort rendered him unable to work full-time or to total capacity. He was declared disabled in 2019.

I had become the backbone of our family, and I did it with pride. I knew this is what others would do for someone they love. The last 8-9 years hadn't been easy, but we made it. Still, I immediately panicked hearing about my own recovery and the financial responsibility of this new illness. I felt strong handling everything and confident in my decision to have a double mastectomy, but thinking about the expenses brought me anxiety.

I knew I couldn't afford to take very much time off from work. We were already living on a tight budget. How could we financially survive this? At the time, we were still recovering from my husband's medical debt.

I was supposed to be the one helping to support our family, and now I was the one in need of support.

This surgery to remove my breasts took so much away from me. It took me a very long time to look at my new body. In the blink of an eye, I had lost an essential element that makes many of us feel like a woman—a significant part of me. I was carrying this heavy physical loss and also dealing with all of the financial weight. I was plagued by anxiety daily, wondering how we were going to make it through each day. But God.

God was always there. He never left us, and He found a way to provide every step of the way.

The October 2022 surgery was a whirlwind of pain and fear, but it began my healing. The physical pain was like being hit by a truck, leaving me weak and vulnerable. But amid the pain, the glimmers of grace became evident. My family and friends rallied around me. In the coming weeks, my acquaintances organized meals, offered practical help, and sent encouraging messages, flowers, gifts, and fruit baskets. This outpouring of love reinforced my belief in human kindness and community spirit.

My husband's support has been a cornerstone throughout this journey. He has stood by my side during my health struggles in the same way I had been there for him during his medical issues. This shared experience deepened our relationship, teaching us the profound meaning of vows and unconditional love.

> *Two are better than one because they have a good return for their labor: If either of them falls, one can help the other up. But pity anyone who falls and has no one to help them up* (Ecclesiastes 4:9-10 NIV).

Amid my health journey, I discovered the incredible power of sisterhood within Women World Leaders Ministry. These women stood by my side, not only in spirit but in tangible acts of love. Their prayers were a source of strength, and their words of encouragement like a soothing balm to my soul. I was overwhelmed by their gestures of kindness—the homemade meals that appeared on my doorstep, the fragrant bouquets that brightened my room, and the thoughtful gifts that served as constant reminders of their support. I am immeasurably blessed and profoundly grateful for this ministry that embodies the true essence of Christian love and community.

Unexpectedly, I had to undergo a series of additional surgeries in the subsequent months. Each time, I again was taken back into the familiar cycle of pain, healing, and recovery. It felt like a continuous battle, but every small victory nudged me toward the end of the tunnel.

He gives strength to the weary and increases the power of the weak (Isaiah 40:29 NIV).

While I believed my reconstructive surgery in March 2023 marked the end of my medical procedures, life had other plans. In April 2023, I discovered an open wound, a grim discovery that spiraled my mind into panic. It was late on a Friday evening when I found it. I was fortunate that my doctor was on call. But, the nurses at the office confirmed my worst fears the following day. The implant had to be removed and replaced. I needed another surgery.

Then, a series of misfortunes unfolded. The scheduled surgery was postponed from Tuesday to Thursday due to delayed authorization. And, as if to mirror my health issues, our home's water heater broke just before my surgery, leaving us without hot water for a few days. Although the events were discouraging, I held onto my joy and hope, standing firm in the faith that carried me through.

There came a moment when I needed to make a crucial decision. I went to see a different plastic surgeon who gave me hope again. After enduring multiple surgeries, I had reached a point where I didn't know what I wanted anymore. Should I keep the breast implants or have them removed? I questioned whether it would be more beneficial to have something artificial in me that would, perhaps, allow me to live as a "normal" woman or if it would be better to embrace my natural self.

The uncertainty was daunting, and I was just grateful to be healthy and alive. My new surgeon, recommended by my oncologist, had over 35 years of experience as a chief surgeon. His care provided me with a glimmer of optimism and hope. He didn't rush me and took the time to listen and understand my concerns.

While nothing in life is guaranteed, I felt a newfound confidence that this third try to rebuild what had been taken from me by cancer could indeed be a charm. The surgery date was scheduled for January 22, 2024.

The hospital's corridors echoed with a mix of anticipation and apprehension as I made my way to the surgery ward. Surrounded by the medical team's professionalism and my loved ones' unwavering support, a sense of calm enveloped me. Little did I know the day would unfold into a defining moment of self-discovery.

In the quiet moments before the surgery, prayers echoed in my mind, a chorus of hope intertwined with the scent of antiseptic. As the moment approached, a surge of courage prompted me to reconsider the path ahead. Tearfully, I made the agonizing decision to forgo the implants.

The journey back home was marked by a tumult of emotions, yet a profound peace accompanied my heart. Despite the pain, I found solace in the conviction that I made the right choice. The new doctor, undoubtedly skilled, understood the gravity of my decision,

This unexpected turn became more than a medical episode; it morphed into a poignant chapter of resilience and self-discovery, In the face of adversity, I discovered an unyielding strength that could serve as a guiding light for others. The intricate dance of faith and uncertainty unfolded, revealing a purpose beyond my own struggle.

Now, with the echoes of prayers still resonating, I embraced this unforeseen path as an opportunity to share my testimony. A narrative of triumph over personal tribulations, a testament to the unwavering support of those around me, and a call to extend a helping hand to others navigating their own pits of despair, my story, a mosaic of pain and perseverance, became a vessel to pull others out of their own abyss.

Amid these decisions, I drew strength from an unexpected source. A family member who is near my age and with whom I am close had already walked this challenging path. She had been diagnosed with the same type of cancer in November 2021, preceding my diagnosis. Her wisdom and experience were invaluable to me. We shared advice and supported each other through every twist and turn of our respective journeys.

Our shared journey allowed us to rely on each other for support. We exchanged advice and found solace in the fact that we weren't alone in this battle. Together, we discovered the power of resilience, faith, and the importance of cherishing every moment of life.

Yet, beyond our own experiences, I became acutely aware of the broader impact of breast cancer within my community. Unfortunately, I learned of other family friends who had also received breast cancer diagnoses after my own. They had endured the grueling path of chemotherapy and radiation, opting not for a mastectomy. But one childhood friend, whom I've known since I was six years old, also opted for a mastectomy.

Another family member was diagnosed just three months after I was. Thankfully, she didn't require chemotherapy but opted for a lumpectomy and radiation. It felt like a series of interconnected stories, each unique yet bound by the common thread of breast cancer.

Tragically, it seemed more and more women I knew were facing this daunting diagnosis. A good friend of my mom passed away in August 2023, merely two weeks after being diagnosed with cancer. Her swift departure served as a stark reminder of the urgency and unpredictability that cancer can bring into our lives.

Amid these challenges, a particular Bible verse brought me comfort and strength. *Trust in the Lord with all your heart and lean not on your understanding; In all your ways submit to him, and he will make your paths straight* (Proverbs 3:5-6 NIV).

I healed from this unexpected surgery, hoping it was the final one. But May 2023 brought the chilling familiarity of another open wound—this one even more extensive. My doctor was not on call when I made the discovery, so I covered the open wound as advised and managed to maintain my calm.

My husband, witnessing my predicament, was filled with panic. We ended up at the ER, and I underwent surgery the following day.

In the face of these repeated trials, I remained hopeful and steadfast. I began to understand that this was part of my story, a significant chapter in my life's book. These trials shaped me, honed my character, and helped me grow into the woman God intended me to be. Despite the challenges, I learned to embrace my situation. I found strength and resilience in my pain.

That is why, for Christ's sake, I delight in weaknesses, in insults, in hardships, in persecutions, in difficulties. For when I am weak, then I am strong (2 Corinthians 12:10 NIV). My ordeal became a testament to this scripture, manifesting God's power.

The journey through multiple surgeries and recoveries also taught me to be patient with my healing process. I understood the importance of giving my body time to heal. And I experienced God's provision firsthand. His love was apparent in the support of my loved ones, the expertise of the doctors, and the inner strength He gave me.

And we know that in all things God works for the good of those who love him, who have been called according to his purpose (Romans 8:28 NIV). My experience bore testament to this truth.

Amid my ordeal, I found an unexpected gift—the ability to live life more fully. Every day became precious, and every moment was a miracle. I began to appreciate the small joys of life, the mundane moments, and the everyday blessings. I learned to live in the moment, valuing the present and letting go of unnecessary worries.

Therefore, do not worry about tomorrow; tomorrow will worry about itself. Each day has enough trouble of its own (Matthew 6:34 NIV).

As I have recovered and reflected on my journey, I have felt a growing urge to give back. I offered to support and pray with others going through similar struggles, and I realized sharing my story could inspire others, giving them hope and encouragement.

> For we are God's handiwork, created in Christ Jesus to do good works, which God prepared in advance for us to do (Ephesians 2:10 NIV).

As painful and challenging as my journey with cancer has been, it has helped deepen my faith. The physical pain, emotional distress, and mental agony have all brought me even closer to God. I've seen His hand in my life more clearly and felt His presence more deeply. He has become my refuge, my strength, and my hope. No matter what I went through, I was joyful—all the glory to God.

My journey led to a profound transformation in my spiritual life. I've found solace in prayer, meditation, and worship. I am leaning on my faith now more than ever. My relationship with God has evolved into a deeper, more intimate connection as I've wrestled with questions and sought understanding.

> But those who hope in the Lord will renew their strength. They will soar on wings like eagles; they will run and not grow weary, they will walk and not be faint (Isaiah 40:31 NIV).

My experience offers essential lessons for others, including emphasizing the importance of regular medical check-ups, trusting one's intuition, and finding strength in faith and community. My story is a powerful reminder that light, love, and power can emerge even in the darkest times.

Consider it pure joy, my brothers and sisters, whenever you face trials of many kinds because you know that testing your faith produces perseverance (James 1:2-3 NIV). My story is a testament to human resilience, faith, love, and community. My journey, filled with unexpected twists and turns, brought me to a place of deeper understanding and purpose. It's a story that hasn't just ended with healing but has evolved into a life mission, an inspiration for others, and a renewed appreciation for every day.

> *And we know that in all things God works for the good of those who love him, who have been called according to his purpose* (Romans 8:28 NIV).

If you are going through a similar journey, remember you are not alone. God is with you. He is holding your hand, strengthening your spirit, and guiding you through the storm. No matter how bleak the circumstances or insurmountable the challenge is...

Do not lose hope.

> *God is our refuge and strength, an ever-present help in trouble* (Psalm 46:1 NIV).

Finally, remember Romans 15:13, *May the God of hope fill you with all joy and peace as you trust in him, so that you may overflow with hope by the power of the Holy Spirit* (NIV).

In your pain, find hope.

In your fear, find faith.

In your journey, find His purpose.

Hope in the Waiting

By Connie A. VanHorn

I often share with others that one of the first noticeable changes I observed in myself after I got saved was an increase in my ability to cultivate patience. Over time, I transformed into a very patient individual, but this growth was a gradual process.

I vividly recall a moment after I was saved when I was in the pastor's office praying about a particular concern. I was eager for change and hoped to see immediate results. However, the pastor mentioned that it could take at least two years for that specific prayer to be answered. Initially, I was taken aback and thought, *Are you kidding me?* I believed that once you accepted Christ, God showered you with blessings and promptly fulfilled your requests. However, I learned that God's blessings come in His own timing, which may not always align with our expectations. This waiting period taught me the valuable skill of patience, which I have since applied to various aspects of my life. As a mother, my children often commend me for being the most patient person they know.

When we have a relationship with God, He instills in us a spirit of peace, joy, and calmness, even as we patiently await the answers to our prayers. During my early journey with Christ, I heard a sermon titled, "Be Still and Quiet Your Noisy Soul," a message that has stayed with me. Whenever I feel anxious or worried, I remind myself to quiet my noisy soul.

I can agree that one of the most challenging yet rewarding lessons we learn is the art of waiting. The thought of "Hope in the Waiting" is a reminder that God's timing is perfect, and He calls us to be still and trust in Him. Scripture tells us in Psalm 27:14 (NIV), *Wait for the Lord; be strong and take heart and wait for the Lord.* God wants us to be strong and have courage. Waiting is not easy; waiting takes having daring faith in God's plan—a plan we can't always see.

I remember a time of impatience when I gave my heart to Jesus in August 2014. I expected instant fulfillment of my desires, believing my newfound faith would usher in immediate blessings. However, God had other plans. Over the years, He taught me the invaluable lesson of patience and the importance of growth in the waiting. Every day in this season of waiting for my miracle, I seek God's guidance and ask Him to reveal the lessons He wants me to learn. In the waiting, God shapes us, molds us, and prepares us for the life and purpose He has in store. Just as a seed is nourished in the soil before becoming a beautiful flower, we must endure our waiting season before experiencing God's miracle for us.

In the waiting, our faith is tested, refined, and strengthened, preparing us to receive God's promises when the time is right. As you walk through your seasons of waiting, remember to BE STILL before God, trusting in His perfect timing and wisdom. Embrace the lessons as He grows your faith and character. Waiting can be a time of blessing filled with hope when we remember that God is faithful to fulfill His promises in His time.

> But those who trust in the Lord will find new strength. They will soar high on wings like eagles. They will run and not grow weary. They will walk and not faint (Isaiah 40:31 NLT).

I am currently in a period of waiting, anticipating a significant breakthrough in my life. At times, this waiting process can be hard, but I walk soundly, knowing that God will finish what He has started. He will fulfill every promise He has made in my life, and He will fulfill every promise He has made in YOUR life. I choose to have HOPE and trust in Him each day as I wait, knowing that He is aware of the desires of my heart and has a perfect plan for me. Let us join in prayer for a calm spirit and the ability to patiently wait on God, to find peace in knowing that no matter what we are facing, He is by our side.

Dear Heavenly Father,

Teach us the art of waiting patiently on You. Grant us the strength to trust in Your perfect timing and the wisdom to learn and grow in the waiting season. Help us find hope and encouragement in Your promises, knowing You are faithful to fulfill them. Help us to be still, to be patient, and to wait on You with bold faith.

In Jesus' name, Amen.

. . . .

Haley Walker

Haley Walker lives in Panama City Beach, Florida, with her husband and two toddler daughters. She has a Media Communications Bachelor's degree (emphasis on Graphic Design) from Asbury University. Haley worked the 2012 Olympics in London, England, before embarking on her career at the Navy Base in Panama City, FL, where she worked for the Department of Defense for over a decade. Her focus now is being a mom and wife.

She loves her church family and enjoys volunteering and finding ways to serve in the local and global church. She also loves community outreach—praying each conversation and encounter could be a seed planted displaying the love of Christ.

One of her favorite quotes is from St. Francis: "Preach the Gospel at all times; when necessary, use words."

In her free time, Haley enjoys her and her wonderful husband's newfound hobby of camping. She is a freelance photographer and also enjoys fitness, studying God's Word, and time with family and friends! In her lifetime of journaling, her dream has always been to write a book!

Email Haley at walker.haley@outlook.com or find her on Instagram and Facebook!

Pray Big

By Haley Walker

You'd give up your entire career? A six-figure salary and over a decade-worth of education and hard work?

Rewind ten years.

I just turned 19. I was about to travel 12 hours away from home to attend my dream college, Asbury University. I had an amazing college experience, some of the best years of my life. Friendships, experiences, and classes prepared me for my future career path.

On graduation day, I proudly walked across the stage and obtained the degree I had dreamed about since I was ten years old. After graduation, I was offered a permanent position where I had been interning—my dream job. It was a government position that was not open to the public or easily obtained (another God-orchestrated story!) The pay was higher than the average for my field and had great benefits. I knew this was what I wanted to do. At 22, I embarked on my career—encountering admirals, including the 4-Star Chief of Operations (one of the President's Joint Chiefs of Staff), preparing for events, and traveling to D.C. I worked many twelve-hour days, but I loved the fast pace.

Two years later, I met the man who would become my husband. We dated for six months and then were engaged for six months. Four years later, my husband and I couldn't be more ecstatic to have our first baby. I felt so blessed by God's unsurmountable blessings.

We did all the things to prepare for our baby girl: put together the nursery, took maternity photos, attended classes, and read all the books. But of course, as any parent will tell you, nothing can truly prepare you for birth or motherhood. One evening, my contractions began. The advice *many* people gave constantly replayed in my mind: "Labor at home as long as possible." So we did—until it was almost too late. When we arrived at the hospital, I was eight centimeters dilated. I was appalled to have the news broken that I had progressed too far for an epidural to be administered, as I originally intended. Thankfully, we got a room, and thirty minutes after arriving at the hospital, our precious baby entered the world. Despite the pain and no epidural, she came quickly and beautifully. There were no complications. We had a healthy seven-pound baby.

I loved being a mom from the very first moment. Even though sleep was almost nonexistent, it was the most indescribable feeling. The bond I had with my baby was unlike anything I had experienced. I felt such a connection and desire to care for my helpless child. I loved breastfeeding, snuggling, and the smells of my tiny human. The little fingers curling around my finger, the tiny toes kicking the air, and the adorable outfits. And then there were all the cute photos. I am a professional photographer, so you can imagine how many pictures I took.

Growing up, I always dreamed I'd get married to the man of my dreams and have children. I thanked God every day for this incredible gift of being a wife and mother.

However, my maternity leave clock was running out of sand. I was debilitatingly burdened by the fact that I'd be back in a cold corporate office 8-9 hours a day while my child was being cared for by a stranger. Her first steps. Saying her first words. My heart couldn't handle it. I was devastated every time I thought about it. I couldn't simply quit my job, as I was well-established. And we didn't know how we would survive financially. I had health benefits and many other job perks that were absolutely unmatchable. I felt completely stuck. I felt hopeless and out of options. What was there to do? Pray.

While on maternity leave at Christmastime, holding my precious three-month-old baby, during naptime I had a few spare moments to watch the Hallmark channel with the best feel-good, sappy, happy-ending Christmas movies ever. One day, I watched a show featuring an interview with the author of a newly released book, *Pray Big Things*. The author, Julia Jeffress Sadler, is the daughter of Pastor Robert James Jeffress Jr., Southern Baptist pastor, author, radio host, and televangelist. He is the senior pastor of a megachurch in Dallas, Texas, and a Fox News Contributor. Was it a coincidence that I caught that exact interview between my baby's cries, diaper changes, and feedings? Since I usually had one free hand, I hopped on Amazon and ordered the Kindle version of the book.

In the book, Julia talked about how she and her husband finally came to the point where they decided to stop limiting themselves by their human minds and started dreaming and *praying big!* Julia and her husband wrote down a list of their hearts' desires, many of which seemed impossible. Then they prayed.

This book spoke to me so *deeply*. Often we are troubled and burdened and debilitated but stuck in our near-sighted, restricted human vision. Why don't we go to God with the impossible? Why don't we pray to Him for bigger things than our minds can fathom?

The key verse that I clung to was, *Now to him who is able to do immeasurably more than all we ask or imagine* (Ephesians 3:20 NIV).

How do you measure the immeasurable? How do you fathom immeasurable? God can do the impossible.

> *Trust in the Lord with all your heart and lean not on YOUR OWN UNDERSTANDING* (Proverbs 3:5 NIV, emphasis added).

> *Jesus looked at them and said, "With man this is impossible, but with God all things are possible"* (Matthew 19:26 NIV).

Although I loved my job and career, I began to have a new dream. My deepest desire and prayer was: *God, how can I keep my job but also be with my baby?* Quitting wasn't an option.

Impossible.

In my own human strength, I worked every scenario on our Excel budget spreadsheet to see if I could somehow make the numbers work. I wondered if maybe I would feel differently when my baby girl turned one. Was that what I needed? Would my heart then be ready? What were my options?

I didn't know how we would manage if I didn't stay at my job. My husband had an *amazing* job and was in the early stages of a 4-year progression plan.

So... I *prayed big things.* That became my mantra of that year and the years to come.

It often feels like sometimes you pray the hardest when you're in a tough season, a difficult circumstance, or facing a hard decision or unknown situation. I know we should always pray fervently, but situations like mine tend to bring you to your knees.

Six months later.

Plot twist.

COVID-19.

Sorry folks...yes...due to my prayer, I single-handedly caused COVID, a nationwide pandemic. I really am sorry! I didn't know God would answer my prayer this way.

It was a normal work day— a beautiful spring day in March 2020. Mid-morning, my boss walked into my cubicle. "I'm going to need you to work from home. Telework. There is some unknown awful virus going on, and with you having a six-month-old baby, I want to send you home first."

Excuse me? Keep my full-time job and be with my baby! Did I hear this right?

Daycares closed. Everything shut down. My parents helped with my baby through the summer while I worked at their house.

This was my exact answered prayer! It was exhilarating to realize my *impossible* prayer was answered! My prayer was to keep my job while also being with my baby. Are you kidding me!?

My Florida sunshine summer days were better than ever. I didn't have to get up extra early to get ready for work and drive to the office. I teleworked in my childhood bedroom. I was so thankful for the telework opportunity to allow some reprieve as a working mom. Prior to COVID, telework was not an option in my particular position.

I could glance out the window at my parents walking around and playing with my almost one-year-old. I could hear her laughter from downstairs. I was able to take lunch breaks with my parents, nurse my baby when needed, and put her down for midday naps. I didn't have to pick her up from daycare and instead was able to take a refreshing afternoon walk. I then headed home to start dinner when my husband got home. None of this would have happened otherwise. *This was beyond my wildest dreams.*

Pray big.

A few months later, in the fall of 2020, businesses started opening back up. My baby girl turned one, and shortly after, she began daycare. Another answered prayer was that the daycare she attended through my church was a very great one.

I still worked full-time and yearned to be home with my baby. My heart and dream changed—I wanted to be home with my baby.

Excerpts from my prayer journal in January 2021:

"Our future: Lord, you have blessed us [me and my husband] so immensely with our jobs and careers! Please guide our path and make it clear if one day I am to be a stay-at-home mom (SAHM). If so, please provide financially with one income. If it's your will, please give a sign. MAKE A WAY!"

And in March: "I believe it's my heart's desire to be a SAHM one day! And I can't help but think it's the Lord's desire since He places desires in our hearts."

He will give you the desires of your heart (Psalm 37:4 NIV).

Financially, it still didn't add up on paper. So, with God's strength, we continued on, taking one day at a time. My husband, baby girl, and I got into a good routine and were surviving. I tried the meal-ordering service plans because I couldn't find the time or stamina to do all the meal planning, shopping, and cooking after work. My daughter seemed to enjoy and thrive in school despite our family being plagued with daycare sickness every other week.

Inspired by the *Pray Big Things* book, my husband and I wrote our New Year's list with fervent prayers for the upcoming year.

Journal entry, January 5, 2021: "We want to be pregnant again and have another precious child. Lord, please allow us to have another sweet baby this year! Our baby girl is such an incredible joy! Children are truly a gift from you!"

It didn't seem real when the two pink lines appeared only a couple of weeks later. Another girl! That fall, we had our beautiful, healthy baby. Again, the intense maternal bond between mother and child led me to tears at how thankful I was for these precious gifts from God.

Once home and settled, juggling motherhood with a busy almost 2-year-old toddler and an infant who seemed to nurse around the clock, I was plagued thinking about returning to work again. I dreaded the thought of shifting my focus from "Mommy" back to "Employee." My mind was clouded and debilitated by the mere thought.

Life was a whirlwind, and I felt like I couldn't stop to enjoy the moment. We were sleep-deprived with two children under two, daily getting up at 5 AM to have coffee (ALL THE COFFEE.) We tried our best to fit in devotions and quiet time and still get ourselves ready for the day. We had to feed and dress our children and be out the door by 7:30 AM so my husband could take our toddler to daycare on his way to work.

I say all this from my personal feelings only; I completely understand that *many* families do this, including families with single parents. I know God gives us all different walks in life and abilities to handle more than we can imagine! I share this as an encouragement to you, whatever your path in life, PRAY BIG.

Again, I prayed. More than anything, I wanted to be home with my babies. I know this isn't everyone's dream or desire, but I believe God specifically placed this deep desire in my soul. It was ALL I could think about. I placed my hope in Christ.

But the enemy continued to have his say through the words of others:

> "I could never stay home with the kids. I'd go crazy! I need to work and have adult conversations."

"What about the risks? What if your husband loses his job?"

"What about finances?"

"I never had that opportunity. I always had to work."

"The kids need social interaction."

"What about ALL your hard work and education for your career?"

"You're crazy to leave a government job!"

Even the silence of other people's opinions was disheartening.

The enemy also had his say by putting thoughts into my own head:

Was I giving up everything? Most people would never get these sorts of opportunities. Was I ungrateful?

Could I actually do this? Be at home all day with a 6-month-old and 2.5-year-old?

Would I completely lose my sanity?

Was I even cut out for this?

Would my children be better off with a skilled daycare worker?

I completely BASKED in every moment of my glorious maternity leave. Another blessing with my second child was that my job granted paid maternity leave, something I didn't have with my first baby. I held my precious tiny baby, breastfed, pumped, tended to the household chores, and, of course, watched Hallmark Christmas movies. Yet again, despite enjoying maternity leave, I couldn't shake the *intense anxiety* and constant worry of knowing one day soon I would be away from my girls. My precious angel babies that were *mine*. My heart literally ached. I began to dwell in hopelessness and dread. I felt debilitated.

But God kept reminding me to *PRAY BIG THINGS!* Really, what did I have to lose?

Christmas came and went. After the New Year, I would be returning to work.

I cried.

I didn't know how I would manage everything: work, dinner, groceries, being a wife, keeping up the house, and caring for a toddler and infant. (Quick note: my husband is incredible and helps with all of this as well! And we are blessed to have a local family who help.)

Thankfully, I arranged a schedule where my parents helped keep my baby two days a week. And for the other days, I was able to telework or use my saved annual leave or leave-without-pay. This got us through until our second daughter got closer to the one-year-old mark.

One winter day, my husband and I, *once again,* revisited the budget. We reviewed our Excel spreadsheet and numbers for the millionth time, including our salaries, bills, and spending.

All of a sudden, it worked.

God unexpectedly revealed that what hadn't worked on paper two years before would now be okay. God had blessed my husband's job *exceedingly more than we could have ever imagined* (that's a story for another day!), and finally, despite forfeiting my six-figure salary and health benefits, we trusted God's future provisions.

We took a leap of faith with abundant hope for our future.

It's humbling to recognize we never know what God is doing in the background.

March 11, 2022, was the day. I'll never forget having the discussion with my boss, notifying him when it would be my last day. I did give them over a month's notice.

"I'm not surprised," he smiled. He emphasized how sad they were to see me leave from a business and employee standpoint, but as a father himself, he understood.

It has now been nearly two years, and I could not be more thrilled. I thank God every day for the opportunity to do the greatest job I ever and will ever have. *Motherhood.* I will say that it's more difficult than I expected. But it is also more rewarding.

He can do IMMEASURABLY MORE! (see Ephesians 3:20).

My encouragement to you is this: if there is something burdening your heart or that your heart desires deeply, lay everything down and PRAY. Print scriptures, dive into the Word, and SEEK GOD.

I am DAILY grateful to God. There have been so many blessings and confirmations that this was the right decision. *Pray Big Things* has been a life-changing book for me. I highly recommend adding this to your Amazon cart as soon as possible.

If you are facing an area in your life that feels impossible and debilitating or if you have areas where you are seeking God to move, in addition to *praying big,* I recommend journaling. Writing helps me process my thoughts. I also enjoy looking back on how God has answered my prayers and worked through different situations. There are many prayers I've forgotten about and many times when I didn't recognize that God was already orchestrating the outcome through various situations.

I look back on my stay-at-home-mom journey and see why He had me wait two years. With His guidance, I grew and now am able to appreciate the outcome even more. That realization helps me get through the tough days of being a mom (especially those trying times of toddler ages 2, 3, 4!) and remember that I am living my God-given answered prayer.

Pray. Big.

Hope in Prayer

By Connie A. VanHorn

Do not be anxious about anything, but in every situation, by prayer and petition, with thanksgiving, present your requests to God. And the peace of God, which transcends all understanding, will guard your hearts and your minds in Christ Jesus (Philippians 4:6-7 NIV).

Praying big and trusting God's promises allows Him to flood our minds and hearts with hope. Prayer is an essential aspect of our Christian journey and a powerful tool that can bring us hope as we develop a closer relationship with our Father in heaven. It is critical to our spiritual growth, offering us a pathway to connect with God, find strength, gain perspective and guidance, and receive encouragement and hope.

God has given us endless opportunities to communicate with Him. We can pray while driving, doing household chores, walking, or exercising. God simply wants us to engage with Him, whether we stand in praise or fall on our knees in moments of desperation. I sometimes pray belly-down on the floor. God desires a relationship with us and wants us to be our authentic selves with Him. He seeks our hearts above all else. When our hearts are focused on Him, God will lead us and teach us how to communicate with Him through prayer.

Prayer is one of my favorite things to do with God. I just talk to Him. Having this closeness with God gives me so much hope, no matter what I face. Still, I'm pretty sure I have missed out on numerous opportunities because I didn't pray with faith. We all have experienced moments where it takes a lot to pray, especially when faced with challenges. There are days when it may be easier to surrender to pain and accept that some situations may not improve. It might even feel "safer" to settle for low expectations and anticipate disappointment instead of appreciating what is right in front of us and investing the effort in hope and prayer.

Friend, God has you reading this for a reason. Let me be His mouthpiece as I encourage you to pray big with daring faith and live with the hope that only He can offer.

> *Those who hope in the Lord will renew their strength; they will soar on wings like eagles; they will run and not grow weary; they will walk and not be faint* (Isaiah 40:31 NIV).

After surrendering our hearts to Jesus, we are drawn to know God intimately. Going to Him in prayer is the best way to nurture that relationship. But opening that relationship and praying in front of others may feel uncomfortable. As you seek a deeper relationship with God, He will give you the courage and strength to grow in the gift of corporate prayer. As a new believer, when I was alone I could talk to God as if He were a loved one or a close friend; however, when it came to praying in front of others, I would feel nervous. Talking to God is a deeply personal and intimate experience; He is our loving Father, and it is natural to desire those one-on-one moments with Him—and one-on-one time with God is what He longs for. But as we become more comfortable in His presence sharing our inner thoughts, He will awaken in us a desire and strength to help others do the same. You see, by praying out loud with others, we have the privilege of ushering someone else into God's presence!

Our hope is anchored in the unchanging character of God, whose love and faithfulness never waver. Through prayer, we can tap into the wellspring of hope that flows from God, finding strength and protection in His presence. And by praying with others, we can help them do the same thing.

One powerful way to find hope through prayer is through the practice of gratitude. By expressing thankfulness for God's blessings, both big and small, we shift our focus from our difficulties to His goodness and purpose for our lives. We can pray prayers of gratitude, acknowledging God's faithfulness in the past and trusting in His promises for the future. In doing so, we are reminded of His love and care for us, filling our hearts with hope and gratitude.

Another way to find hope in prayer is through lifting up the needs of others before God. When we pray for those who are struggling, hurting, or in need, we become vessels of hope and compassion, extending God's love to those around us.

Additionally, prayers of surrender can be a powerful way to find hope in God. When we release our worries, fears, and anxieties into His hands, we make space for His peace and presence to fill our hearts.

In all these ways and more, prayer becomes a lifeline of hope, connecting us to the source of all hope and light. Our hope is alive in God, for He is the One who sustains us, strengthens us, and guides us through every season of life. May we continue to seek Him in prayer, trusting in His love and faithfulness to bring hope, healing, and restoration to our lives and the world around us.

> *Rejoice always, pray continually, give thanks in all circumstances; for this is God's will for you in Christ Jesus* (1 Thessalonians 5:16-18 NIV).

Maria Termotto-Horwitz

Maria Termotto-Horwitz resides in Palm Beach Gardens with her husband, Josh, and their cherished daughter, Genesee. They form an unstoppable team in their personal journey and their thriving real estate business called "Best Home Ever," where they enjoy "Connecting Blessed Families with their Best Homes." The couple also manages "Village Management Services," a property management company.

Maria is unwavering and dedicated, infusing faith into every aspect of life. Her faith remains her cornerstone as she hosts heartfelt Home Church gatherings, nurtures discipleship groups, and actively participates in nonprofit work. She also enjoys traveling, investing, gardening, and writing. Her book, *Blessed Life Ever: Biblical Affirmations for Victorious Living*, offers a fresh perspective on the most cherished Bible verses in order from Genesis to Revelation, rewritten in first person.

Maria's mission is "To inspire and empower young people in living their Blessed Life Ever for the glory of God." Her dedication to this cause is evident in every endeavor, making her a true beacon of faith, family, and purpose in an ever-changing world.

Maria can be contacted at 561-779-9452, on Instagram at Maria_blessedlifever, on Facebook at Maria Christina Termotto-Horwitz, or by email at BestHomeEverTeam@gmail.com

From Broken Beginnings to Living My Blessed Life Ever

By Maria Termotto-Horwitz

The year was 2005. My younger brothers and I were sitting in the backseat of the car when my mom gazed at us through the rear-view mirror. She asked us a question that would change our lives forever.

"Would you guys be okay if I died?"

I looked up at her. After a pause, I said, "We would survive, but why are you asking us, that's never going to happen?"

Two days later, at 6 am on November 28th, 2005, I awoke to my brothers pounding on my door. They were shouting, "Mom's dead!"

In a daze, I walked over to my parents' room, where the sickening smell of gun smoke filled the air. I saw my dad on the phone with the paramedics and my mom on the bed. Her chest heaved in and out. My mom had shot herself in the heart.

My dad shouted at me to get towels, but I could barely hear him. Everything was a blur.

My brothers and I then went outside. We were crying as we waited for the paramedics to come. By the time they arrived, she was gone, and we were taken to the police station for questioning about what had just happened.

When we returned home, my dad revealed to us that our mom was suffering from depression and had been suicidal long before we were born. When she was 13, her father walked out on her family with another woman, leaving her mom in a deep depression. My mom's brother and sister fell into the drug and party lifestyle, which later took both of their lives.

My mom met and married my dad at a young age to escape her family. Outwardly, she was the most happy, talented, beautiful, God-loving, and people-loving woman I knew. On the inside, she was suffering from depression, bipolar disorder, and sadness.

As my brothers and I grew up, we often saw my mom in bed for long periods of time. We were told she was "just sick." Now, we learned the truth. I was 13, my brother Michael was 11, and my brother Max was 6.

I considered my mom my best friend, and my best friend was gone. I was now the only girl in the house, and it was a lonely road. One day, I was sitting at the kitchen table with my dad and brothers, and to my horror, my dad told me to get my diary. My heart was beating so loudly as I got up to get it, knowing that I had written about a boy I liked. He then proceeded to read my diary out loud while my brothers laughed. It was humiliating.

We had gone to traditional school but, after a few years, switched to homeschooling. I spent my days cleaning, cooking, praying, and taking care of my brothers. I wanted to be a nun and escape the world. My form of religion was not attractive to anyone looking in. I fasted a lot, kept to myself, prayed for long hours, and judged everyone and everything as sinful. I thought of myself as a "stay-at-home nun," but in reality, I was probably more like a "modern-day Pharisee."

My family rarely talked about my mom for years following her death. I bottled up what happened and stored it away. As an adult, my biggest fear was that the same thing would happen to me that happened to my mom. I feared getting married, having children, and my hormones going out of whack like my mom's. What if I decided to end it all? It wasn't until my relationship with my husband that I discovered this fate would not be my future. I can be the mother who would make my mom proud.

Before meeting my husband, I found myself in two back-to-back relationships. I compromised my beliefs and gave into premarital sex, even though my mom had instilled in me a healthy desire to remain pure. Then I met Josh. He was the first boyfriend who respected my desire to wait until marriage—even though I eventually messed that up.

In our first week of dating, I took Josh to my mom's burial site and "introduced them." I looked past the fact that he wasn't a Christian believer and had a Jewish background with an agnostic outlook. I asked him early on, "What will it take for you to believe in Jesus?"

He said, "Jesus would have to come down here, hit me upside the head, and say, 'Hey, it's me!'"

I was confident He would show up. And I was determined to lead Josh to the truth and into a relationship with God.

Everything was fine until it wasn't. Months into our new relationship, I was suddenly plagued by fear and uncertainty in every area of my life. *Is this the right man for me? Is this the right job for me? Am I on the right path?* It was a really difficult time. I was depressed and unsure of myself. I was inspired to fast and pray for clarity, which lasted nine days in total: a three-day juice fast, leading into a three-day water fast, and then another three-day juice fast. Josh joined me in the last three-day juice fast. By the end, I had the clarity I was seeking. Yes, this is the right man for me. Yes, this is the right career. Yes, this is the path God has for me. Keep walking.

My dad wasn't so convinced and said he wouldn't give us his blessing to be married unless Josh came to believe in Jesus. Josh and I had a heart-to-heart conversation in which we agreed to go on a journey to re-discover God together. Up until that point, I was holding tight to my Catholic beliefs, and he was holding onto his Jewish upbringing.

We started reading the Bible together daily and watched the movie *The Case for Christ*. Josh also read the book *The Case for Christ* and the Hebrew Gospel of Matthew. We realized that Jesus was actually Jewish (Go figure!). And we found ourselves growing closer and closer together as we grew closer to God.

We prayed for purity, doing a 93-day purity fast leading up to our wedding. Josh repented for his porn use and publicly confessed it to others, which made such an impact! We watched the movie *Brain, Heart, World*—which helped us both understand the harmful effects of pornography on the brain, the heart, and the world. This also helped me understand that his addiction was not an offense against me but a deep-seated stronghold that plagues the world and requires God's grace to overcome.

As we were worshipping in church one day, Josh heard the Voice of God tell him that his mission was to bring together the Jews and the Christians as one. Josh was so touched by that message. He remembered the vision he had the previous year and knew it had finally come full circle. We had taken a pilgrimage to Israel, visiting all the meaningful sites, when Josh did something special at the Western Wall—he read aloud a heartfelt letter his father had written him the day he was born, read a chapter out of Genesis, and then prayed. After doing this, Josh touched the wall and saw a bearded figure full of light speaking to him. Though he couldn't make out the words, Josh knew the figure was Jesus. Now, with the Voice, he knew what Jesus had been saying to him, and he was ready to receive it.

This is the day which the Lord hath made; we will rejoice and be glad in it (Psalm 118:24 KJV).

The Best Day Ever finally arrived! We got married at a picturesque outdoor venue on a lake with beautiful sweeping trees and desert rose flowers everywhere. My dad walked me down the aisle. A bouquet of sunflowers was placed on a prominent seat to honor and welcome my mother's presence. We had many meaningful moments in our ceremony—such as Josh blowing the shofar before I walked down the aisle. Our beautiful day also included the washing of feet, the tying of three cords (representing the bride, groom, and God), the breaking of the glass, and the Hora song, which was when we were raised up overhead on our chairs with friends dancing around us. It was a most blessed day!

Soon after the wedding, we went on a marriage retreat at the Glen Eyrie Castle in Colorado Springs. It was a prayer and Bible-focused retreat. Our room was the "King's Suite"—the highest room in the tallest tower. We enjoyed the gorgeous 180-degree views of the mountains. One of our tasks was to find a meaningful rock together and tell the story of why we chose it. Josh and I hiked up the highest nearby mountain (over 5,000 ft in elevation!). At the top of the mountain was a pile of rocks with one perched on top. We took that rock, broke it into three pieces, and left the piece that signified God on the rock pile. On the retreat, Josh fully forgave himself for the past abortions in prior relationships, and we prayed to be blessed with a child.

Leaving the retreat, we went to stay with our friends on Genesee Mountain in Golden, Colorado. When I saw the sign on the side of the mountain, I thought, *If I'm pregnant right now, Genesee is the perfect name for a baby girl.* Genesee means "Beautiful, pleasant valley" in Native American and

Ancient Hebrew. It also reminded me of Genesis, which was significant because a child would solidify the beginning of our family. We soon found out that I was pregnant! We chose to be surprised on the delivery day with the gender. Nine months later, we had a beautiful baby girl who we named Genesee. She is an answered prayer and gift of God!

When Genesee was one year old, we went on another pilgrimage—to Israel with the Kevin Sorbo group. Leading up to this pilgrimage, I had asked Josh many times when and where he would like to be baptized. Josh would look at me and put both his hands up as if weighing his responses on a scale, "Being baptized in a kiddy pool on the church lawn...or being baptized in the Jordan River where Jesus was baptized." His answer was clear. On May 22nd, 2023, Josh was baptized for the first time in the Jordan River—the same river where Jesus was baptized! Hallelujah—all glory to God!

When we returned from Israel, we started hosting home church gatherings after being prompted by a friend who does mission work. This grew into monthly gatherings, which also grew into a weekly discipleship group. We had food and fellowship, live worship music offered by a talented worship leader, and a powerful message. Then, we closed out in prayer, followed by more fellowship. I was so proud of my husband for sharing his testimony of being an agnostic Jew who became a believer in Yeshua (Jesus)! I love that we are doing exactly what believers in the early church did. *They devoted themselves to the apostles' teaching and to fellowship, to the breaking of bread and to prayer...They broke bread in their homes and ate together with glad and sincere hearts, praising God and enjoying the favor of all the people. And the Lord added to their number daily those who were being saved* (Acts 2:42, 46-47 NIV).

Around the same time, God put a strong desire in my heart to glorify His Name and Word by compiling a book titled *Blessed Life Ever: Biblical Declarations for Victorious Living*. I was unsatisfied with the many Bible verse books separated by popular themes in no particular order that always relied heavily on the epistles. I saw the need for a Bible verse book that encompassed the best verses of the entire Bible in order from Genesis to Revelation and rewritten into first person. There's a reason Psalm 23 is so popular—it's written in first person. By newly reading these verses in first person, God's Word comes alive in even more incredible ways. My favorite verse is from Proverbs, which is modified in the book to read, *I trust in the Lord with all my heart and lean not upon my own understanding. In all my ways, I acknowledge Him, and He directs my paths* (from Proverbs 3:5-6, modified from ESV).

I am so excited for all God has already done and is continuing to do through the power of His spoken Word!

Today, we have a non-profit in my mother's honor called Amanda Termotto's Right From the Heart Foundation, whose mission is to encourage and empower young people to live out their *Blessed Life Ever* for the glory of God. We do this through our discipleship groups, the Blessed Life Ever book, supporting two Ugandan Orphanages, and partnering with other local non-profits such as Fellowship of Christian Athletes, Little Smiles, A Different Shade of Love, Lutheran Services Florida, Women World Leaders, and many others. I believe it's important to support and stand with other believers. If we will be spending eternity with each other in heaven anyway, we might as well get to know each other on earth!

I love the family we are growing and how we are doing it as naturally as possible. We used a midwife and doula for our first pregnancy, which we are doing again as we are currently expecting another bundle of joy in April 2024! When people ask us how many kids we want, our answer is always, "As many as God blesses us with!" I love that we get to do life together as a family. From day one, Genesee has been with us everywhere, from real estate closings to walk-throughs to Christian concerts and travels throughout the US and to the Holy Land. I feel so blessed to be a mother and to raise our children on a biblical foundation. I'm currently working on my next book titled *Blessed Beginnings: Embracing Pregnancy and Parenthood through Biblical Wisdom.*

Behold, children are a heritage from the LORD, the fruit of the womb a reward (Psalm 127:3 ESV).

I reflect on my life with such gratitude to God. He led us through the hard time of losing my mother and the years of loneliness. I remember all the times I sat in a Catholic church alone, looking around at all the big families together and praying, "All I want is for my family to go to church together and have a united faith." My prayers have all been answered. Not only does my husband look forward to church, but most of our immediate family now comes, too!

Reflecting on my years of loneliness, I now realize I was never alone. Jesus was always right beside me. He says to me, "Fear not, I am with you. I have always been with you. You are never alone. You are mine. I love you with an everlasting love."

My hope is alive. I've come from debilitated to exhilarated with God. All glory to Him!

Hope in Your Future

By Kimberly Ann Hobbs

As we look around our world and see the various changes and people who are weary about their future, Jesus calls us to keep our eyes on Him. Although it is easy to become overwhelmed by despair and fear for our future, we can find lasting hope when everything may seem hopeless by meditating on what God says in His promises from scripture.

In my own past, having made terrible choices by not honoring God, I was on an emotional roller coaster. I had moments of grief that swept over me during a period in my life that set me up for failure. I lost all hope in my future until God radically changed my life by rescuing me. He pursued me, and my heart began opening to His desire to have a relationship with me.

> *The sufferings of this present time are not worth comparing with the glory that is to be revealed to us* (Romans 8:18 RSV).

When I entered a relationship with Jesus Christ, God opened my eyes, illuminating all that was in front of me. He changed who I was and took me off the roller coaster that was headed for ultimate disaster. He never left me alone, giving me His power and wisdom to address each situation I encountered. And He blessed me with a great family and a Christian community support system that set me up for a future of success in so many situations.

We may not always understand the circumstances God puts in our path, but how we respond to those circumstances truly defines us—either drawing us closer to God or further from Him. God has a plan for your future and will put you on the path He has paved for your life if you continually put

Him first. Through the power of the Holy Spirit, you can look forward with joy to God's destiny in your life. God's life-changing Word overflows with His promises of real love, forgiveness, salvation, peace, hope, and joy for everyone who trusts in His Son, Jesus.

> *May the God of hope fill you with all joy and peace as you trust in him, so that you may overflow with hope by the power of the Holy Spirit* (Romans 15:13 NIV).

When I completely surrendered my life to Christ, He gave me hope for a future.

> *"For I know the plans I have for you," declares the LORD, "plans to prosper you and not to harm you, plans to give you hope and a future"* (Jeremiah 29:11 NIV).

God continues to lead me every day. And He will lead you if you allow Him to be the cornerstone of your life, seek His perspective on issues that arise ahead of you, and look for His guidance through even the toughest times. A quote I often look to is, *Trust in the Lord with all your heart and lean not on your own understanding; in all your ways submit to Him, and He will make your paths straight* (Proverbs 3:5-6 NIV).

God has given me so much hope for the future! I feel so blessed that I get to spread His Word through books such as this. He has blessed me with so many earthly things that make me so grateful. When I was in those bleakest moments, I could never have imagined my future would look anything like it does today. I cannot thank Him enough for the eternal life He gave me through Jesus Christ, who gave His life for me. All my hope in what was to come for me came the day I bowed my knee to my Savior in repentance. I cannot wait to see what God has in store for the rest of my journey as I continue to walk with Him.

May you look to your future by holding God's hand in yours and embracing Him fully, with great anticipation, knowing that He is with you always, even to the ends of the earth.

> *Your future is bright and filled with a living hope that will never fade away* (Proverbs 23:18 TPT).

Ana Taffe

Miss Ana Taffe is a fearless warrior of God and a mum to three teenage daughters. She recently relocated to New York, where she is an Army reservist and a full-time student online at Liberty University, majoring in Christian counseling. In her free time, Ana enjoys writing, studying Scriptures, spending time with family, and being out in nature and doing God's Kingdom work.

Ana also designs Christian apparel (available at discipleship-apparel.creator-spring.com) for Rising Up Ministries. Part of the proceeds are donated to Children Of the Night, which is a safe haven for boys and girls who have been trafficked.

Ana's life's mission is to help others and to show them the love of God and how beautiful a relationship can be with Father God and Jesus, our Lord and Saviour.

To connect with Anavay, you can e-mail her at taffeanavay@gmail.com

www.risingupministries.org

Finding Freedom in Yahshua

By Ana Taffe

Life has an interesting way of unfolding during our quest to discover who we are and why we are here. Somewhere along the way, we encounter a beautiful gift called "faith," and we come to realize that there is more to life than just existing. The maker of faith is Yahweh (Yahweh is God the Father; Yahshua is His Son—Jesus); only through Him can we truly understand what faith means. And with faith comes hope.

My faith journey started long before I realized I was on a faith journey. Growing up, the only time I stepped foot inside of a church was when I visited my grandmum. I thought it was boring, but I did enjoy the free food and the Bible she gave me. It was the *Psalty Kids Bible.* Thinking of it now brings a big smile to my face. Oh, how I loved belting out (out of tune, I might add) the songs in that Bible. Perhaps the seeds my grandmum planted were the beginning of my faith journey, or maybe it was when my mum sang hymns to me and my sisters when I was a toddler.

When I was 19, I met and married a man who had grown up in an overtly strict religious environment. He wasn't practicing religion when I met him, but he decided he wanted to start going to church with me after we became husband and wife. I really don't remember what those early days were like. It seems my memory is flooded with simple things like going to church, playing house, and trying to please my husband the best I could.

Throughout my nine years of marriage, I became pregnant five times, but only three of my babies survived. My girls were my happy place. I did not know who Yahweh was, nor did I understand what it meant to have hope in Him. I was following religion and the unhealthy cult-like indoctrination that, in my case, came along with it. I was clueless about the relationship I could have with Yahshua because I had never learned who He was in the eyes of Yahweh, so it was impossible to envision the future He had for me and nearly impossible to walk in faith and full obedience.

Jesus said to him, "I am the way, the truth, and the life. No one comes to the Father except through Me" (John 14:6 NKJV).

I always felt strange that I was just living day to day with nothing to look forward to. I dreamed of a life filled with hope but doubted it would ever come to fruition.

I struggled to make Yahweh the head of my marriage, which was plagued with infidelity from the very start—beginning with my husband's actions and soon followed by mine. My husband also physically and mentally abused me. Because of the trauma, I don't have a lot of memories from our marriage. But I do know that as the years went by, my depression worsened, and the need to be loved by someone else consumed me.

I eventually met a man who was also married. We started an affair that continued for four years, both divorcing our spouses. It was yet another toxic relationship that I had no business being in.

I eventually left religion and its teachings, taking time to process the strict adherence to the specific religious doctrine I had adopted. I felt the only way to heal from what I had gone through for the sake of religion and sin was to sever what little relationship I had left with Yahweh.

Four years post-divorce and newly single for the first time in my adult life, I was at a crossroads. I knew I needed a change, so when Holy Spirit told me to move out of Florida, I did just that. I wasn't a Christian, nor had I given my life to Yahweh, though I prayed to Him every day, asking for His guidance in my life and holding onto hope that a better tomorrow would come.

The decision to leave Florida wasn't easy because I had three young daughters who still needed me. I was desperately grasping onto the small, remaining pieces of who I was; I knew I could no longer be the mum or woman I needed to be if I stayed in Florida. But moving out of state meant leaving my girls behind with their dad and seeing them less.

Trusting in Yahweh, I made that leap of faith. What happened in the days leading up to my move and the months after is nothing short of miraculous. Yahweh's hand was written all over it.

In January 2018, I was staying at a boutique hotel on Hollywood Beach when a massive migraine hit me. I attempted to drink a glass of wine, but it tasted bitter on my lips. It wasn't until I started driving out of town that the migraine began to subside. I trusted in Yahweh's plan but didn't realize He was orchestrating the direction of my life as He took away my desire to drink and listen to secular music, particularly classic rock, which had been a part of my everyday life.

I moved to Connecticut as planned; my twin sister had just moved from there, so I took over her studio apartment and clients. It's not easy to share that we were courtesans, that is, prostitutes. We were both trafficked at the age of fifteen; that was the life we had known ever since.

A few months later, I was visiting my sister in Buffalo, New York, when Holy Spirit gave me a call to move there, which I obeyed.

One day in May 2018, while my sister and I were driving, we shared visions we had each received from Yahweh. I told her about the vision Yahshua had given me many years earlier, right before I decided to walk away from Yahweh. In the vision, I was sitting outside when Yahshua started descending from the clouds in the form of a bright white light. He said to me, "The time has come," meaning His second coming. I understood that He didn't mean He was arriving right then and there but that this was a message for me to get right with Him. Unfortunately, I was terrified and did just the opposite, going on my four-year journey of defiance.

As we drove, we suddenly came across a "T" in the road with a sign above it that said "Pastors Walk and Wilton." My sister and I immediately looked at each other, fully knowing Yahweh was speaking to us, saying we needed to give our lives to Him right then and there, so we did.

We stopped at the "T" in the road and gave ourselves to our Lord and Saviour—Yahshua Messiah (Jesus Christ). It was an invitation I wasn't going to miss. I greatly accepted the beautiful gift of hope that came along with it. It was the kind of hope that helped me to envision and believe in a future for myself. It was the kind of hope that helped me see Yahshua in a different light; thus, a new kind of faith was born in me.

You see, when I claimed to be a "Christian" in previous years, even though I had been trying my best, I lived for religion instead of seeking a relationship with the one true Elohim. Despite my efforts, I didn't really know who Yahshua was, nor did I understand the depth of His saving grace. My newfound hope now helped me truly see Him. I finally understood that the only way to the Father is through Him, which is why when we pray, we pray in His name.

"And in that day you will ask Me nothing. Most assuredly, I say to you, whatever you ask the Father in My name He will give you" (John 16:23 NKJV).

After giving my life to Yahweh, I knew I could no longer live my life in sin, nor did I want to. And I trusted He would provide for me. I stopped working as a courtesan, and I severed ties with a man who was helping financially support me, knowing that I could not walk in the ways of Yahshua while also living a life of sin. It just doesn't work like that. I trusted that Yahweh would make a way, and He did—by sending me a husband just a few short months later. In that marriage, Holy Spirit showed me the purpose and calling for my life.

You might think that is where my faith journey ended, but that would be far from the truth. It was just the beginning. The seeds that had been planted since my childhood started to bloom. And my first big mission was revealed to me in December 2021. Yahweh called me into the military, really putting my faith to the test. My husband gave me an ultimatum—choose him or the calling that Yahweh had put on my life. If I chose to go into the military, my husband said he would divorce me because He didn't believe that Yahweh would call a woman into the military—even the Army reserves, which is what I eventually signed up for. But having chosen man over Yahweh before, I wasn't about to do that again.

I knew that when I gave my life to Yahweh, I would be called into ministry somehow, some way—that I would ultimately be led to serve outside of the home. I also understood that the only way for Yahweh to reveal what He wanted for my life was for me to be still. When I entered into my second marriage, I did just that: I was still. I continued to evolve spiritually and heal from the pains of my past, so who I was when I first met my husband had changed, as did certain views and beliefs I once held onto. When I first met my husband, I said I would never join the military and had strong opinions that supported this belief. Oh, how walking in faith and in the ways of Yahweh will change the very makeup of how we see things, right?

Therefore, if anyone is in Christ, he is a new creation; old things have passed away; behold, all things have become new (2 Corinthians 5:17 NKJV).

It's so much easier to hear from Yahweh when we make an effort to slow things down in our lives and silence our minds long enough to listen. Sadly, after my second marriage ended in 2022, there were times when I allowed the busyness of my life to get in the way of doing what Yahweh was calling me to do. He is the One who gives me guidance from the control tower of my soul and shows me my next steps. However, when I allow the busyness of life to take over, a cloud blocks the rays of the sun, and depression sets in as Yahweh's voice becomes muffled.

After I graduated from job training with the Army in 2021, I moved back to Florida. I grew impatient and frustrated because I knew what I needed to be doing in my walk as a believer. Like Jonah in the Bible, I altered Yahweh's plan by not obeying Him when He told me what to do next. There was a time when I wasn't hearing from Him like I used to, but that didn't stop me from the faith journey that I was on. Yahweh made me well aware that the two years of struggle I went through after I moved back to Florida was because of my disobedience and lack of faith in Him. That motivated me to do what He called me to do.

All praise be to Yahweh. After many attempts to do it on my own, He showed me that to keep hope alive, I had to push past the "I don't feel like it" mindset and stop living in my feelings. He also reminded me to discipline myself and read His Word every morning before everyone else in the house would wake up.

That discipline was fully instilled in me when I met Miss Kimberly Hobbs, founder of Women World Leaders, in May 2023. I had reached out to her, wanting to use their publishing services for an autobiography I just finished writing. While we were talking, she asked if I read the Bible every day. I realized I didn't, and I felt guilty. Sure, I cherry-picked a few verses here and there throughout the week for the sake of reading the Word, but I wasn't really immersing myself in it the way I had before I moved back to Florida. The divine encounter with Miss Kimberly brought me a much-needed dose of hope.

Hope comes in many different forms and can help us feel more joyful, giving purpose and meaning to our lives. It can also make us more productive and feel more balanced.

Before Kimberly and I spoke, I had recently finished reading one of Women World Leaders' books, *Victories: Claiming Freedom in Christ.* I've always been an avid reader. For most of my life, my genre of choice was fiction, which gave me hope for a better tomorrow. Fantasy stories were my escape from reality. As I got older, however, the Bible became my book of choice, and I also enjoyed a few hidden gems written by women of faith along the way. From these writings, a new type of hope would arise, allowing me to no longer dwell on the pains of my past and, instead, look forward to tomorrow, imagining a future I wouldn't have to escape from.

Given this, you'd think that when Miss Tina Kadolph gave me the book *Victories* in 2022, I would have read it right away. Instead, it got shuffled around as I moved from place to place for over a year. A part of me wanted to read this book that I had been blessed with, but something was holding me back. In hindsight, I now understand that when I went to that event where I met Miss Tina, I was still dealing with unresolved trauma from being trafficked as a teenager. It took time and work with God to embrace the healing that came with reading that book.

While I have come a long way, all praise and glory be to Yahweh, I'm still a work in progress. I'm still learning daily how to survive as I unpack and work through certain areas of my trauma in a healthy way. I've learned that the only way to do that is to give it all to our Creator, Yahweh.

When I finally read the powerful messages in Victories, I immediately understood through Holy Spirit's wisdom that the enemy was doing everything in his power to keep my faith journey from evolving. I was in awe of how Miss Julie Jenkins and the other ladies penned their thoughts. Their words, experiences, vulnerability, and courageous faith in Yahweh gave me a new dose of hope.

When I was growing up, life didn't make sense to me, and I had no clue who I was. I have never felt like I belonged to the human race. I longed to go to a place that was not on earth and to be around people that I felt connected with, but I didn't understand why that was. Now that I am a believer, I understand that our real home is with our Creator. Perhaps that is what my soul was longing for.

I had a great disconnect toward mankind in general, but especially women (including professing Christian women) because I felt like I could not relate to them on any level. I felt like I was an alien from another planet dropped here on earth. That all changed, however, when I read Victories. It literally transformed my mind and how I view women and, overall, the human race. In those pages are stories of Spirit-filled women—other authentic believers of Yahweh living their lives for Him based on a personal and intimate relationship with Him, not based on religion. I was in awe.

I realize now that finding other authentic believers with a relationship with Yahweh was what my soul had been longing for. Holy Spirit helped me understand that my next season of life and faith journey would involve meeting other women and building healthy, Spirit-filled relationships with them. The time of Yahshua's return is soon upon us, my friends, and we need each other more than ever.

It is my prayer that as I am writing this chapter for *Hope Alive*, I can bless you all with the same inspiration and hope that these ladies have given me, and I can encourage you to walk by faith, not by sight (2 Corinthians 5:7). I know, it is difficult to do at times, especially when we are trying to make sense of our lives and understand who we are as Yahweh's children.

I am looking forward to the continuation of my healing and spiritual journey and building beautiful relationships with other women of faith. It's amazing to watch the puzzle pieces of Yahweh's kingdom work coming together.

Praise Adonai for these fresh doses of hope and His promises for a better tomorrow! Not every day will be sunshine and rainbows, but don't let that stop you from stepping out in faith and finding hope in Yahweh. You will be blessed by the beautiful friendships and experiences He gives us along the way.

> *For I know the thoughts that I think toward you, says the LORD, thoughts of peace and not of evil, to give you a future and a hope. Then you will call upon Me and go and pray to Me, and I will listen to you. And you will seek Me and find Me, when you search for Me with all your heart* (Jeremiah 29:11-13 NKJV).

Hope in God

By Kimberly Ann Hobbs

> *"But blessed is the one who trusts in the Lord, whose confidence is in him. They will be like a tree planted by the water that sends out its roots by the stream. It does not fear when heat comes; its leaves are always green. It has no worries in a year of drought and never fails to bear fruit"* (Jeremiah 17:7-8 NIV).

When we are in Christ Jesus and when we put our faith and trust in His work on the cross for our sins, we are connected to the source of all living water. In surrendering your life to Christ Jesus, YOU become planted beside the life-giving water.

Have you ever walked near a stream and listened to the trickle of the water as it sweeps by the rocks and pebbles? Or listened to the hanging limbs that dangle from the trees above, gently brushing and penetrating the water's surface? If you have, you will understand the calm that can take over your moments of thought while you are lost in the beauty of God's creation. That is the exact place we need to be to prevent anxiety.

God's river of life provides hope. When we place our hope and trust in Him, God says our strength will be renewed. Our stress and worries will dissipate, and we will soar on eagle's wings. When we discover the life-giving power of Jesus' promise, He provides the living water that will renew our soul with hope, strength, and complete rest.

But those who hope in the Lord will renew their strength. They will soar on wings like eagles; they will run and not grow weary; they will walk and not be faint (Isaiah 40:31 NIV).

God wants us to patiently trust in Him and keep our covenants. He blesses us with divine help when we need it most. He is a sustaining God, and He promises in His Word that when our hope is in Him alone, we will find rest with Him.

Yes, my soul, find rest in God; my hope comes from him. Trust he is my rock and my salvation; he is my fortress; I will not be shaken (Psalm 62:5-6 NIV).

In a world that often leaves us feeling drained and exhausted, we know we can find renewal and refreshment in His springs of living water. Whether we need to release from the demands of work, the stresses of relationships, or even the weight of our own expectations, we find relief with encouragement when we place our hope in the Lord. As the water that is living is never stagnant or temporary, you will find that it is a continual source of POWER and guidance, giving you hope and restoration during some of the heaviest of life's challenges.

. . . .

Emily Wheeler

Emily Wheeler is a passionate servant to the Lord, called to bring His children back home to Him.

Her life experiences give her a unique perspective on humanity and who King Jesus calls us to be. She uses that perspective and passion to pour into others.

Emily resides in Buffalo, NY, where she is a wife, mother, bonus mother, and first lady of her church, as her husband is a pastor. She is also the co-founder of Rising Up Ministries (www.risingupministries.org), an online ministry focused on the end times, which is currently launching a new project—Operation Tivkah ("hope" in Hebrew)—that will create healing retreat centers throughout the United States.

Emily only knows how to use her whole heart, and now that she has been saved by the grace of King Jesus, she takes being an ambassador of Christ very seriously!

Emily's love language is food—she loves cooking, baking, and serving others. She often uses her passion for food as a catalyst to help others work on their whole health—body, mind, and soul. She lives by the belief that our bodies are the temple of the Messiah, and we honor Him by taking care of our health.

Finding Hope in Jesus

By Emily Wheeler

If I go up to the heavens, you are there; if I make my bed in the depths, you are there (Psalm 139:8 NIV).

Like many folks, I grew up in a broken home. I dealt with many difficulties, including emotional neglect, addictions in the family, sexual abuse, and losing my mum in a car accident when I was just four years old. At the time of her passing, we were living in Georgia, and although I was young, I remember the day she passed as if it were yesterday.

I am the youngest of four siblings, all girls. When my mum died, our eldest half-sister, Sarah, went to live with our grandmum on our mum's side, while my second eldest sister Grace, my twin sister Anavay, and I went to live with our estranged dad, both back home in Washington state. By this time, my dad had been remarried to a woman who was the textbook evil stepmother.

Like any child who loses their mum at a young age, I experienced emotional trauma. But my sisters and I also had to deal with the sexual abuse we endured at the hands of my mum's boyfriend just before she died. Could my mum have known about the sexual abuse when she was alive? It's hard to say. If she had, she could've been too scared to confront him about it because he was physically violent, once even sending her to the hospital after nearly beating her to death.

When mum died and we went back to live with our dad, there was no room for healing. Rather, a new kind of hell began with our stepmother and new trauma from the emotional and physical abuse we endured. My twin sis and I rebelled more than Grace did, often leading us to get into the most trouble. There was an incident when we were seven years old where I coerced my twin sis to start the bathroom on fire once everyone had gone to bed. The plan backfired. As soon as the bathroom began to go up in flames, the smoke alarm blared. My dad and stepmother rushed out from their bedroom, and they quickly extinguished the flames. After this incident, my stepmother had enough of my twin and me and gave my dad an ultimatum: either he would get rid of "the problem" (us), or she would divorce him. He chose her over us.

My grandmum from my dad's side decided to take my twin and me in and raise us the best she knew how. However, she and her long-term live-in partner were both alcoholics.

At age thirteen, I moved to Idaho with my twin sis, grandmum, aunt, and my aunt's husband, who began to abuse me sexually. Ashamed and confused, I kept quiet all summer about the abuse until I went back to my grandmum's for the school year. My aunt and grandmum heard of the accusations toward my uncle from my twin sis, whom I confided in confidentially. However, when they both angrily confronted me about the abuse, I was afraid I had done something wrong, so I lied and said it didn't happen. Not long after that incident, my grandmum sent me back to live with my dad and stepmother again.

At age fourteen, I began to experience depression for the first time. I felt like I couldn't relate to anyone, and I had this unexplainable feeling that I wasn't from this world and this earth wasn't my home. It was a thought I couldn't comprehend. It wasn't until I was in my early thirties and saved by the Lord that I truly understood what this feeling meant.

If you belonged to the world, it would love you as its own. As it is, you do not belong to the world, but I have chosen you out of the world. That is why the world hates you (John 15:19 NIV).

When I began to experience depression, I attempted suicide for the first time by getting into a bottle of my stepmother's prescription medication. From there, I was sent to Fairfax Mental Hospital in Kirkland, Washington, for eight months. During my stay, I was groomed by a male orderly who was more than three times my age.

By the time I was fifteen, I was raped by someone I briefly met at a bus stop, who I ignorantly decided to trust when he offered me the opportunity to use the telephone at his home. That same year, I was sex-trafficked by a pimp in Seattle, Washington, and Oregon. Just before my 16th birthday, whilst being trafficked in Oregon, I ended up getting arrested at a motel for prostitution. At the time of my arrest, I had a john in the motel room with me whom the police officers told to get dressed and leave, even though they suspected I was underage. They were more interested in my criminal offense; they arrested and held me in a juvenile detention center for three months before they could find a foster home placement. I was only in foster care for one month before I ran away, getting sucked right back into being trafficked across the country by a different pimp for the next few years.

At the age of eighteen, I broke free from my trafficker because of his arrest. I was still stuck in the vicious cycle of the adult industry, bouncing back and forth between escorting and dancing in adult clubs, as no normal job would hire me without prior work experience. I would spend more years dealing with depression and PTSD, thus my second, near-fatal suicide attempt. I had taken a bottle of Tylenol and was unconscious until the following afternoon. I know now it was by the divine grace and mercy of our Lord that I came out of that alive.

Although I lived an alternate lifestyle, I still longed to be a wife and mother, far away from the adult industry. When I was nineteen years old, I thought I had met the man who would take me away from it all. However, he also happened to be a 41-year-old married client with three adult kids and lived in New York City. I knew I shouldn't mix my personal life with work, but I pursued a relationship with him anyway. He was charming and said all the right things. It wasn't long before I was pregnant with my son, and we were making plans for marriage. My son was born just before my 21st birthday, and a few months later, my son's dad cheated on me. Because of the infidelity, I decided to leave him and take my son to Florida, where my twin sis was living with her husband. I fought hard to keep custody of my son; however, because my son's dad was a wealthy man, he was able to drag it out in court long enough to where I was ultimately pressured into signing over my rights. After having almost full custody, I only had weekend and other sporadic unsupervised visits.

In the first year of visitations, one evening while I was staying at my son's dad's place, his father put a roofie in my drink and date raped me. I didn't go to the police out of fear of not being believed. I tried my best to be there for my son, flying back to NYC every month to spend time with him; however, out of spite, anger, jealousy, and control, his dad sometimes wouldn't allow me to see him once I arrived in town. When I did get the chance to visit my son, things between his dad and I only grew more hostile. After the date rape incident and growing hostility, I started to drink and dabble in recreational drug use, spiraling even more into depression and suicidal thoughts. At that time, my son was the only thing keeping me alive.

In December of 2012, I attended a 3-day "self-help/empowerment" conference in West Palm Beach, Florida. During this time, a friend of an ex-boyfriend recommended that I try Ayahuasca to help treat my depression and PTSD. I readily agreed because I felt I had nothing to lose.

For those of you who aren't familiar with Ayahuasca, let me give you a little background. The word Ayahuasca means *vine of the soul*. It comes from the caapi plant, native to the Amazon region. The shaman brews the plant into a tea; it is considered "plant medicine" to help treat mental health disorders such as depression and PTSD.

I first used Ayahuasca in the summer of 2013 to help relieve the pressures of my past. During this time, I was not yet a Christian believer. I had been following New Age ideologies and believed in a "higher power" but didn't have any concept of who Yahweh (God) or Yahshua (Jesus) were. The only Jesus I was familiar with was from the New Age, who is claimed to be an ascended master, which I now know is pure deception.

My testimony on how I came to know the real Yahshua begins on November 11th, 2017. I was attending a weekend Ayahuasca retreat in the rural parts of central New York when one fateful night would forever change my life. I was harshly awakened by the truth of who Yahweh and Yahshua are, what heaven and hell are, and the reality we live in.

The retreat was a 2-night ceremony, not much different than the nine other ceremonies I'd done in the past, except this would be the first time I was participating in back-to-back ceremonies over the course of two nights. The first night ceremony went without incident; however, the second night proved more fateful.

On the afternoon of the second day, another facilitator was staying in the house administering kambo (frog poison), which is used to cleanse the body from toxins. No one at the house told me that I shouldn't be taking kambo if I was planning to attend the second night ceremony because of how the two "medicines" would interact with each other.

That night, as I lay on the living room floor, waiting for my turn to go up to the shaman to drink the tea, I heard a voice in my spirit, loud and clear, tell me not to go up and drink it. I'd heard this voice since 2015, but I chalked it up to being nothing more than my "spirit guide" because that's what I learned in the New Age. Now, I clearly knew that the voice guiding me all those years was the Lord's.

I did not heed that voice and went up to drink from the cup anyway. With all the previous ceremonies, it had taken about 45 minutes for the tea to start taking its effects. However, I had barely made it back to my spot on the floor when I blacked out and "woke up" in the spirit realm. I found myself to be of sound mind and sober in thought, more alert in my senses than I had ever been in the physical world. Everything in the spirit world—thought, vision, sound—seemed magnified tenfold. Quickly overcome with fear, I knew I had crossed over and heard a deep, loud, booming voice right behind me saying, "You knew this time would come."

Afraid, all I could think about at that moment was, "No, no, no, this can't be!"

I was aware that it was Yahweh speaking to me; however, it wasn't until some time later, when I was back in the physical world, that I realized the magnitude. I was in the presence of the great I AM.

After He spoke those words to me, He told me that even though I was a "good" person, I did not know Jesus. Now, I know what the Bible says about how not one of us is good (Romans 3:10-12). However, I think He was meeting me where I was—I did try to live my life treating others kindly and putting others before myself.

I was then shown my life in review, like a picture slideshow, to include the times I used to mock Christians. After this, I was shown prophetic visions of war that is to come in our own country. Ironically, they were the exact same visions I had seen in a dream a couple of years prior, which I chalked up to being nothing more than a dream at the time. Following the visions of war, I was shown two more visions as if they were being played out in real time, and I could feel what was happening to me as these visions played out.

The first vision I had was at the ceremony. I was lying unconscious on the living room floor; the ambulance had come to the house. I was looking down onto the living room from the ceiling as the paramedics came and rushed me to the hospital. Then, I was suddenly above the hospital room, looking down at my own body as the doctor frantically tried to resuscitate me after going into cardiac arrest. The doctor solemnly looked at the nurse and said, "I'm sorry, there's nothing more we can do for her."

In the second vision, I was driving back home from visiting my son in NYC to Buffalo when I got in a car accident. I was lying on the side of the road as a passerby was holding my head in her lap as I bled out from my injuries and died.

After the visions, I was then cast into a black abyss where the psychological torment began. It's hard to put into words what I felt because the feeling in the spirit realm is magnified tenfold compared to what we experience here on earth. Demons were tormenting my mind, almost like a merry-go-round, rapidly intensifying, then slowing down, only to speed back up again. I could hear another soul somewhere in that abyss wail out in their own torment, although I did not see them.

Somewhere amid my torment, feeling very weak, I felt the urge to call out to Jesus, which took all the strength I had to utter His name. It was as if the forces of darkness were keeping me from speaking His name; however, I mustered the energy to call out to Him. As soon as I did, I felt something spiritually begin to shift. I called out His name again, this time having gained a little more strength to call out to Him a little louder. I began to see a pinpoint of white light in the distance. It felt as if I was "waking up" again. I felt the darkness lift, and I understood what was happening. It was like I fell asleep on a raft in the lake and woke up from drowning, realizing that I had to fight to survive. I pleaded with Yahweh to let me come back—that it wasn't yet my time to go. I told Him if He allowed me to come back, I would tell the world that Jesus is real.

The louder I cried out to Jesus, the closer I began to drift toward the light, which grew brighter and bigger. As I approached the light, Yahweh showed me that the world is spiritually asleep and needs to wake up because Jesus is coming back soon. I entered the light, now a vast white space, brighter than any shade of white I have ever seen. I was ushered toward heavenly voices that were singing and praising the name of Jesus, and I joined them as I trembled in amazement. About 20 people were standing there, all dressed in the same pure white, looking in my direction and acting as if they were celebrating as they kept singing, "Jesus, Jesus, Jesus...." Then that's when I realized they were celebrating me! My birth. My awakening. They had all been praying for me when I was in the black abyss of torment. The urge I felt to cry out to Jesus from the abyss was the prayers of those Saints being answered.

I was led in front of the crowd and baptized. As soon as I was baptized, I returned to my physical body; I was in utter shock and disbelief when I returned. As soon as I came to, the Lord showed me that if I hadn't cried out to Jesus from the abyss, my fate would've been sealed with that first vision he had given me with the paramedics coming to the house.

Remember that second vision I had about the car accident? That came to pass in June of 2020; however, the outcome was not fatal, as in the vision. I was heading back to Buffalo from visiting with my son when, just before sunrise, I hit a deer almost head-on, going 75 mph. As I survived the impact after my car spiraled out of control on the highway, Holy Spirit reminded me that if I hadn't given my life to Him when I did, I would have died in that accident.

If I hadn't given my life to Jesus, I wouldn't be here today, testifying that Jesus is very much real. We need Him now more than ever.

It's possible that people may read my story and excuse my sins because of all I endured. But no matter what we have gone through, God holds each of us accountable for what we do. Thankfully, He has already paid the price for our sins and stands ready to forgive us. He has made a way for us to live in the light with Him for eternity. But we must turn to Him and call out His name. There is hope in knowing Jesus.

Your life can be over in the blink of an eye. You don't have all the time in the world to get right with Jesus. He is the only way, the truth, and the life. The only way to the Father is through Him.

Jesus said to him, "I am the way, and the truth, and the life. No one comes to the Father except through me" (John 14:6 ESV).

Say yes to the hope that only Jesus can offer.

Hope in Jesus Christ

By Kimberly Ann Hobbs

For to this end, we toil and strive, because we have our hope set on the living God, who is the Savior of all people, especially of those who believe (1 Timothy 4:10 ESV).

Have you ever asked a person who seems to be joy-filled all the time why they are always so full of contentment? I have, and it never ceases to amaze me that the answers I receive often have to do with having Jesus in their heart and being alive another day on this earth.

Before I had Jesus living in my heart, I would fight back against my emotions. My daily concerns about my future were a constant battle. Would I wake up to a day dealing with depression over things I could not change? Often, I would. My hope waned because of things I strived to do in my own power; I lacked the ability to control the circumstances around me, so I allowed myself to take on the weight of the world. I needed to meet the God who would not desert me in tough times. I needed to see the Jesus who would come alive to me in His scriptures and speak into my heart the truths I needed to hear. I needed a source of POWER that could help me. In the scriptures, I read about His presence bringing hope even in the darkest of places, but I did not seek Him.

God understands that sometimes our anxieties or depression can put us in a place of complete grief. But He provided His Son, Jesus Christ, as the antidote for our suffering and the ultimate sacrifice for our sins—we need only trust His work on the cross accomplished for each of us. Give yourself permission to seek God, trust Him as your Creator, and believe His living Word as a manual for life.

> *For this is how much God loves the world—He gave his one and only, unique Son as a gift. So now everyone who believes in him will never perish but experience everlasting life* (John 3:16 TPT).

God offered true hope by loving us enough to be born into this world as a human being named Jesus Christ and then giving up that life—experiencing death Himself—in order to save anyone who trusts in Him from sin and death. What a scripture—the best scripture that gives us hope in Jesus Christ.

I can now honestly say Jesus Christ has brought me everlasting hope so that each day I wake up, I have the joy of my salvation through Jesus Christ embedded in my heart. I have surrendered my life to Him and completely repented of my sin—trusting His work on the cross has granted me full forgiveness. And now, all my sins are cleansed through His shed blood. I believe by faith that the God of hope has given me POWER through Jesus. He has brought me joy that never ceases.

We can find so much hope in scripture through the gift of eternal life brought to us and made possible through Jesus Christ. No matter what anxieties, trials, temptations, or pain we suffer from, we can be confident in the hope God extends to us.

> *I've written this letter to you who believe in the name of the Son of God so that you will be assured and know without a doubt that you have eternal life. Since we have this confidence, we can also have great boldness before him, for if we present any request agreeable to his will, he will hear us* (1 John 5:13-14 TPT).

Celebrate with praises the God and Father of our Lord Jesus Christ, who has shown us his extravagant mercy. For his fountain of mercy has given us a new life---we are reborn to experience a living, energetic hope through the resurrection of Jesus Christ from the dead. We are reborn into a perfect inheritance that can never perish, never be defiled, and never diminish. It is promised and preserved forever in the heavenly realm for you! Through our faith, the mighty power of God constantly guards us until our full salvation is ready to be revealed in the last time. May the thought of this cause you to jump for joy, even though lately you've had to put up with the grief of many trials (1 Peter 1:3-6 TPT).

For by grace you have been saved by faith. Nothing you did could ever earn this salvation, for it was the love gift from God that brought us to Christ! So, no one will ever be able to boast, for salvation is never a reward for good works or human striving (Ephesians 2:8-10 TPT).

In Jesus, God determined that we would be able to do the good works He planned for us and walk in them. That should bring us tremendous hope and a joy-filled spirit.

. . . .

Shirley Stewart

Shirley Stewart is a passionate lover of Jesus Christ and a daughter of the Living God. For over thirty years, she has spent countless hours journaling in the presence of God as her Heavenly Father speaks to her. Today, those journals stack over two feet tall. As she spends intimate time in the presence of the Lord, her very being reflects His glory. Shirley loves sharing the truth of God and His Word with others, ministering to them as the Lord sets them free.

Shirley lives in Chesterland, Ohio, and has been married to her husband, Tom, for almost 35 years. They have three wonderful adult children and two beautiful grandchildren, with a third expected soon. Shirley works alongside her husband, stewarding a small, prosperous business that the Lord has blessed them with.

Shirley has served the Lord, ministering to both men and women for over 25 years. She believes a relationship with Father God is one of deep personal intimacy. Her heart's desire is to see others connect to Him in a deep, meaningful way that allows the Lord to transform them in His presence.

A Hope That Does Not Disappoint

By Shirley Stewart

> When hope's dream seems to drag on and on, the delay can be depressing. But when at last your dream comes true, life's sweetness will satisfy your soul (Proverbs 13:12 TPT).

*HOPE: (biblical definition) "a strong and confident expectation";

(worldly definition) "to wish for, to expect, but without certainty of the fulfillment; to desire very much" *[Bible.org]

Have you ever hoped for something only to be disappointed? I know I have, time and time again. I had worldly hope. As a child, I grew up in a home where my parents made promises but rarely kept them. My earthly father was emotionally distant from me. Being a workaholic, he was far removed from my life.

When I was born again in 1994, I came to know Jesus as my Lord and Savior. It was through the testimonies of His people that I heard about Him. I chose to put my hope in Him to save me from the disastrous circumstances

I found myself in. At that time, Father God seemed distant and far removed from me. I didn't realize that I was relating to my Heavenly Father through the experiences I had with my earthly father. Through those experiences, I learned that hoping and dreaming only ended in disappointment. Father God knew that the foundation of my life had to change, and that foundation was what I believed deep in my heart about Him. My beliefs came from my experiences with my earthly father and the things I heard and was taught. What we hope for or who we put our hope in is based on our beliefs. What we believe is the foundation of hope itself.

My beliefs from my childhood experiences did not reflect the truth of who my Heavenly Father is. God knew I had to learn through new experiences with Him that He is the Living Hope of my life, He is a good, good Father who loves me unconditionally and cares about every aspect of my life, and He is intricately involved and present in everything I am and am living through. I also had to learn in my heart that God's Word is true and can be believed and that He is a promise keeper. Father God needed to reveal the lies buried in my soul that distorted the truth about who He is. He had to show me what I believed in my heart, not just in my head, to uproot those lies and plant the truth.

When we believe in the One who is hope, we will never be disappointed. I have walked this journey with God for over 20 years. Only recently have my eyes been fully opened, and I have begun to develop a deep understanding of who God truly is.

> *You kissed my heart with forgiveness, in spite of all I've done. You've healed me inside and out from every disease* (Psalm 103:3 TPT).

When I was born again, I learned about God. I heard Him through reading the Bible, listening to preaching and Christian radio, talking and listening to His people, and by the revelation of His voice speaking to my heart. The voice of God is revealed to us by the Holy Spirit, which we receive upon salvation.

About a month after I accepted Jesus as my Lord and Savior, I was diagnosed with Lupus, an autoimmune disease in which the body's immune system attacks healthy cells. Currently, there is no cure, and it ends in death. Over the course of the following five years, I continued to listen as the Lord spoke to me. He showed me the "root" of the disease was in my soul—it was self-hate. As I walked this out with Him, repenting and renewing my mind daily to receive His love and learning to love myself, He changed my heart and destroyed the root. At the end of that five-year journey, God miraculously healed me, actually changing my DNA. I came to know the Lord as Jehovah-Rapha, The Lord Who Heals. Even meeting Him in this way, however, did not uproot the deep lies planted in my heart that made me susceptible to hearing the enemy's voice.

There is no fear in love; but perfect love casts out fear, because fear involves torment. But he who fears has not been made perfect in love (1 John 4:18 NKJV).

A few years later, I began having symptoms of another autoimmune disease, Multiple Sclerosis, or "MS" for short. Again, there is no cure, and eventually, it will end in death. After having an MRI (a type of x-ray) done on my brain, the neurosurgeon told me that the result was negative; I did not have MS. All my symptoms ceased after that. But during this time, the enemy of my soul, Satan, ingrained in me accusations that God had not healed me the first time. I heard his lies, which planted fear in my heart because I had come to believe from my childhood experiences that I couldn't trust those who cared for me.

About eight years after that, I was in an automobile accident. I had an MRI done to make sure my neck and back were okay. The results showed signs of MS. The doctor assured me that what she saw on the MRI was definitely

MS. Of course, fear rose up in me, and Satan said, "See? I told you so."

The doctor sent me for another MRI of my brain; the results came back clear—there were no signs of MS. She apologized and said, "Well, let's just say that you are highly susceptible to getting MS." This reinforced the fear in my heart that something was wrong with me, and the lie Satan spoke to me that God hadn't really healed me. Once again, I listened.

During that time frame, I was also diagnosed with degenerative disc disease in my lower back, something I have been enduring for over 20 years. This disease is a loss of cushioning of the discs between the vertebrae in my spine. It has caused me chronic pain that has gotten progressively worse over time. I also developed pain and weakness down my legs, with the most recent symptom being my right leg not functioning correctly.

> When you are half-hearted and wavering, it leaves you unstable. Can you really expect to receive anything from the Lord when you're in that condition? (James 1:7-8 TPT).

Now, it so happens that MS also affects the muscles, nerves, and use of the legs. Over the years, I kept pushing out of my mind the thought that my leg problems were symptoms of MS. The Lord kept telling me that there was nothing like that wrong with me. But how could I deny the symptoms that were progressively getting worse? Satan was right there saying. "See? See? I told you so. It IS MS".

My motor functions, especially in my right leg, continued to decline noticeably. In 2019, upon the urging of a friend, I had another MRI done on my back. I made appointments with three different back surgeons who told me, "No surgery. You could end up worse than you are". They did not address the weakness and malfunctioning of my right leg. At that time, I was afraid to even mention the word "MS" to the doctors because, deep down, I was afraid I had it. The doctors directed me to do physical therapy focused on strengthening, balancing, and stretching. I also joined a hospital wellness center to use the weight machines and the therapy pool.

> *I waited patiently for the Lord; And He inclined to me, And heard my cry* (Psalm 40:1 NKJV).

During all those years, I kept crying out to God to heal me. I knew He could because He had healed me from Lupus all those years ago, and I know that nothing is impossible for God. But I kept wondering why He didn't do it. Again, Satan's lies came into my mind, saying that God didn't really heal me back then and that I actually had MS. I pushed those thoughts away and, being very determined, kept going to the gym four to five days a week. I truly believed that God would help me through exercise and stretching to regain my strength in both legs, especially the right one, which was so weak. I believed it would just take time.

> *But when he saw the wind, he was afraid and, beginning to sink, cried out, "Lord, save me!"* (Matthew 14:30 NIV).

In late spring of 2023, the symptoms in my right leg became terribly worse. My right foot began to drag, and I would trip and break my toes and often fall down. At times, my right leg would not move along with my body, and I would have to drag it along with me. By then, I had been going to the gym for over three years. One day, Satan said to me, "Look at your symptoms. They're getting worse even though you're working out almost every day. That's because it IS MS, and you're in denial. God isn't helping you or healing you. JUST LOOK AT WHAT'S GOING ON WITH YOUR BODY!" Suddenly, I looked. I took my eyes off Jesus, and I saw the symptoms. I saw the downhill decline. The fear that was in my heart rose up, saying, "Maybe it IS MS."

As I looked at the symptoms all around me and listened to the lies being spoken to me, I began to sink into a deep pit of hopelessness and depression. I began to believe that nothing could be done to help me. God wasn't answering me. He wasn't healing me. Depression overtook me; I had no desire to do anything or go anywhere. I had no desire to keep pressing on. All I could do was sleep; I was so tired all the time. I dragged myself to the gym, becoming a slave to it. My whole focus became working out so I could make myself better, so I could fix me. But it wasn't working. Nothing was working.

> But in the day that I'm afraid, I lay all my fears before you and trust in you with all my heart (Psalm 56:3 TPT).

Once again, I cried out to the Lord for help. I admitted I couldn't fix myself, no matter how hard I tried. I was in a pit of depression, and I needed help out of the pit. I had lost all hope. I became desperate and began not to care what the source of my problems was. I said to myself, "If it's MS, then it's MS. I'm no longer going to be afraid. I want to face this, Lord. I need your help."

> For we live by faith, not by what we see with our eyes (2 Corinthians 5:7 TPT).

It was hard for me to admit to anybody that I was suffering from depression. There was so much shame attached to it for me. Depression runs in my family line, but it was never talked about and always covered up. I made an appointment with my primary care doctor, but I kept beating myself up over making it. I thought that it meant I just didn't have enough faith for God to heal me. But then the Lord said to me, "Shirley—it took faith just to MAKE the appointment." Hearing that set me free. Opening up and sharing the fact that I was depressed with my doctor unloaded its power over me.

> *He lifted me out of the pit of despair, out of the mud and the mire. He set my feet on solid ground and steadied me as I walked along* (Psalm 40:2 NLT).

Once the Lord helped me out of the pit of depression, I began to hear Him more clearly. My back doctor scheduled a new MRI, suspecting I had developed spinal stenosis—a condition where pressure is put on the spinal cord and nerves within the spine. It causes pain, numbness, and muscle weakness. I became hopeful that the root of my issue would be revealed, and if it took back surgery, then so be it. I was no longer afraid to face anything. I just kept asking God to make the hidden things known.

> *Call to Me, and I will answer you—I will tell you great and hidden things, which you do not know* (Jeremiah 33:3 TLV).

The MRI results showed my spinal cord free from any stenosis. I couldn't believe it because my symptoms were so severe. The doctor's assistant told me there was nothing wrong with my back; I could get nerve block pain shots, or they could put me on a prescription for pain. Once again, there were no answers. I still had all the symptoms. I thought then that it must be the autoimmune disease MS because I definitely had a nerve/muscle issue. I made an appointment with a neurologist who couldn't see me for five months. At that time, I was also scheduled for an EMG. The test results were negative/normal—again, no answers.

> *Stop striving and know that I am God; I will be exalted among the nations, I will be exalted in the earth* (Psalms 46:10 NASB).

During those two months, I kept listening for God. I kept asking Him to reveal the hidden things. I had a memory of telling my dad as a child that I couldn't see the chalkboard at school. His response was, "You just want glasses because your sister has them." He didn't listen or believe me. After a year, the school contacted my parents and told them I needed glasses. Suddenly, God helped me understand I had come to believe that my earthly father never listened to me. He didn't believe me when I told him anything that was happening to me. The Lord showed me that belief had infiltrated my relationship with Him. Deep down, I believed God didn't listen to me when I cried out for help. That lie was the foundation of my relationship with my Heavenly Father, and I didn't even know it. In that moment, I forgave my earthly father, and I asked God to forgive me for judging my father and believing this lie. The Lord wanted to reveal Himself to me as El Shama: A God who hears, a God who listens. God is not an absentee father who is far removed from my life, but a good, good Father who is completely involved in my life.

> And you shall know the truth, and the truth shall make you free (John 8:32 NKJV).

After this revelation, I went to see a second surgeon to get a second opinion. I prayed in the office before he came in, "Lord, you are the Great Physician. You are the Lord who heals me. Expose the hidden things. Open the ears of the surgeon to hear me. You know what's going on; nothing is impossible for you, Lord. You are here with me and within me. You never leave me or forsake me. I'm trusting in You, Lord, not in doctors or their reports. I am trusting in You and Your report for me."

When the surgeon came in, He had looked at the MRI and already knew what was going on. He showed me I had lumbar stenosis, a condition where the nerves running down my right leg were being choked out. He knew this condition was the cause of all my symptoms. He said that with a minimally invasive back surgery, he could fix me. My heart leaped for joy, and I said, "Are you saying there's hope for me?" I believe the Lord Jesus spoke through him in his response, "Shirley, there's always hope."

God used this situation in my life to expose the lies I believed about Him, of which I was unaware. He showed me a few other memories from my childhood that had also planted lies in me, not only about Him but about myself. Repentance and forgiveness cleaned out my childhood memories and cleaned out my heart, too. Father God wants us to know Him as He truly is. He wants to reveal His character and nature so we can know Him intimately. And He will use every situation and expose every lie to ensure we see Him.

> *Now may the God of hope fill you with all joy and peace in believing, that you may abound in hope by the power of the Holy Spirit* (Romans 15:13 NKJV).

The truth is, I do not have an autoimmune disease. I was healed from that almost 30 years ago. Satan lied to me, and when I listened, he planted fear in my heart founded on lies. Only God's perfect love can cast out fear.

I now know God not only as my healer but also as my good, good Father who hears me and listens to me. He cares about me and loves me beyond measure. He wants me to know Him intimately, and He doesn't want anything to prevent that. He will make the hidden things known—in His way and in His time.

God's ways are higher than our ways. He sees and understands what we cannot. God knows the plans He has for each us—His plans are to prosper us and not to harm us, to give us a hope and a future (from Jeremiah 29:11). Hope in Him will not disappoint, for He truly is Elohim Yachal, the God of All Hope.

Hope in a New Day Dawning

By Kimberly Ann Hobbs

When times are dark, it can be difficult to see beams of light, let alone look for the dawning of a new day. But with God's presence, there is always beauty; He gives us hope for tomorrow. Although looking beyond what is happening in tough and uncertain times can be difficult, the silver lining of the Son will always usher in hope.

Spring is a time of refreshment and renewal, with flowers blooming and the sun staying out for longer periods of time. Our spirits are lifted, and our days seem brighter as plants burst out of the ground and vibrant colors and fragrances bring fresh new beginnings. But we don't have to wait for spring to experience renewal. We can live with the newness of life each time we open the Bible. The Bible is a place that will show us the dawning of a new day. In it, we can find scriptures that spark hopefulness in even the gloomiest of days.

Because we don't focus our attention on what is seen but on what is unseen. For what is seen is temporary, but the unseen realm is eternal (2 Corinthians 4:18 TPT).

We cannot see what is ahead or what tomorrow will bring, and as human beings, we can get stuck as we fix our eyes on only what is currently happening. But God gives us hope when He tells us that what we see is only temporary, but what we do not yet see ahead is eternal. God instructs us not to worry about tomorrow because tomorrow will worry about itself, and every day has enough trouble of its own. And the Gospel of Matthew shares in chapter 6, verse 34, that when we put our hope in God and believe that

He exists, we have an anchor for our soul and hope for our tomorrow.

> *"For I know the plans I have for you," says the Lord. "They are plans for good and not for disaster, to give you a future and a hope"* (Jeremiah 29:11 NLT).

When you go your own way and put all your hope in things that disappoint you, you can give everything over to God. You can ask Him how to live in confident expectation to face tomorrow. He will make Himself known to you and show you where to walk. The God of hope is only a prayer away; a new day dawning is on the horizon.

Placing our faith and hope in God not only gives us help, strength, and power for today, but it also gives us hope for life after death. There is no more confident expectation of the ultimate tomorrow than to know that your eternal destination is secure in Jesus Christ.

> *Now may God, the inspiration and fountain of hope, fill you to overflowing with uncontainable joy and perfect peace as you trust in him. And may the power of the Holy Spirit continually surround your life with his super-abundance until you radiate with hope!* (Romans 15:13 TPT)

It is natural to talk about our tomorrows and think about things we plan to do, but no one knows for sure if tomorrow will ever come. We do know that everyone has a day appointed unto death, so we best be assured that we have the right relationship with God. The Bible tells us to seek God first, before everything else, then your tomorrows can be added to you.

Therefore, do not worry about tomorrow, for tomorrow will worry about itself. Each day has enough trouble of its own (Matthew 6:34 NIV).

By placing your trust and faith in God alone, the God of your today is faithful to be your God of tomorrow. He has been faithful to every generation—past, present, and future. He is even faithful to us when we are without faith. He tells us that He has a grand plan for each of our lives, and He is in control of them. And just as spring is a new season and a fresh start, tomorrow is a new day dawning. God has your future placed in the strong hands of Jesus Christ if you surrender your trust and control to Him.

Romans 8:24 says, *Hope that is seen is no hope at all. Who hopes for what they already have?* (NIV).

There is your answer. When you cannot see the good or the light at the end, look to tomorrow. God's light is shining on a new day dawning. Jesus' power is shown through our weakness, and our greatest strengths are found through Him alone. As the sun rises every day on time, so will tomorrow with a fresh start upon you. Because Jesus, the Son, gives us hope for a new day dawning.

. . . .

Lynn Strickland

Lynn Strickland grew up in rural North Florida in the town of Perry. After meeting her husband David, they settled in Lake City, FL, and raised their family. Recently, she and her husband relocated to beautiful North Carolina. Lynn's greatest accomplishment is being a mom and Gigi. They have five beautiful children and seven grandchildren. She enjoys spending time with her family playing board games, having cookouts, or traveling. Her family is only second to God in her life.

Lynn has been a nurse for 30 years, most of them focusing on home care. Currently, she is the VP of Education for Concierge Home Care. She also serves in her local church on the praise team and has worked many years with the youth and as the camp nurse.

God has been a part of Lynn's life from a very young age thanks to wonderful grandmothers; although there have been many trials and troubles, she believes that her faith and relationship with God is the only reason she is still here and able to tell you her story. Lynn's desire is that when you read about her journey with COVID, you will find hope in whatever your story is.

Faith to Fight

By Lynn Strickland

I've spent the last 24 months on an extraordinary journey with God—a beautiful journey of healing, restoration, and miracles that I believe God wants me to share with the world. I've documented my journey along the way so I can share my story of what God has done and continues to do in my life.

My early years were full of trauma and abuse but also love. I was raised mainly by my two wonderful grandmothers, who taught me about the love of Jesus and made sure that I was in church on Sunday. Because of these two amazing women, I know God and have been able to endure trials and be here today.

I remember praying as a small child, asking God to help me. I often felt alone and afraid but always had hope that God was with me. He became my best friend and my only source of strength. The first 20 years of my life were not easy. I learned at an early age to be independent and rely only on my grandmothers and God. I can look back now and see the amazing people God brought into my life to help shape who I am today. In the midst of chaos, I learned to cling to God and His promises. My story is about holding tight to those promises and believing God for miracles beyond what you could ask or imagine.

> Now to him who is able to do immeasurably more than all we ask or imagine, according to his power that is at work within us (Ephesians 3:20 NIV).

In March of 2020, COVID-19 hit the world. I work for a home care company, traveling the state of Florida to provide education at the offices. During that season, I trained everyone to care for COVID patients and educated them on infection control. Of course, none of us had ever been through a pandemic of that magnitude. I remember staying glued to the TV and the daily press conferences in between the continuous conference calls we provided to keep our staff and patients safe. It was excruciating to watch the number of deaths climb daily with no answers. We were only told to remain home when possible, wear a mask, and stay six feet away from others.

When the pandemic hit, my daughter was home from college on spring break and could not return to school that year. My son lost the last few months of his junior year in high school and went through his senior year with restrictions. Being isolated from his friends caused him to struggle with depression. He would take long runs to get his adrenaline going and to feel better. My other daughter was in nursing school when COVID hit. Her class was forced to switch to online learning, which is not the best for nursing students. By the time she graduated, she was in full throttle taking care of COVID patients.

My husband could not remain home during the height of the pandemic. He was a grocery store manager, a job considered to be "essential." This meant he had to work with the public daily, potentially being exposed to the virus and bringing it home to us. The risk was high, but our story is not unique. There are families all over the world who experienced the same or much worse. During this time, our world suffered mentally, physically, and financially. The fight-or-flight response was always engaged, and the long-term impact was devastating.

I found comfort in the presence of God and on my church praise team. Even though the church had moved to online services only, I was on the team that made this possible. Some lessons learned through those early months of the pandemic were life-changing. Before COVID, I often took relationships and attending life events for granted. During the pandemic, many missed birthdays, holidays, and even funerals. I personally gained perspective on what is most important in my life and learned that when a crisis strikes, all I have is others and God. With all the distractions of the world and life taken away, God had so much in mind for me to learn.

A few months into the pandemic, I was needed in South Florida to assist our company in merging with another. Honestly, I was so ready to get out of the house. I was a little concerned but was obsessed with cleaning everything and avoiding exposure. In all my travels for work, I was fortunate to avoid COVID for 18 months.

This is where my personal world came to a grinding halt!

I wasn't feeling well for a couple of weeks and took many COVID tests, which were all negative. On August 15, 2021, I visited my daughter while still not feeling great. I tested again; that time, it was positive.

My first instinct was to panic. My overall health was not that great. I weighed 337 pounds and had type 2 diabetes with frequent bouts of bronchitis and asthma. I knew in my gut that this was not going to be good. I immediately called one of my best friends, who instructed me to go to the hospital to receive early intervention. My sweet husband drove me to the University of Florida and dropped me at the emergency room door. He was not allowed to come in and sat in the parking lot for hours. Unfortunately, I was not a candidate for the antibodies as my oxygen saturation levels had already started to go down, and I was admitted that day. While I was waiting to be moved, God and I had a chat. I had prayed on the way to the hospital and continued praying throughout the night.

I have experienced God's presence before and felt the Holy Spirit move, but this was different. As I was lying in the ER alone and scared, I felt His presence from the top of my head to the bottom of my feet.

I audibly heard God say, "I got you, my daughter. You will go through tough times, but hold onto your faith and know that I will fully heal and restore you."

> "But I will restore you to health and heal your wounds," declares the LORD (Jeremiah 30:17 NIV).

God assured me I would be okay. I believed His promise and held onto it with every fiber of my being. I wouldn't go on a ventilator.

> Let us hold tightly without wavering to the hope we affirm, for God can be trusted to keep his promise (Hebrews 10:23 NLT).

I stayed in the hospital for one night and then was sent home. I was certain I would have to return at some point, but the beds were full. It was complete chaos. Sick people were piled in rooms and every space of the hospital. After my release, I did everything I knew as a nurse to stay healthy and try to heal.

About a week later, I thought I was feeling well enough to ride to Nashville and take my son to college. The night we arrived, my oxygen levels were decreasing. When we got to our Airbnb, I could barely make it inside. When I did, I just went to bed. I was in respiratory failure but did not comprehend it was that bad. The next morning, I couldn't move and wanted to be left alone to sleep. A friend, not knowing I was that sick, called me about a work question. I messaged her back, "Can't talk, can't breathe, resting." She called my daughter and my boss (best friend) with concern. They called immediately and, in no uncertain terms, told me to get to the hospital immediately.

My husband and son were with me. My son stepped into immediate action. He said, "You are not going to bully us into not taking you. We are going to the hospital right now."

At that moment, I knew my son was a man. It took me five hours to get ready. I just couldn't breathe. My husband again had to drop me off at an ER door, this time at Vanderbilt Hospital in Nashville, Tennessee. He didn't know if he would ever see me again. I couldn't imagine what he was feeling as he had to drive away and leave me there. I would not get to hold his hand again for 21 days.

I was taken to the hospital's garage, which had been turned into a holding area, until they could get me a bed. I spent one night in that garage and then one night on the regular COVID floor. The next day, I crashed and went to the ICU for the following 56 days. For the next few weeks, I was in a fight for my life. However, I knew I was going to be okay. God and I had a secret. He had told me I would face something difficult, but I would be okay. I knew I had to go through this journey for His glory to show the world what a promise-keeping and miracle-working God He is.

I held His promise close and denied the ventilator on several occasions. God had said I would be okay.

I was in respiratory failure, and at any moment, they said I was going to go into multi-organ failure. I told them that no, I wasn't. I would live.

They said I had a pulmonary embolism. It took them three days to get me stable enough to have a CT scan. I told them it wasn't an embolism, and it wasn't.

I was on bi-pap (a mask to force air into my lungs) and high amounts of oxygen and steroids. They were doing everything they could to save me. In the 92 days I was in the hospital, I made sure to tell EVERYONE who entered my room about God's promise to me and how He was working miracles!

> Therefore, since we have been justified through faith, we have peace with God through our Lord Jesus Christ, through whom we have gained access by faith into this grace in which we now stand. And we boast in the hope of the glory of God. Not only so, but we also glory in our sufferings, because we know that suffering produces perseverance; perseverance, character; and character, hope (Romans 5:1-4 NIV).

At one point, I was not doing well, and my family was told to prepare for the worst. My daughter flew to Nashville for the second time. During those first few weeks, I could only have one visitor for two hours each day. They could sit outside my ICU door and Facetime me. My husband, children, and brother took turns staying with me. To this day, my heart breaks for them; I knew I would be okay, but they did not have that same reassurance. They believed what I said but didn't have the same encounter with God that I had.

The doctors tried on multiple occasions to put me on the vent. One night, they were around my bed in gowns and with shields on their faces. It looked like a scene from a horror movie. They said, "Mrs. Strickland, you need to go on the ventilator as your oxygen levels are in the 70s and 60s."

I looked at them and whispered with the little air I had left, "God is busy down the hall and will be back to me in a minute. Wait. If I become unconscious, do whatever you have to."

They said I could have ten minutes.

I reminded them that is all God needs.

Blessed is she who has believed that the Lord would fulfill his promises to her! (Luke 1:45 NIV).

After they left the room, I felt myself going in and out of consciousness. Suddenly, I felt my bed shake, and I heard the word, "Breathe."

I saw two people in my room, and I knew with my entire soul that it was Jesus at the foot of my bed and my daddy, who had passed exactly two years earlier, to the left of me. Jesus had saved me many nights before, but the miracle that night was extra special. He brought my daddy. He knew what I needed at that exact moment.

The doctors and respiratory team came running back in as my oxygen levels started climbing. They had been preparing the crash cart and the ventilator. The respiratory therapist was getting things ready, and I said to her, "Well, Jesus showed up and made things better."

Some would say that I was hallucinating that day—that my brain had been deprived of oxygen, and I wasn't in the best shape. But I know the truth. I know with full clarity and certainty I was in the presence of God as He showered many miracles over me.

I had moments of frustration and sadness throughout this entire ordeal, but I was never afraid. I know it's hard to believe, but after the first night at the hospital, I knew God would keep His promises. There were many ups and downs in the 92 days in the hospital, but God showed up for every single one of those days. He reassured me through my daily devotions, prayers, calls, and visitors that I was okay.

Sometimes, God will purposely stop us in our tracks with a big train to remind us that we have to depend fully on Him. My life is a perfect example of this. I had been going to church, working constantly, and thought I was fully leaning on God, but He showed me I wasn't. I was coasting.

He performed miracles for me, not just physically but also spiritually and mentally; He performed miracles in my health, family, and marriage. I will never take my sweet husband for granted. He meant the vows that he had made years before.

I fought hard to get home for Thanksgiving. The hospital didn't want to release me, but I'm stubborn and got my way. I was in a wheelchair and on oxygen, but I was going home. I had not been outside for 92 days. I had not felt the sun on my face for 92 days. The world seemed more alive, vibrant, and colorful than I remembered. I will never forget the first night I pulled up to my house. A friend had placed a big sign in the yard that said, "Welcome Home, Lynn." The tears just flowed.

For the next six months, I fought to regain my strength. I ended up in the hospital two more times due to lung damage and pneumonia. I continued my therapy, and I was determined to get out of that wheelchair and be present when my newest granddaughter was born. And although I was still in the chair, I made the trip back to Nashville to see our sweet granddaughter be born.

In October of 2022, I said goodbye to my oxygen. I went on a women's retreat and refused to be tied down to it. I reminded God that He promised me healing and took it off. My next lung doctor's appointment was right after that trip. I walked into his office—with no wheelchair, no oxygen, and with a new CT scan that showed marked improvements. "See? They had told me I would never get off oxygen, that I had pulmonary hypertension, and I would most likely need a lung transplant."

The doctor said, "Your will to survive is remarkable and has gotten you this far."

But I told him God was healing me and that I didn't do any of this on my own. It was God; He healed me as He promised. I'm not sure if the doctor was a believer or not, but he was very aware that he couldn't fix me.

I have now lost over 120 pounds. I am walking, working, and living life to the fullest with family and friends—because God kept His promise. He got me to that hospital in Nashville. He put people in my path so I could witness and tell them how great our God is. The healthcare workers were tired from the death all around them. They needed a win, and I was their win—right when they needed it.

That was God, y'all.

He led me to pray with so many in that hospital and through my journey. He has shined His glory. And if one person has been saved or if one person has come to know Him more, then my life has counted. My journey has been worth it. He is a good Father, and He wants all people to know His love.

God gave me the vision to write a book and tell the entire world what He did for me—this is my first step. He has provided more opportunities than I could wish or ask for—I have spoken at women's retreats, given my testimony at church, shared on a podcast with Women World Leaders, and am now writing in this book. God brought me from debilitated to exhilarated. And He wants to do the same in your life. No matter what your journey is, God wants to walk through it with you. He is there in illness, addiction, disease, divorce, brokenness, trauma, abuse, depression, and anxiety. All of it. God can restore everything. And He loves you and desires to have a relationship with you. God is so, so good!

Now may God, the inspiration and fountain of hope, fill you to overflowing with uncontainable joy and perfect peace as you trust in him. And may the power of the Holy Spirit continually surround your life with his super-abundance until you radiate with hope! (Romans 15: 13 TPT).

Hope in Healing

By Kimberly Ann Hobbs

How do we find hope during the tough times when we are praying for healing? The key is allowing our situations and emotions to take on a biblical perspective. When we look to the sources that provide the right answers, we experience a paradigm shift that will not only provide a brighter outlook but will also allow our natural bodies to heal.

> *My son, pay attention to what I say; turn your ear to my words. Do not let them out of your sight, keep them within your heart; for they are life to those who find them and health to one's whole body* (Proverbs 4:20-22 NIV).

I know there are some reading this book right now who are in need of healing. We all cry out to be fixed in different ways. Whether we need physical healing, emotional healing, or even spiritual healing, we look for a solution and try to find it wherever we can.

Be on guard, as the enemy of your soul wants to use your troubled situation to bring up negative emotions. It is a tactic of Satan to speak lies to you. He may utter words such as, "Jesus has forgotten you," or "God is delaying His healing for you because of something you did wrong." Or even more drastically, he may say, "Your end is near," or "The end of the life of someone you love is near." Remember, no one knows the day Jesus will call any one of us home to be with Him, especially not the devil. There is a counter-response that will put those lies to death.

Heal me, Lord, and I will be healed; save me and I will be saved, for you are the one I praise (Jeremiah 17:14 NIV).

God provides us with so many scriptures that counter the lies the enemy wants us to believe. Scripture is therapy to our souls that offers us tremendous hope in healing. Cry out to the Lord in your trouble and praise Him in your storm. I know it may sound difficult to praise God when all we want to do is curl up in a ball and give up. But when we praise God by proclaiming His Word, we remind ourselves of His goodness. His holy scriptures are filled with instructions for us even when we are suffering and in need of healing. If you or someone you know is going through a difficult illness of any kind, take comfort in reading God's scriptures on healing.

> *Then they cried out to the Lord in their trouble, and he delivered them from their distress...Let them give thanks to the Lord for his unfailing love and his wonderful deeds for mankind, for he satisfies the thirsty and fills the hungry with good things* (Psalm 107:6, 8-9 NIV).

"I have heard your prayer and seen your tears; I will heal you" (2 Kings 20:5 NIV).

> *My son, pay attention to what I say; turn your ear to my words. Do not let them out of your sight, keep them within your heart; for they are life to those who find them and health to one's whole body* (Proverbs 4:20-22 NIV).

"He will wipe every tear from their eyes. There will be no more death or mourning or crying or pain, for the old order of things has passed away" (Revelation 21:4 NIV).

> *Lord my God, I called to you for help, and you healed me* (Psalm 30:2 NIV).

> *But he was pierced for our transgressions, he was crushed for our iniquities; the punishment that brought us peace was on him, and by his wounds we are healed* (Isaiah 53:5 NIV).

Jesus wants us to see Him as the source of hope in our healing. We can find so many scriptures that point us to the hope that lies within our Savior. We can truly experience this healing now and not in the distant future. Focus on the words of Jesus scattered in abundance within His Word, His living Word, the Bible.

Find a community that will speak truth from the Word of God into your life and allow them to pray with you. Look for scriptures you can memorize that will allow you to grasp hope and cling to it. God does not want you to suffer alone. The enemy wants you to believe that no one cares about your sickness and you are alone without hope. Please do not isolate; understand you are not alone because God has given you hope in healing through your relationship with Him.

The scriptures speak truth, and God confirms that truth through other believers who will help you, pray with you, read with you, and point you to God.

. . . .

Kat Pennington

Kat Pennington and her husband have three children, several grandchildren, and a liver-colored mini-schnauzer named Trooper.

Kat was a professional photographer for over 30 years, specializing in photographing children and high school seniors. She began her business in a small building adorned with a brightly colored striped awning on the town square.

Later in her career, after marrying her military husband, Kat began to specialize in weddings. She freelanced for several photography businesses when they were assigned to various locations, and she and her husband jokingly called her "The pro on the go."

While her husband was stationed in Louisiana, she enjoyed teaching graduate-level photography as an adjunct professor at Northwestern State University.

A member of WWL (Women World Leaders), Kat has been a chapter writer for three books: the International Amazon #1 Best-Selling book *Miracle Mindset, Unshakable,* and *Hope Alive.*

Kat is a Stephen Minister, trained to provide one-to-one care for those experiencing a difficult time. She and her husband currently lead their church's Marriage Mentoring Ministry, sharing their passion for living marriage God's way.

When the Answer Is Yes

By Kat Pennington

I believe God's answer to every prayer is Yes. But wait a minute...don't we often learn God's answers come in a variety of Yes, No, or Wait? I would like to propose a different viewpoint.

How would our prayer perspective change if we expected God's answer to our every prayer to be something like, "Yes, of course," or "Yes, when the time is right," or "Yes, your prayer will be answered, but in a way you can't understand now." With any of those Yes answers, faith is exercised and hope is born.

Family Blessings

As a little girl, I daydreamed about what it would be like to have children. What would they look like? What would they enjoy? What would they grow up to be? I wanted to have loving, lifelong relationships with my children and grandchildren someday. I also wanted to provide the family stability I missed when I grew up in a dysfunctional family.

God exceeded my childhood dreams by blessing me more than I could imagine with two precious sons, Tommy and Tony. I raised my sons in the church's embrace, and from their youth, their hearts sought a relationship with God.

As the boys were growing up, I prayed that they would choose Christian wives, a request that God wonderfully fulfilled. One of my favorite Bible verses was, *Train up a child in the way he should go; even when he is old he will not depart from it* (Proverbs 22:6 ESV).

Just as my mom had taken me to church to learn about Jesus and belong to a Christian community, I took my boys to church for the same reasons. I hoped that they, in turn, would pass on this legacy to their children.

After both boys were married and established their own families, asking God for grandchildren was an addition to my prayers. Tony, the youngest of my sons, was the first to share the joyous news that we would have a grandchild—a granddaughter! It was an unforgettable day for my husband, Lee, and me.

We prayed that our granddaughter and future grandchildren would come to know Jesus Christ as their Savior. Now that we had entered the season of being grandparents, my heartfelt prayers were petitions that the boys and their wives would raise their children in a church community where they could be a part of a family of God-followers. Fast-forwarding a few years, that's just what happened. God is good.

Tony and his wife, Ryann, named our first grand Hadley Grace, affectionately nicknamed Had. We grandparents took turns passing her back and forth, showering her baby face with kisses. It was love at first sight on a truly "grand" scale!

Selecting grandparent names was a fun chore and a meaningful process for Lee and me. I decided on Oma, the German word for grandmother. This choice held a special significance for me because I was born in Wiesbaden, Germany, where my dad was stationed. Additionally, I have German ancestry, so Oma felt like the perfect fit.

Lee opted for Base as his grandparent name. This unique choice originated from a family story of a misunderstanding involving Lee's older brother. Their mom used to call their dad Babe, which Lee's brother heard as Base. The name stuck throughout Lee's dad's lifetime. So, Lee adopted Base as his new granddad name.

I have the sweetest memories of those early moments with Hadley Grace. Her melodious little voice would call out to me when we were playing, saying, "C'mon, Oma!" with a big smile accompanying my name. Had would smile and laugh a lot—as if God had given her an extraordinary zest for life. She found joy in almost everything; her speech was enthusiastic and harmonious. Even when she said the blessing before meals, listening to the lively inflection in her voice was a joy!

A Rising Storm

When Had was born, a nurse in the hospital noticed a tiny bruise on the upper part of our newborn granddaughter's right arm. At the initial follow-up, her doctor said not to be overly concerned, explaining that the bruise, now a little bump, would likely disappear as Hadley grew older. With a smile, he said not to worry.

By the next checkup, the size of the lump had not reduced. This time, the conclusion was that some children have small areas of nerves bunched up under their skin, and it takes a little while to straighten out.

But, during another checkup eight months later, a different doctor ordered a biopsy of the lump. Quickly thereafter, the doctor requested a second biopsy to investigate the initial test results further.

When we all, parents and grandparents, gathered to receive the test results, Hadley's doctor delivered the news that none of us had ever imagined hearing: *it was cancer.*

We were stunned. The doctor advised us not to turn to the internet due to the frightening and negative information that could be found there. Of course, we couldn't resist, and we immediately went online. I dove into researching everything I could that related to Rhabdomyosarcoma (Rhabdo for short), and the doctor was right. The information was alarming.

So, our precious Hadley was diagnosed with Rhabdo when she was just nine months old, and she started chemotherapy right away. The doctors implanted a port into Hadley's tiny body—a tube-shaped device beneath her skin on the front of her chest—so she could take 40 weeks of chemotherapy, blood transfusions, and other treatments.

As she was treated, Had believed everyone else was going through similar experiences; her innocence was endearing. One day, she tugged on Lee's shirt, pulling it away from his chest and asking, "Base, where is your port?" It was a heartwarming question that led to warm hugs and smiles.

Unfortunately, instead of improving, things got worse. Soon after Had's first birthday, her right arm, where the cancer was, was amputated just below the shoulder because the cancer was spreading.

On the day of the amputation, I entered the dim hospital room where she was taken after the surgery. I felt like the air had been sucked out of the room as I watched Had, despite the medication, crying due to the pain she was enduring. As he held her, Tony managed to smile at me and shared that his precious child was now cancer-free for the first time in her life. He expressed how he envisioned walking her down the aisle when she married. It was a strong testament to the power of hope.

During her recovery from the amputation, Had re-learned some basic skills, like how to balance herself when she was walking. She also discovered new techniques; for example, she picked a ball up by rolling it up her leg and learned to color while sitting up since she didn't have an elbow to lean on. When she became tickled and laughed, she would clap by tapping her left hand on her leg or chest. Even through the challenges, nothing dampened the joy she had for life.

Had was a frequent visitor in the oncology ward and lived in a world within a world, blending with all of the other children who were also missing their hair from the side effects of chemotherapy. Because of possible infection, her blood counts were usually too low for her to go out in public, and she mostly stayed in the hospital or at home.

Sometimes during her hospital stays, Had was too weak to walk, so we pulled her through the halls in a wagon so she could enjoy the decorations. When she did have the strength to walk the halls on her own, she usually managed a little jig of a dance, carrying a smile on her face as music swirled in her head. What pure joy to watch!

She loved going to the ocean; occasionally, her parents would take her to the beach, where she could roam without public contact. When she reached the age of two years and two months, it seemed that Had had triumphed over cancer. It appeared that brighter days were on the horizon.

The media heard about Hadley's zest for life; through news coverage, her story reached many people. Our family was blessed to hear testimonies of how her life was witnessing to and comforting other families going through difficult times.

The Raging Storm

Unfortunately, during another checkup, the doctors discovered a spot on one of Had's lungs, which led to another surgery to remove one of the lobes from her lung. But even through that surgery and despite feeling sick from yet another round of chemo treatments, Had remained happy and forward-focused, asking, "What are we going to do tomorrow?"

When she was two and a half years old, Hadley underwent a second round of chemotherapy with added radiation treatments. Given her age and the necessity to remain still during the radiation treatments, Had would be given anesthesia so her body could be placed in a specially created plaster cast that kept her immobile, ensuring the accuracy of the laser. Still, Hadley's unwavering spirit in the face of adversity during the treatments was truly remarkable.

Joy in the Storm

The Children's Hospital in Birmingham, Alabama, has an extraordinary program called *Hand in Paw*. As part of this program, a trained dog accompanies the child into the radiation room, jumping up on the table while the child drinks a glass of "magic milk" to induce sleep. After the radiation treatment, the dog is waiting on the table to greet the child as they wake up.

Hadley was paired with a salt-and-pepper-colored mini-schnauzer named Ellie. Hadley was excited about seeing Ellie every day, which, in turn, made her eager to go to her radiation treatments. During her radiation season, whenever she woke up, Hadley asked her parents if she would get to see Ellie that day. This was a heartwarming blessing.

Had and her parents lived a three-and-one-half-hour drive away, and although no one at the hospital knew, waiting for Hadley at home was her own salt-and-pepper-colored mini-schnauzer the family had raised from a puppy. Can you guess her name? Yes, it was Ellie! What a comfort it was to have what my family calls a "God wink."

By the time she reached the age of three, Hadley had endured a series of biopsies, two rounds of chemotherapy, an amputation, many blood transfusions, lung surgery, radiation, platelet transfusion, several medications, and shots almost every day. Another blessing was that Hadley's mom, Ryann, had nursing training in college and displayed remarkable skill in administering shots and providing expert nursing-level care for Hadley at home.

Home for Christmas

When Hadley was three years and two months old, her medical team administered a potent, one-time drip treatment with the instructions that if the drip worked as expected and she felt like it, she could go home the next day. We were ready for her to come home because it was Christmastime, and we had presents prepared for her under the tree.

But God had a different plan for Had's Christmas. Despite the efforts of skilled doctors from all over the country and Canada, shortly after midnight on 7 December 2006, with her family anxiously sitting in the hospital waiting room, our Hadley Grace went home to live with Jesus.

Just minutes after she transitioned to heaven, a line of doctors and nurses on call came to comfort our family and say farewell to their favorite little patient. Some told us how Had's life had touched their lives, and several wept.

Hadley lived surrounded by family and beloved pets and was bathed in love and affection every day of her life. From the first week she was diagnosed with cancer, her dad—my son Tony— faithfully documented an online diary. I requested Tony's permission to share his *Final Update* in this chapter, and he graciously agreed. The following paragraphs are part of an excerpt of Tony's last diary entry, written by my child about his child:

Final Update

It breaks my heart that I won't be giving any more updates on this site. Hadley's previous update seemed as if everything was okay. The truth was that it wasn't. Hadley has been a really sick little girl her whole three years of life but she has had such a remarkable spirit that it never showed.

A few short hours after posting the last update, Hadley began complaining that her tummy was hurting. We started to console her when she stopped responding. Her lips turned purple so without thinking, we grabbed her and sped to the hospital. We are so blessed by the apartment we had been given (loaned) only two blocks from the hospital. We were there in less than a minute. The doctors grabbed her right away and they began working on her. They got a tube down her throat and she began to respond well.

She was put in PICU, the pediatric intensive care unit, so they could find out what happened. She regained her color and got her complexion back. But every attempt to take her off of the machine failed because her body wasn't strong enough. They found the right side of her heart was enlarged so they began tracing what the problem could be. They found a clot in a vessel in her left leg. The doctors contacted the number one pediatric clot team in Toronto, Canada. Because of the severity of the clot, they begin to administer a clot buster called TPA. There was a 5% chance this could do fatal damage but doing nothing was fatal as well.

At midnight on 7 December the visiting hours opened and Ryann and I were the first parents to go back. We thought the previous night was the scariest moment of our lives, but when we went through the double doors, a team of doctors was around Hadley doing CPR. After 45 minutes the doctors stopped. What we know is that it was very fast. Hadley felt no pain and she wasn't alone.

Hadley had been taken Home. I find peace in the fact that I can't imagine the relief Hadley felt when she was cradled to Heaven. In my heart of hearts, I know Hadley knew she was going home. Until a couple of weeks ago Hadley had a typical three-year-old's list for Christmas. Hadley saw the statue of an angel outside the hospital and it had a harp.

From that moment on all Hadley asked for Christmas was a harp. I imagine she has it now. Hadley never complained in the hospital, and whenever home was mentioned, she always talked about (her pets) Peanut, Ellie, Oscar, or Sunny.

In the past week whenever we asked Hadley if she wanted something she said,

"No I just wanna go Home." No mention of an animal. I didn't know she meant Heaven. Rest assured, we have no regrets. Knowing what we know we would do it all over again for the blessing of Hadley.

Before time began God knew that a little girl named Hadley Grace would live three years and bless everyone she met. Everyone who knew this little girl would be encouraged, and they would learn something valuable about life and what really mattered. I am honored God allowed me and Ryann to be the parents of this special little girl...

... Please don't ever feel like you can't mention Hadley. We may at times tear up or cry, but we never want her forgotten. She will live on through the lessons she taught and the stories we will tell. Love to you all.

Life after Death

In the Bible, Paul quotes from the book of Hosea, *"O death, where is your victory? O death, where is your sting?"* (1 Corinthians 15:55 ESV). As a Christian, I'm confident that death is not an end but a doorway to a new beginning with eternal life—without suffering. I do not doubt that Hadley's last earthly breath was immediately followed by her first breath in heaven.

God gifted my family with treasured memories, and we continue to tell "Had stories"—there are many to tell. I would love to share with you a few of my favorite memories:

• Pink was her favorite color.

• Chicken strips and fry-fries were her favorite foods.

• She loved to say the blessing at mealtime.

• *Dora the Explorer,* a TV show she watched in the hospital, taught her how to say a few words in Spanish.

• She delighted in throwing rocks in the pond and exclaiming, "Baloosh!"

- She giggled when she jumped on the bed.

- Playing dress-up was always fun.

- She liked the big, shiny stars on top of Christmas trees.

- She had a joyful, high-pitched voice.

- She had pets, lots of them! Two dogs, one cat, one miniature horse, and some goldfish.

God's promises of a joyful reunion with Had, in His presence, clothe me with hope. Though I miss her like mad, I take delight in having her as my granddaughter and am certain I will see her again.

When the Answer Is Yes

From the time I received news about Hadley's illness, along with many other people, I asked God to heal Had completely. He did heal her. Completely. In *His* way and in *His* time. I know it was perfect because I trust Him. I leaned on His will and His wisdom and...

God's answer was Yes.

Hope in Suffering

By Connie A. VanHorn

Years ago, I found myself in a profound and excruciating hardship. The weight of suffering seemed unbearable, and I stood at a crossroads where pain threatened to consume me. In that dark place, where hope seemed lost forever, I discovered a glimmer of light that changed everything ... God's unwavering hope. I like to call this "Sprinkles of Hope." God found me belly down on the dirty floor of a Quality Inn. When I look back on that time, I can see the little droplets of gold that He showered on me, even in the darkness surrounding me. It was at that moment that my hope started to grow. I collected each one of those tiny droplets and placed them in my heart.

> Not only so, but we also glory in our sufferings, because we know that suffering produces perseverance; perseverance, character; and character, hope (Romans 5:3-4 NIV).

In the depths of my pain, I found a paradoxical truth—suffering, though agonizing, had the power to shape and refine me. Each trial and tribulation became a stepping stone towards a deeper understanding of resilience and hope.

The suffering I endured during that dark period of my life was temporary in comparison to the eternal glory that is waiting for me in heaven. God changed my perspective, allowing me to see beyond my suffering and embrace the promise of a brighter future.

This race. This life. It's a journey that leads us towards our final destination—

home with Jesus. Our hope is knowing that heaven is our ultimate goal, a place of eternal peace and joy beyond all suffering. We are going to suffer. Suffering is part of life; it is a refining fire that molds and shapes us into who we are meant to be. It can propel us into our purpose. God can and will use our suffering to bring others into relationship with Him. Even in our suffering, we are called to persevere, to hold onto the hope that God's plan is unfolding even in the dark places we travel.

It wasn't always easy to keep going. Some days were darker than others, and I remember vividly the days when the light at the end of my suffering seemed dim and distant. It was a terrifying and agonizing journey, but in the dark places, I found light, walking through the shadows with faith and following the trail that God lit up for me.

After I was saved, I prayed and asked God to reveal Himself to me. I needed hope and a miracle during that time. I didn't ask for anything specific, but God knows His children and what we each need to endure the race. The race that leads us home to Him. So, God revealed Himself to me through butterflies. These beautiful creatures became a constant reminder that GOD IS ALWAYS WITH ME! He lit up my path to keep me on course so I could stay focused on Him. He knows I am easily distracted and would need a constant reminder of His love for me. I look back on my time of suffering, and I wouldn't change a thing about it. It was in that place that I found God, and He restored my hope.

Have I not commanded you? Be strong and courageous. Do not be afraid; do not be discouraged, for the Lord your God will be with you wherever you go (Joshua 1:9 NIV).

This verse became my constant reminder that I was not alone in my suffering. God's presence is a continual source of courage and comfort, guiding me through the darkest of places.

Keep moving forward. Believe in the miracles that God can work in the midst of your suffering. Every trial and hardship is a canvas for God's glory to shine through, transforming our suffering into beauty.

This race.

This life.

It may be messy, painful, and heartbreaking, but if we can rise again and allow God to work in and through us, our lives can become a masterpiece of His grace and redemption. Be grateful for the scars and brokenness, for it's the proof of the faithfulness of God and the strength we have gained because of it.

> For our light and momentary troubles are achieving for us an eternal glory that far outweighs them all (2 Corinthians 4:17 NIV).

Keep pressing on, knowing each step brings you closer to the day Jesus will welcome you home with open arms. In the end, the transformation of suffering into triumph, of brokenness into wholeness, is one of God's greatest miracles. So come as you are, give your all to this race, and let your heart be filled with all the sprinkles of hope and excitement for the day Jesus will look upon you and say,

"Welcome Home."

Cindy Edgett

 Cindy Edgett is a wife, mother, teacher, and author of *Hear God's Voice Everyday*. Over the past forty years, she has served the Lord in multiple ministries such as Worship Team, Women's Bible Studies, Small Group Bible Studies, Inner Healing Prayer Ministry, Intercessory Prayer, Children's Ministries, and Youth Ministry.

She has a heart for this generation to be well-trained and equipped for the work of the Kingdom of God. She is passionate about teaching others to hear the voice of God. Cindy loves to facilitate workshops and help train up the next generation.

Quote: "Give a man a word from the Lord, and he will be edified; teach a man to hear God's voice, and he will have faith that produces hope for a lifetime."

Cindy and her husband, Curtis, will be married 43 years this year. They currently reside in beautiful South Florida.

A New Season Is Coming!

By Cindy Edgett

I am in a hard season as I write my story to share with you. My mother just passed away, I'm caring for my stepfather in hospice, and I still have the normal daily challenges that we all have in life. Despite my present circumstances, I am not hopeless! I can still hear the Lord's voice, which comforts me and gives me wisdom and hope for my future. But I haven't always had that hope—I gained it when I began to hold tight to my heavenly Father and trust in His plan.

> *"For I know the plans I have for you," declares the Lord, "plans to prosper you and not to harm you, plans to give you hope and a future"* (Jeremiah 29:11 NIV).

My father died when I was three years old. I was raised in a Christian home by my mom and grandparents until my mom remarried when I was ten. I knew of God and learned Bible stories from my grandparents and mom. Having lost my father at a young age, I longed for a father's love. As I heard the stories of God, I desired to know Him more, have a relationship with Him, and be close to Him. Even as a child, I grasped the concept of the Trinity of the Lord—Father, Son, and Holy Spirit. But I wanted the Lord to speak to me; I wanted to hear His voice. Through my early years, I tried to silence my desire to know God with things like drugs and alcohol. Thankfully, God was more in control of my life than I was.

Whether we recognize it or not, we all crave a relationship with God—not any god, but with the God of Creation, the Savior of the world. How do I know this? Because the Bible says: *He has made everything appropriate in its time. He has also set eternity in their heart, without the possibility that mankind will find out the work which God has done from the beginning even to the end* (Ecclesiastes 3:11 NASB).

Regardless of who we are and what we believe, God has set eternity in our hearts. That's how He created us—with a desire to be with Him. That is why we all look for something to fill the void in our lives. Ecclesiastes 3:11 makes so much sense to me now. The desire I had when I was younger and the desire I still have today can only be filled by God Himself.

Growing up in a Christian home did not protect me from the evil of this world. Even with some of the best family members to watch over me, Satan slipped in to bring pain into my life. At an early age, he brought fear, hopelessness, and despair. I had heard the stories of Jesus and how He delivered His people, and I began to wonder why He did not spare me from the pain of this world.

Pain can cause some to turn against the Lord, but something deep in me wanted to know Him. I wanted to talk with Him and have a relationship with Him, but I really did not know how. People would tell me I only needed to have faith. The thing is, I already had faith—at least as much as a mustard seed. What I needed was to trust Him and give myself to Him fully. I desired to hear the voice of the Lord, but it would be years before I would hear His voice like a friend talking to me.

My sheep hear My voice, and I know them, and they follow Me
(John 10:27 NKJV).

I met my husband Curtis while attending college and working three different part-time jobs to pay rent. We dated for two and a half years and were then married. Even while dating, Curtis and I knew we wanted children. We talked about our dreams and future together, and having a family was at the top of the list. Soon after getting married, we decided it was time to start a family. I never thought I would have a problem getting pregnant. Watching other friends and family, it seemed as if they talked about it and were pregnant the next month. As time continued, each month I started my period, I would feel the disappointment of not being pregnant. Months turned into a year. And then a few more years passed.

I began to think it was my fault for not being able to get pregnant. You know the lies—had I not used drugs, alcohol, or done some of the other terrible things I did, I would be able to get pregnant. I started to believe this was my punishment for the sins I had committed. Yes, I was young and not mature in the Lord. I know now that is not how God disciplines His children. It would be like me putting my child's hands on a red-hot stove and saying, "Now that will teach you not to touch." That is absurd; we all know that's not how you instruct a child. Yet somehow, when negative circumstances arise in our lives, we can begin to see God as a tyrant who would teach us a lesson by bringing more pain.

This is ABSOLUTELY NOT TRUE! If that is how we see God, we don't know Him very well. That is not the character of God!

The scripture tells us the Israelites were afraid of God to the point that they did not want to hear His voice. They knew of the signs, wonders, and miracles He had performed, but they did not know Him. The Israelites thought they understood God's ways. They told Moses to go and hear God's voice for them because they were afraid. You see, Moses knew God, not just who He was. Moses heard and listened to God's voice, which changed his life.

> *He made known His ways to Moses, His acts to the children of Israel* (Psalm 103:7 NKJV).

I had not yet encountered God as intimately as Moses did, yet that story made me long even more to hear my Father's voice.

For the next few years, every time I heard that someone else was pregnant, sadness would overtake me. It wasn't that I was not happy for them; it was just that I was sad that it wasn't me. This hopelessness continued in an up-and-down cycle of anguish, others not knowing my personal pain. After four years of not being able to get pregnant, Curtis and I decided we would start fertility tests. After four fertility tests and one attempt at a medical solution, I went to the doctor's office for a consultation.

As I sat across the table from the doctor, he stated that the results of the fertility tests indicated there were problems. He calmly looked at me and, citing the test results, said, "You'll never have children of your own. It is not possible." Then he added, "It's no big deal. You can always adopt."

I don't think I heard anything he said after that. All I heard over and over in my mind was, "You'll never have children of your own." I was devastated. I left the office sad, crying, and hopeless.

My husband, pastors, and friends continued to pray for me to get pregnant. I can remember Curtis saying that he knew in his heart that we would have a family of our own. He knew I would become pregnant. Unfortunately, I did not have the same assurance within me. I continued to hear those words from the doctor, "You'll never have children of your own. It is not possible."

Finally, I was late. We all know what that means! Four weeks turned into eight weeks, and everything was good. I was finally pregnant! God had heard our prayers! Suddenly, at about two and a half months, I began to bleed.

We called the doctor, who told me to stay in bed for a couple of days and see if the bleeding would stop. But no matter what I did, it got worse. I went to the doctor's office for an examination. Words I did not want to hear echoed from the doctor's mouth, "You've lost the baby." I began sobbing.

I had waited for this baby for at least four years, and now, after being told I would never have any children, he told me the baby I was carrying was dead, and that I would also need a D&C procedure to help recover. As I lay there devastated by this experience, I heard these words in my head, "You'll never recover from this."

Those words felt true at the time and continued to feel true throughout that season of my life.

I felt so sad about the loss and was so hopeless that nothing would change in my situation. My thoughts were everywhere. Getting pregnant had been a miracle. But in losing her, I believed I lost my only chance to have a child, and I would never get pregnant again. I felt God had forgotten me. Surely, I must have done something wrong, or He would not have allowed this to happen. And if it was not for that reason, then He must not genuinely love me as much as He loved others. I felt so alone with so much sadness. Satan took full advantage of the situation and fed me lie after lie, which I began to believe.

I have always considered myself a strong woman who could manage her emotions and whatever life threw at me. It is amazing, however, how this specific life circumstance turned me into a hot mess. I felt so crushed in my spirit and in my emotions that I began to lose hope that I would ever have my own children. I remember sitting in parking lots away from everyone and just crying until I could pull it together to keep going. My scripture for that season was Psalm 34:18—*The Lord is close to the brokenhearted and saves those who are crushed in spirit* (NIV). I knew God was close to me in all my pain.

About six months after losing the baby, my little brother, Chris, who was thirteen at the time, came to live with us. He, too, had been brokenhearted in life, but he responded not with sadness but with anger. We gave our attention to Chris to help in every way we could. Over time, his walls of resistance came down, and God began restoring his heart right before our eyes. Our lives began to change. You could sense that peace and joy were returning to all of us. I could finally understand God's timing a little bit. Chris took every bit of love and energy we had to help him, and a baby at that specific time would have been difficult.

However, let me say this: I do not believe God took our baby, but I do believe He used the situation to give me hope that I could get pregnant. About a year after Chris came to live with us, I became pregnant again. I was excited but didn't want to get my hopes up. You see, life experience had taught me that I could lose that baby as well. Of course, thoughts bombarded me, telling me I would lose this baby, too. So, we spoke only to a few people, holding our breath, so to speak, until I was nearly past the first trimester. Six months later, God gave us our first child—Brandon! We were so excited! It was truly a miracle! We went on to have two more boys, Reid and Keith. Again, two more miracles!

At that point, we felt three boys were enough for us, so we decided I would have my tubes tied after the birth of our last child, Keith. All three boys were delivered by cesarean section, so I had a tubal ligation after the delivery. As the doctor performed the procedure, he stood over me and said, "How in the world did you get pregnant? Oh, well, obviously, something worked." Snip, snip, and then he laughed.

After having three boys, even the doctor was surprised that I was somehow able to get pregnant. You and I know how! Our boys were truly miracles from God!

Despite my prayers and cries to God, I had carried the lies of that miscarriage with me, waiting for the other shoe to drop. Yet God always had my best interest at heart. His desire was for me to be free of the lies the enemy told me. But even after I had a family, the pain of miscarriage still lingered. It would be another ten years before inner healing would come my way.

There was a deep pain in my soul that only Jesus could heal. As I embraced inner healing, God began to put His finger on the lies I believed, and then He would speak truth to each lie.

Therefore, if the Son makes you free, you shall be free indeed (John 8:36 NKJV). I now understand this scripture.

Not only did God speak to the lie that I would never recover, but He showed me how I had already begun to recover. He promised He would complete His work in me if I would allow Him.

Being confident of this very thing, that He who has begun a good work in you will complete it until the day of Jesus Christ (Philippians 1:6 NKJV).

Not only did we have three children of our own, but God also brought our daughter, Thayse, to us when she needed a family, and we were so ready for her. My family was now complete—that is, until they got older, and their spouses were added to our family. We now have another daughter, Melissa, and another son, Tom. We look forward to the other spouses and grandchildren coming into the family. Our legacy has just begun, and we are grateful!

When I look back over my life, I can see how God was always working in my life, always present even if I didn't see Him. The Bible says that He will comfort us with the comfort we've been given. I have always believed that in one moment with God, one Word from Him, one touch—everything can change instantly.

> *Praise be to the God and Father of our Lord Jesus Christ, the Father of compassion and the God of all comfort, who comforts us in all our troubles, so that we can comfort those in any trouble with the comfort we ourselves receive from God* (2 Corinthians 1:3-4 NIV).

After a few more years and many inner healing sessions, not only did God bring healing to me, but I later trained to become a Theophostic Facilitator for inner healing. My desire was to help others receive the comfort and healing I'd been given. It is such a blessing for me, personally, when I facilitate for others. I "get to" watch God do the miraculous in their lives! I see the comfort and peace of God fill them, and many people are never the same again.

This October, I will be celebrating 42 years of marriage with my husband, Curtis. I am so grateful he's in my life! We can sense a change in our present season, and we are excited to move into it together. One of the reasons people love the northern states is because they can tangibly watch the change of seasons. They can be in the middle of winter and know that spring is coming. They see the subtle changes coming, and before they know it, they are in full-on spring season.

Through the years, I have learned that life moves in seasons. I have not stayed in just one season my whole life, and neither will you! Just like the seasons on the earth, our lives continue to change. This gives me hope for my future. I may not see hope while I'm in the winter season, but I know the snow will melt. And when my situation or circumstances begin to calm down or dissipate, I sense a new season is coming. I believe God uses the natural seasons to remind us of this principle: Seasons come and go. Though I may feel stuck, He will not allow me to stay there. There's always hope for a new season. The Bible says weeping may endure for a night, but joy comes in the morning.

> For His anger is but for a moment, His favor is for life; Weeping may endure for a night, but joy comes in the morning (Psalm 30:5 NKJV).

After walking through the painful seasons of infertility and the loss of a baby, a new season began. Brandon was born. Then Reid. And then Keith. Years later, God brought Thayse to us. After a painful, childless season, God brought many children into our lives.

God is faithful to complete the work He started in me, and that means I'm not staying where I am at this present moment; I'm moving on with Him!

If you are in a season of weeping, hold tight to God and remember He has great plans for your future. Take time to know Him, and you will learn that He will never let you down. For joy truly does come in the morning!

Hope in the Pursuit of Purpose

By Connie A. VanHorn

"For I know the plans I have for you," declares the Lord, "plans to prosper you and not to harm you, plans to give you a hope and a future (Jeremiah 29:11 NIV).

One of my favorite topics of discussion is purpose. Purpose is a huge part of Women World Leaders' ministry, and it was through God and this ministry that I found mine. Finding my purpose filled my soul with so much hope at a time when I desperately needed it. Hope fuels us for what is coming next. God wants to reveal His purpose for your life.

We are all given gifts and talents. It can be tempting to believe we are not equipped or good enough for the calling God has given us, but don't believe those lies. You are capable of achieving great things for God! When God first revealed His purpose for my life, I wanted to run and hide. I didn't feel qualified and constantly said things like,

"I'm not good enough."

"I'm not smart enough."

"I'm not educated enough."

I reminded God of all the reasons why I was unqualified and unprepared. Do you think He listened? Yes! But He constantly reassured me and found ways to reveal His plans for my life. Through constant prayer and devotion, God showed me that although the purpose He was calling me to was impossible in my power, it was very possible through HIM.

God has a purpose for each and every one of us; it's up to us to pursue that purpose with passion, determination, and BELIEF. Don't ever lose sight of the fact that we are all uniquely gifted and called to make a positive impact in this world. Trust in God's plan for your life and have faith that He will guide you toward your purpose. God wants you to stay hopeful and never give up on the journey to fulfill your purpose. You are capable of achieving great things with God by your side.

Don't lose hope. Even when the path seems unclear and the challenges seem insurmountable, remember that God is always with you, leading every step of the way. You can find hope and joy in the journey, knowing that each experience—good or bad—shapes you into the person you are meant to become. Your purpose is not just a destination but a continued process of growth and transformation. Trust in God's timing and have faith that He will open doors and opportunities that align with the purpose He has given you.

Now to him who is able to do immeasurably more than all we ask or imagine, according to his power that is at work within us (Ephesians 3:20 NIV).

In my own moments of doubt as I work toward my divine calling, God constantly reminds me to KEEP GOING! He has the same message for you: Keep persevering, keep believing, and keep trusting in the hope God has placed within your heart. Your purpose is worth pursuing; with God, you can achieve the extraordinary. God can turn any mess into a message, and let me tell you, I was the definition of a mess. BUT GOD! God can and will turn it all around. He is looking for a willing heart to be His hands and feet. It doesn't matter what you have or where you come from—God can and will use you to do amazing things for His kingdom.

To everyone reading this, please hear this message: Keep going. Let go of any doubts or fears that may be holding you back and step boldly into the calling that God has placed on your life. You are uniquely equipped with so many special qualities that will impact the world. Have bold faith.

Believe God is bigger.

Believe in the impossible.

Believe in yourself!

Remember, with God, all things are possible. He will never leave you nor forsake you. Keep pressing on, keep shining your light, and keep trusting in the promises of God. Your purpose is waiting to be fulfilled. So go forth with courage and confidence, and never let go of hope.

> *The LORD himself goes before you and will be with you; he will never leave you nor forsake you. Do not be afraid; do not be discouraged* (Deuteronomy 31:8 NIV).

. . . .

Sarah Probst

Sarah Probst is a Christian Licensed Mental Health Counselor Supervisor with a passion for helping the Church understand trauma through a biblical lens. In the past decade, she founded Pneuma Counseling, Brain Parlor, and, most recently, Trauma-Informed Christians.

Soon after her birth in Italy, Sarah moved to the US as a toddler and grew up in the New Orleans area until she was displaced to Portland, Oregon as a result of Hurricane Katrina in 2005. Since then, Sarah has earned two Master's Level degrees and studied trauma recovery all over the globe, including an internship in Cambodia with young girls recused from sex trafficking, as well as at the Portland Rescue Mission.

Sarah has a passion for synthesizing Biblical Theology with Clinical Psychology and enjoys speaking engagements where she teaches her curriculum to ministry leaders. Her latest project, Trauma-Informed Christians, exists to create online courses to help churches worldwide understand trauma through a biblical lens.

When she's not in sessions with clients, Sarah enjoys worship music, theology, and creative outlets, including writing and digital content creation. She also loves spending time socially dining out or walking her Maltese pups, Barbara and Laverne.

When Hope Feels Abusive

By Sarah Probst, LPC-S

Kimberly Hobbs, founder of Women World Leaders, and I were wrapping up a phone call when she asked, "How can I pray for you?"

"Pray for my hope. It is dead." I was surprised by my painful words, for which I had zero explanations.

"We just started a new book, and you won't believe the title!" she said.

I joked, *"My Hope is Dead, and So Am I?"*

"No, it is called *Hope Alive!* I've got goosebumps. Would you pray about writing a chapter?" she exclaimed.

"I'm not sure I could write an entire chapter on *Hope Alive* considering how DEAD my hope is. Hope and I are in a big fight; it has beaten me up for the last time with its relentless disappointments and trickery. Hope is downright abusive, and I won't fall for that again! I have nothing to contribute to that book!"

That was several months ago, and as I sit here writing, I am in awe of the events that only God could have orchestrated since then. In His infinite mercy, He has taken years of disappointments and painful struggles and wrapped them all up into this pretty little chapter. He never wastes pain.

Childhood

This story begins long ago. Hope began torturing me in the earliest days I can remember. It can be very dangerous for little girls with big imaginations and even bigger insecurities.

I grew up as a chubby, hopeful, insecure dreamer who was yearning for acceptance through countless unattainable fantasies.

My hopes deferred are far too numerous to list here, but I'll share the highlights:

I *hoped* to be accepted by my popular peers.

I *hoped* to make various cheer and dance teams, attending tryouts galore.

I *hoped*, from junior high through high school graduation, that just once, a boy would invite me to a prom or homecoming dance!

And after my childhood, I began the longest and most painful of all my hope-deferred journeys: the *hope* for a husband and family of my own.

The Past Five Years

When I turned forty-six years old, I subconsciously thought I had achieved the maximum deferred hopes for one lifetime. I decided the time had come for God to make it all better because, by my calculations, my springtime was past due. But I could not have had more flawed expectations. Little did I know, just when I thought I was on spring's doorstep, I was entering the darkest winter my soul had ever seen.

God escorted me as I entered with my big hopes.

It's impossible to describe the series of relentless struggles and disappointments I have experienced over these past five years—great ones like cancer, the global pandemic, and a 3000-mile move back home. Plus, there were small ones, like driving into my garage door and a broken fridge. It would take much more than a chapter in a book to recount them all. I was confused, stressed, and exhausted. As soon as one struggle passed, another began.

It felt like my soul gradually died. I couldn't smile and rarely left the house after work. I made some friends, but personal turmoil is not the best purveyor of new relationships. My former *hostess-with-the-most-est* vibrance had become a walking-dead woman.

Well-meaning people took their stab at why things had been going so horribly wrong, saying, "You're cursed," "Your bloodline is cursed," or "Maybe you sinned and don't know it."

And they offered advice that seemed impossible to follow: "Just be positive!"

In the Bible, when Job went through unimaginable trials, his friends sat with him in silence for seven days before they began their attempts at explaining his *dark night of the soul* (Job 2:12-13). Perhaps his friends should have just stayed silent.

Trying to understand the reasons for my struggles was exhausting, and hoping that things would change had become terrifying. I deflected any fantasy of experiencing springtime.

I talked to God and read the Bible but couldn't translate the words to my soul. Even going to church felt like a trigger. I prayed the words of Elijah, *"I have had enough, Lord,... Take my life"* (1 Kings 19:4 NIV).

After five years in the hopeless dark, there I was on the phone with Kimberly being asked to write in this book, ironically titled Hope Alive. Still, I gave God a reluctant "yes" to write this chapter, and a week later He began releasing a new spirit of wisdom and revelation over my life.

One Tuesday, I was sitting in my beautiful home with everything a woman could possibly need, yet feeling completely dead and hopeless inside. I logged onto Zoom to greet my therapist, Jessica Gondalfo LPC-S. "What would you like to work on today?" she asked.

"I just feel dead inside, and I stupidly agreed to write a chapter in a book titled *Hope Alive.* I feel completely terrified to hope about anything."

She lovingly empathized with my pain and offered to reframe my experience. "Sounds like you're in a cocoon," she stated as fact.

"A cocoon?" I felt her words viscerally pierce the deepest cavern of my chest. I knew her words were God's words. "A cocoon, not a coffin," I stated.

The realization that this terrible season had a beginning, middle, and *END* made me feel like someone had cracked a window in my dungeon-like heart and rearranged all my spiritual furniture. I felt *HOPE.*

The metaphor revised the way I saw my situation. I physically felt lighter but realized I had not yet reached the butterfly stage. I was still inside a cocoon, which didn't feel good. While certainly better than a coffin, this spiritual straight jacket had been holding me in the grip of its painful transformation for far too long.

HOPE NUGGET #1: There is a vast difference between a coffin and a cocoon.

The Hope Hornet (Hope Deferred)

The next week, my therapy session was equally productive. I shared that although it had given me great relief knowing I was not dead, I was still trapped in a cocoon, and every time I thought about emerging from it, I got nauseous.

"Let's explore the negative feelings of emerging from the cocoon," she coached. I closed my eyes and entered the darkness of my inner world. "Imagine yourself emerging from this cocoon that has confined you for several years. Reach up for your dreams," she guided.

I saw myself wrapped in the darkness of a very tight silk. I tried breaking out of the chrysalis while envisioning my dreams above me when, so abruptly, a giant hornet appeared and violently punched me. Seeing my body physically jolt, she asked, "What happened?"

I hesitated as the shock dispersed throughout my body and slowly opened my eyes. "A hornet!" I said, puzzled. "A fierce, large, angry hornet just forcefully punched me when I tried to rise out of the cocoon!"

"What does it represent?" Her voice carried a curious weight, as though she could discern the answer buried within the recesses of my soul.

"Hope. The hornet represents hope, and it punched me as I tried to break free from the cocoon," I cried, my voice carrying a mix of devastation and surprise as the revelation had its way with me.

I knew only God could paint such a validating metaphor of the intense pain and shock of so many hopes deferred. Nothing could have symbolized my "fear of hoping" more clearly than that hope hornet punching me.

All the punches I had endured flashed before me. As a fifty-one-year-old, never married, childless woman, this hope-hornet has taken his aim at me regularly. There had been so many things I believed for, hoped for, had faith for, prayed for, and fasted for that ended with spiritual brutality.

But gently, like a faint song in the distance, I started to hear Proverbs 13:12. *Hope deferred makes the heart sick, but a desire fulfilled is a tree of life* (ESV).

"I think I have *hope sickness* from all the deferred hope!" I shared. "My heart is sick, not dead!"

God was slowly opening a window and making sense of my despair. Despite having read that verse countless times, the living words offered a fresh perspective.

The ancient writings of the Holy Scriptures didn't just diagnose me with "hope deferred sickness," they also revealed the *cure* for my disease—fulfilled desire, or in some translations, a *dream-come-true.*

There's a cure!

And the cure, a *dream come true,* is a tree of life. God knew I needed LIFE because I felt so DEAD. I needed Him to choose a dream that would turn out the way I HOPED it would.

HOPE NUGGET #2: – Too many punches from the hope hornet causes hope sickness, but God can bring His healing life to that dead place when He fulfills a dream.

The Conference and the Book

Fast forward a few months. I was attempting to write this chapter while still inside the cocoon.

So now what? I was stuck in this cocoon with hope sickness and was still waiting for God to make a dream come true, not realizing that He was the dream I longed for. I've got lots of dreams. I begged God to please just pick one so I could be cured. I needed His miraculous grace even to hope again. I needed to be healed in my hope-sick heart.

"How long, oh Lord? This chapter draft is due Friday, and I completely forgot I have this darn conference to attend in Nashville. I'm not finished writing!"

"Neither am I." He whispered, and the deadline mysteriously got pushed back a couple of weeks. Whew!

The irony in the midst of all of this is I have been a Christian Trauma Therapist for a decade. My job is literally to instill hope in my clients. Despite my despair, God graciously suspended my own personal darkness and allowed me to witness His miraculous power in my office. He deposited vicarious hope through me, for my clients, which was much less painful than hope for myself.

So, I had more time to write, but it had completely fallen off my radar that I had signed up for the *American Association of Christian Counselors'* Conference in Nashville.

I sensed God had something for me in Nashville. There it was again, *hope*. I still had a fear of hope, but like a balloon in the ocean, it springs eternal. "He's going to make a dream come true at the conference. I'll probably meet my husband," my hope assumed.

"Wait a minute!" The hope hornet didn't have to punch me this time. I wasn't cured, but I had learned my lesson, and I wasn't going to hope for anything specific.

So, I went to Nashville, secretly hoping a husband would be my cure. The conference was the icing on my four-month resurrection cake.

I checked into the beautiful Gaylord Opryland Hotel. I wasn't surprised when I saw my first session was titled *Working with Spiritual Struggles*. In that session, an article from the Journal of Psychology and Christianity was presented by Siang-Yang Tan Ph.D., a professor from Fuller Theological Seminary in Los Angeles. It was entitled *Dealing With Spiritual Struggles in Psychotherapy: Empirical Evidence and Clinical Applications From a Christian Perspective* (2022).

The speaker presented six types of Spiritual Struggles: divine struggles, demonic struggles, interpersonal spiritual struggles, struggles with doubt, moral struggles, and struggles of ultimate meaning. I stared in disbelief as I realized I had been experiencing *ALL* of them in my cocoon! I was astonished that my struggles were summarized so profoundly.

Dr. Tan went on to discuss the "mystical aspects of the life in Christ such as the Dark Night of the Soul" and said, "Its purpose is not to punish or afflict us, but to set us free." And "Suffering is a means by which God imparts *hope* to us."

Every word validated and provided language for my five-year cocoon experience. I couldn't believe God brought me to an entire teaching on *Hope Sickness.*

I ran into Dr. Tan later and let him know that everything he said resonated with me because I felt so dead and hopeless inside. His face lit up. He immediately walked me over to a table full of books and picked up *The Night Is Normal* by Alicia Britt Chole. "You need to buy this," he insisted.

"There's a whole book about this cocoon?" I marveled at God. First, a workshop, and now a whole book!

As I walked out with my book, I saw a thirty-foot-tall banner that said "Know Hope." I looked around and couldn't believe my eyes. How had I missed this? I have *NO HOPE* and am standing in the middle of countless signs that literally say *KNOW HOPE!* It turns out it was the theme of the conference!

Wow, God! A conference entitled *Know Hope?* A Book entitled *The Night is Normal?* Workshops on Spiritual Suffering? All this while writing a chapter in a book called *Hope Alive?*

It would be impossible to write about all the miraculous things God was teaching me about *hope* at the intensive four-day *Know Hope* conference. Suffice it to say, I started to feel my soul breathing again for the first time in years.

"*YOU* showed up! *YOU* are my dream-come-true and the cure to my hope sickness. *YOU* went to all this trouble for me?"

The fact that the God of the Universe sees me is far too wonderful for me.

HOPE NUGGET #3: When the dawn of the Son touches the horizon, He lights up everything fast. Joy comes in the morning, and so does hope.

The Drive Home

The night before my drive home, I noticed the book in my bag. I was feeling better, but still had questions about the deferred hope and disappointments. I read little more than the introduction that night and knew I had to download it to listen on the seven-hour drive back home.

The next morning, I woke up and got on the road. After a sweet visit with my sister in Franklin, I spent the next eight hours listening to the entire book. God was shedding light on everything I had experienced over my lifetime. He was speaking directly to me through Alicia Britt Chole's words.

God has some grand gestures of rescue! He had orchestrated many things to get that book into my hands to reassure me that my cocoon would end and that there is treasure in my pain and disillusionment.

I felt an overwhelming feeling I hadn't felt in so long—God's presence. He was with me, and I was alive!

Not only was He there, but He was letting me know that the terrible and seemingly pointless season I had been in was somehow *good,* and somehow even *God.*

Chole broke down the definition of disillusionment.

The act (*-ment*) of removing or negating (*-dis*) false ideas (*-illusion*).

Or, in other words, "The painful process of gaining reality."

This sentence summarized every disappointment in my lifetime. I realized the painful punches of the hope hornet are really the disappointment we feel when we put our hope in illusions instead of God's reality.

Disillusionment is the act of removing all *MY* illusions and painfully gaining *YOUR* reality! I had so many illusions. I have been in the 'cocoon of disillusionment' suffering with hope sickness from all the hornet punches. It all made sense.

I felt tears drip as I thought of His love. Even when I was hoping for yet another illusion, He had been watching me all along. He was with me in the cocoon as the hope hornet visited me time and time again, knowing He was painfully removing my false illusions and installing reality.

And boy, was I a chronic illusioner!

I thought that God would...

I thought that people would...

I thought the church would...

I thought that I would...

Jesus knew all along that the greatest dream (cure) of my heart was for me to understand that He is still good and hadn't abandoned me; He had a perfect plan for my life in all the mess. He is the resurrection life, and He resurrected me on that drive home.

Jesus told her, "I am the resurrection and the life. Anyone who believes in me will live, EVEN AFTER DYING" (John 11:25 NLT, emphasis added).

I was alive after dying. God had been performing a painful extraction of illusion while I was in the cocoon. In hindsight, every hornet punch was full of mercy. Mercy was painfully installing reality and removing illusion while surrendering me to His throne where my dreams are His dreams, and His dreams are realities, not illusions.

Everything God used to resurrect me from the cocoon is impossible to list in the brevity of this chapter. But the entirety of God's ways with us are indescribable.

HOPE NUGGET #4: The hope hornet may be painful, but it represents God's mercy and love, removing FALSE hope and making way for truth and something better for His Kingdom.

Conclusion

As God always does, He highlighted my experience through His Word. I have come to realize that spending a lifetime disillusioned and ending up hope-sick inside a cocoon with a hornet buzzing overhead is the glorious dismantling of self that Romans 5 talks about.

> *And we boast in the hope of the glory of God. Not only so, but we also glory in our sufferings, because we know that suffering produces perseverance; perseverance, character; and character, hope. And hope does not put us to shame, because God's love has been poured out into our hearts through the Holy Spirit, who has been given to us* (Romans 5:2–5 NIV).

Real Hope for God's Spirit and in God's future does not put us to shame.

False Hope results in the hope hornet putting us to shame when he punches us with disappointment.

The hope of the glory of God and His Spirit is all I really wanted, but I had to persevere in suffering through the painful shattering of my illusions, which miraculously changed me by producing character.

Through the painful process of disillusionment, FALSE HOPE can be removed and TRUE HOPE can be rightfully placed in the hands of the only One from which good things come.

True hope is a miraculous fruit of the Spirit of God, and He rarely shares all the details in advance. True hope sometimes requires an extended stay in the cocoon before we have enough character to align our visions with God's big-picture plans for His entire Kingdom. He is always working harder than we are at our own stories, overseeing every finite detail in his perfect timing.

God showed me how to identify illusions and stop investing in them. The "character" of Romans 5 allows us to invest all our hope in the glory we will see when we enter eternity where disappointments, death, and evil are not permitted and *every righteous dream comes true.*

Even though the long winter in my cocoon has been a painful season of putting countless illusions to death, winter's death is where spring's new life really begins. We can't have one without the other. God mirrors this profound truth in the seasons of His physical world to mimic the seasons of our spiritual worlds and give us *hope* in every winter.

So, if you are feeling trapped inside a cocoon with hope-sickness after experiencing relentless blows from the hope hornet, know that God has not abandoned you. God is painfully stripping you of false hope and replacing your illusions with His glorious reality, which is your greatest dreams coming true.

He is depositing grace for you to persevere and reshaping your character so that the refined result will be hope in His eternal things instead of temporary illusions. After the turmoil and all the struggle, HOPE will remain.

> *And now these three remain: faith, hope and love. But the greatest of these is love* (1 Corinthians 13:13 NIV).

Now, I can see how my cocoon miraculously reflected Christ's resurrection. My illusions needed to die; there was no other way but through the cross. Our hope is in Christ alone because He alone engraved Himself in our hearts. He rescued the entire human race and prepared a place for us where every dream does come true.

HOPE NUGGET #5: Our ultimate hope is found in the fact that if God never does another thing, He has already done enough!

Hope in the Chaos

By Connie A. VanHorn

The LORD is my rock, and my fortress, and my deliverer; my God, my strength, in whom I will trust; my buckler, and the horn of my salvation, and my high tower (Psalm 18:2 KJV).

Life is hard. It can be even harder when we feel like we are walking through it alone. In the midst of chaos, it can be easy to feel lost and overwhelmed. But remember, there is always hope to be found, even in the darkest times. God is always with us, guiding us and providing us strength and comfort.

Like most of us, I had to learn to hope in the chaos through experience. During my early Christian walk, I faced many hard things and times of uncertainty. God had revealed Himself to me, but my faith still needed to be established. God built my trust in Him through a series of experiences and moments that showcased His faithfulness, love, and presence in my life. Each hard thing I faced and each prayer I said became a stepping stone toward a deeper relationship with Him. In my times of doubt, God showed His love and guidance, strengthening my faith and revealing His plan for my life.

We all have a journey with God that becomes a message of His grace and mercy, shaping our trust in Him as a firm foundation for our lives, even in the chaos. Believe in the power of prayer and the peace that comes from surrendering your worries to God.

No matter what you are facing, know that you are not alone. Trust in God's plan for you, and have faith that He will see you through. Take a moment to breathe, pray, and surrender your worries to Him.

God works in mysterious ways—He has a purpose for everyone and everything. Keep your faith strong and your heart open to hear His voice, even through the muffled clutter. You are stronger than you think, and God will empower you to overcome whatever obstacles and chaos come your way.

Stay positive, stay hopeful, and remember that God is always by your side. You are loved, you are valued, and you are never alone.

When it feels like the world is crumbling around you, do not lose hope. And when the storm finds you, remember that there is also light to be found. We are safe in the eye of every storm. God is our refuge and strength, a very present help in trouble. Lean on your faith and trust that He is working behind the scenes, creating a beautiful life for you. You can be confident and filled with peace knowing that God has you. Hold onto the hope that tomorrow will be brighter.

> *You will keep in perfect peace him whose mind is steadfast, because they trust in you* (Isaiah 26:3 NIV).

God is with you every step of the way, providing you with the strength and courage to keep going. Keep your eyes on Him, and let His love and grace carry you through the storm. Keep going, keep trusting, and keep believing that God is working all things together for your good. You are a child of God, loved beyond measure and destined for greatness. Keep the faith, keep the hope, and keep going even through the chaos.

· ·

Victoria Farrand

Victoria Farrand, born in Wisconsin, grew up in many states due to her stepdad's job promotions. After graduating high school, she returned to Wisconsin and met her husband, Brad. They had a wonderful life and were blessed with two boys they are extremely proud of.

Victoria worked as an HR & Safety Manager for many years, studied for her Real Estate Brokers License, and then started and operated her own Property Management Company. After losing her husband and her two boys were grown, she moved to Georgia, remodeled houses, and studied to become a certified fitness trainer and nutritionist. She developed a passion for helping people with their health so they may have more time with their families.

Victoria moved to Florida for a short time, where she was honored to meet John C. Maxwell and become a Certified Leadership Trainer, Life Coach & Speaker with the John Maxwell Organization. She now owns a business helping coach women who have experienced trauma and loss, become stuck, and need help moving forward. Life is hard, but life is wonderful if you allow yourself to heal and truly live.

Live the Life you Love, Love the Life you Live

Victoria@victorioustransformation.com
www.victorioustransformation.com

Finding True Hope

By Victoria Farrand

There is so much meaning in the word HOPE. Hope is something we cling to during the darkest of days. We all hope for certain things to come true in our lives—I know I have hoped for many things throughout mine. However, I would be completely lying if I said that hope hadn't disappointed me over the years. In fact, I was crushed by hope when it seemed to let me down. We all experience tremendous struggles, pain, and loss at some point. This is my story of learning the meaning of the true Hope we all can count on.

On January 13, 2007, my entire world turned upside down. My husband of 21 years and two sons were at a resort to celebrate our oldest son's 16th birthday. My husband and our son share a birthday one day apart. We celebrated my husband's 49th birthday a day early because the next day, we had 12 kids coming over to celebrate my son.

On the morning of January 13, 2007, my husband got up early while I stayed in bed to rest. Shortly after, I got up I noticed my husband had fallen back to sleep on the couch, which he rarely did. I told our youngest son to be quiet and let his dad sleep a little longer. He joined me in the oversized chair while I drank coffee and rubbed his head for a while. A short time later, I nudged him to go wake his dad. He bounced out of the chair and shook his dad to wake him, but my husband didn't respond. I immediately realized that something was wrong.

My oldest son was startled awake in his bed by all the yelling and came running downstairs. He tried to help me perform CPR, but to no avail. We could not bring my husband back. He was gone.

Life was incredibly difficult for many years after the death of my husband. We had a wonderful marriage and a happy family with lots of laughter and fun. I believed my family and my husband's family would all come together to get through this unexpected, tragic loss, but that didn't happen. My boys did not know how to process the loss of their father, and they became very angry. My in-laws didn't support me as I thought they would. I felt like I lost not only my husband but also my second mother and additional family.

I became confused and angry at God. My greatest dream was to have a husband and family, and now, at the age of 43, it was gone. After my husband passed, my life was consumed with anger and struggles. Everyone was fighting and turning against each other. How could things have gone so wrong? I battled to hold on to hope. How could God let this happen? My husband was such a good man that everyone loved. He always helped others. He was funny and a wonderful husband and father. He was a soccer coach and youth wrestling coach and had directed the youth program for over 20 years.

As time went by, my pain got deeper. The family strain escalated. I was in the middle of selling my business to go into full-time real estate sales when my husband passed away. I had no business to focus on; then the housing market crashed; I invested almost everything we had into the stock market with the belief of setting us up for the future, and the stock market crashed. I was sinking. I soon realized the only way I could survive this was by leaning on God. I had started to see God's hand at work months before my husband passed away when I joined a Bible study and met some incredible women. God surrounded me with the women who would support and carry me through the most difficult time in my life. These amazing and beautiful women became my lifelong friends.

When we are in our darkest days, God is still working His plan for our lives. He is surrounding us with His love through the people He brings into our lives—the people who will become our support and carry us through the hard days. The scripture I held close during my hard days was Jeremiah 29:11. This scripture is still close to my heart to this day.

"For I know the plans I have for you," declares the Lord, "plans to prosper you and not harm you, plans to give you hope and a future" (Jeremiah 29:11 NIV).

I clung to this verse and many others during this time. Although my hope for a future with my husband was crushed, my anger at God eventually subsided. I felt guilty for being so angry at God for taking my husband. I learned that anger is actually one of the steps in the grieving process and is perfectly normal. When we are hurting and suffering great loss, it's okay to be angry at God. Cry out to Him, tell Him how you feel. We are never promised a life without pain, but we are promised a life where God will be with us through it all.

Be strong and courageous. Do not fear or be in dread of them, for it is the Lord your God who goes with you. He will not leave you or forsake you (Deuteronomy 31:6 ESV).

For several years, things were very difficult as the pain surfaced daily. My oldest son joined the Navy right out of high school. I believe this was his way of escaping the pain. My youngest son dealt with the loss differently, holding all his pain inside and demonstrating outward anger. We had a fractured relationship for many years. After he graduated from high school, I decided it was time for a change. I couldn't handle the ache of my broken family and the thought of starting over with someone new in the same place. I had such happy memories with my husband. I didn't want to lose those memories or drown them with new ones. So, I moved to Georgia to be closer to family. I moved 1000 miles away to escape the pain. The only problem is that pain follows you.

Over the years, the relationships mended, and the hurt healed. I became active in a wonderful church and made new friends. My spirit felt renewed once again. I even dared to hope for a future with another man. As time went by and the seasons changed, that hope faded away like the beautiful fall leaves; it turned into bewilderment as to why God hadn't answered my prayers—I wasn't meeting a new man who would be my forever husband.

Finally, after being single for almost ten years, I found a pinch of hope—I met an amazing man. Our new relationship flourished, and everything seemed perfect. My boys liked this man, which was important to me. I felt like I would have a whole family again. I was excited because he had sons of his own. This relationship was ideal. We didn't waste time and were married ten months later. We believed that we were ready and mature enough to make this decision based on what we already knew about each other. Our boys got along and liked each other. We had so much fun together as a family. My life felt complete once again. God blessed me more than I could have hoped. Or at least that is what I thought.

After we were married, I sold my home and moved in with my new husband. We lived in a fun, family-oriented neighborhood. The neighbors all got together for dinners, boating, parties, holidays, and events. We went to church together as a family and became part of the core team to help start a satellite campus. We were both busy volunteering. It was everything that I prayed for. I loved this man with all my heart.

Then, in the blink of an eye, life changed. I started seeing and experiencing behavior that had not surfaced before our marriage. For example, my husband would burst into fits of anger, swear at me, and call me every vulgar name you can imagine. I couldn't say or do things right. I wasn't allowed to bring up money or how much we were spending—that would cause a huge fight, and the fights were always my fault. He was completely different in front of others than he was behind closed doors with me. With others, he was perfect and charming. Everyone, including my family, loved him and raved about what a wonderful man he was and how lucky I was to have found him. I didn't know what to do. No one would believe me if I told them what he was really like. He was so wonderful to others, but inside, I was breaking. I found a way to blame myself for what I was going through.

I expect too much.

I should learn to communicate with him better.

God wouldn't bring this man into my life after ten years if he isn't who I am supposed to be with.

I just need to be more patient and understanding while God works on him and his spirit.

I convinced myself I would see change and believed God was working on his heart. He would tell me how much he loved me and was grateful for me and my walk and commitment with God. He would say I helped him grow stronger in God. But the fighting increased, the name-calling increased, and the destruction of things and property increased. He would empty our bank account, purchase a plane ticket and leave, while I had no idea where he went or when he was coming back.

He took off his ring and said he wanted a divorce more times than I can even remember. Then, he would come back and apologize—being the most amazing man you have ever seen. But then, he would blame me for making him act that way towards me and demand that I go to counseling, as our problems were mostly my fault.

We eventually went to counseling together. He would explode on me after each counseling session. The counselor shared with me the definition of a narcissist as well as the behaviors of gaslighting and being a con man, which was very abusive and manipulative behavior that twists blame, constantly placing all the fault on the partner.

I prayed constantly, asking God what I should do and what He wanted me to learn from this.

> *So we do not lose heart. Though our outer self is wasting away, our inner self is being renewed day by day. For this light momentary affliction is preparing for us an eternal weight of glory beyond all comparison, as we look not to the things that are seen but to the things that are unseen. For the things that are seen are transient, but the things that are unseen are eternal* (2 Corinthians 4:16-18 ESV).

I prayed and counseled with my pastor. God does not like divorce, but God also does not expect a woman or a man to stay in an abusive relationship. In God's commandments, we are to love and respect each other and become one.

In March 2020, my world fell apart, and my hope of having a whole family was shattered once more. My husband emptied a large amount of money from our bank account again and refused to put it back or communicate with me. So, I took the steps needed, and I filed for divorce.

On March 5, 2020, my husband was served divorce papers, which he would not accept. This was only the start of the nightmare to come. The same day, I received a call that my father was in the hospital and not expected to survive. I jumped in a car and drove to Wisconsin with my son to be with my father. My father survived only to be permanently paralyzed.

Then came the announcement of COVID-19 and a nationwide lockdown. This also meant that the courts were shut down. My husband and I were required to live in the same house, which was a total nightmare. I slept in a separate room with my door locked. I had a door stopper under the door and a loaded gun under my pillow every night for six months.

I shared earlier that my oldest son had gone into the Navy right out of high school. In his first year of training, he suffered a severe head injury. He spent many years fighting to get the help he needed and was finally scheduled for surgery. Unfortunately, his four-year run in the Navy had ended, and they refused to approve the surgery. They told him he would have to restart the approval process with the Veteran's Administration. I reached out to our State Congressman, who eventually halted his discharge. My son had several unsuccessful surgeries before being permanently and medically disabled from the Navy in 2015.

In June 2020, after five years of prayers and again working with our State Congressman, my son received approval to have another surgery at the Mayo Clinic in Rochester, Minnesota, from one of the best surgeons in the world. On the day of his surgery, I called my mother to tell her how her grandson was doing. She informed me that my stepfather had late-stage lung cancer and was not expected to survive much longer.

I was shattered. My life seemed so out of control. My next two years were complete agony. How could life possibly get any worse? I was in the middle of a very difficult divorce while living in the same house with a man who thrived on being manipulative and nasty.

The world was dealing with its own kind of darkness. COVID rocked the world, and everyone was locked down. Things were hard in the world but even harder at home. I had no work. My father was paralyzed and in a very bad condition. My son had major surgery on his head for the fourth time, and we were unsure if this time would be successful. My stepfather was dying of lung cancer. And a few months earlier, I lost one of my best friends and an aunt who was like a mother to me.

I felt bruised by HOPE! What do we do when our hope is shattered? What do we do when hope doesn't turn out the way we are expecting? What do we do when we have gone out on those audacious limbs of faith, but life doesn't turn out the way it is supposed to?

We trust in God's plan!!

> We are hard pressed on every side, but not crushed; perplexed, but not in despair; persecuted, but not abandoned; struck down, but not destroyed (2 Corinthians 4:8-9 NIV).

There were days when all I could do to make it through the day was to cry and look to heaven and just say, "I don't understand God, but I trust in you."

> Trust in the LORD with all your heart and lean not on your own understanding; in all your ways submit to him, and he will make your paths straight (Proverbs 3:5-6 NIV).

One particular night in July, I had three different people send me messages asking me if I was okay. They each had their own uneasy feeling for my safety. At this point, I was already sleeping with a gun under my pillow, but I began to feel incredibly anxious. I cried out to God, begging him to help me. I begged Him to protect me from my husband.

I don't hear God speak to me audibly. But I have learned that God speaks to us through people and guides us through His Scripture, nature, and His Holy Spirit that communes with us. That night, I literally felt the Holy Spirit saying, "It's not about the money. It's about your safety. TRUST IN ME!"

I called my attorney the next day and shared my concerns with him. I told him I wanted the divorce finalized no matter what it cost me. Even if it was to be more than what I should give financially. My attorney thought I was overreacting, but I dismissed his comments and told him I was trusting in God. We settled five minutes before we were to go in front of the judge. My husband got more than he deserved, but for me, it was over. My stepfather passed away five days later. Before he passed, I was able to share with him that it was over and that I felt safe again. My biological father deteriorated quickly, so I went to Wisconsin to help take care of him in his last month of life. He passed away six months after my stepfather died. I had lost nine people in two years. Both fathers, two best friends, my aunt who was a 3rd mother to me, two brothers-in-law, another aunt, and an uncle.

Now, I am rebuilding HOPE again. I know that God has not forgotten or abandoned me. I'm not afraid to have hope again. I don't understand everything, but I'm looking for something positive. We can always look for hope in the dark places.

My ex-husband's youngest son and my oldest son still call each other brother. They have become close friends and even lived together for a while. They both served in the military and have several things in common. I do not know God's plan, but I see great beauty in that.

Hope!

My father was the hardest-working man I have ever seen. He taught me the value of hard work and to never give up or quit, no matter how hard things get. He also taught me to always believe in myself.

My youngest son became very close to my father after the death of his dad. When my father died, my son was able to purchase the family farm and owns it today. What a sweet blessing.

More hope!

My stepfather was the most positive man I have ever known. He always encouraged me and always complimented me up until the day he died.

This gave me the strength to be the best woman I could be under any circumstances.

I don't share my story with you to seek pity or to compare our pain. I share my story so you can see that your pain is important to God; He will comfort and care for you in your pain as He did for me in mine. I am sharing my hope just in case you have lost yours.

Don't be afraid to have hope again. Don't be afraid to dream big again. God isn't done with your story yet. I don't know what is next for my future, and I surely don't have all the answers. But I can tell you from experience that we can all trust in God and His perfect plan.

Please believe with all you have that what has been broken can be restored. No matter what you have been through, you are not at the end of your story. This life is not all there is.

> He will wipe every tear from their eyes. There will be no more death or mourning or crying or pain, for the old order of things has passed away (Revelation 21:4 NIV).

Hope is not found in money, family, or friends. Hope can only be found in the One who loves us unconditionally—that is God. Trust in HIM. He is our HOPE.

Hope in Relationships

By Kimberly Ann Hobbs

> *Love each other deeply, because love covers a multitude of sins* (1 Peter 4:8 NIV).

God provides endless hope in relationships through wisdom and help from His Word. Even though we may not see hope for a broken association, especially when pain has been inflicted, God has His ways of providing a future for even the worst of damaged or fractured relationships. Whether a relationship has been severed due to your actions or someone else's betrayal, there is always hope for reconciliation when God is involved.

Giving in to adverse feelings and allowing them to control us can lead to severed relationships. When we choose to end a relationship because of harsh feelings toward someone else, we allow negative emotions such as anger or bitterness to bore through our very core and alter our personality. How do we diffuse the enemy's attempts to destroy our relationships? We remind ourselves of truth.

When you question how a relationship has gone wrong, recognize that God may be trying to get your attention. Although we are often quick to blame the brokenness on the other person, we must examine ourselves, thereby diffusing any of the enemy's authority. When we succumb to the mishap and mayhem of a damaged relationship, we do not allow God to move. God can heal any broken relationship and bring hope for a different outcome if we look to Him for direction.

He heals the brokenhearted and binds up their wounds (Psalm 147:3 NIV).

To allow the miracle of healing to begin, we must first go to God in prayer. God knows where our relationship went wrong. He knows what started and is sustaining the angst. God says we have not because we ask not. Ask Him to help you remember the closeness and the goodness you once had in the severed relationship and put away any lies the enemy tries to speak into your ear. Pray for a covering while both of you heal. God really does care about your relationship. Pray about taking the initiative to reach out to the other person in love.

If the relationship is important to you, it is important to God. Try to sympathize with the other person's feelings and look out for their interests, not just your own. If your prayer for the other person aligns with God's perfect will, it will be done. Healing will happen.

> Humble yourselves, therefore, under God's mighty hand, that he may lift you up in due time. Cast all your anxiety on him because he cares for you (1 Peter 5:6-7 NIV).

Confess all your own limitations and issues that may have been the cause of the broken relationship. Please understand that God's Word tells us first to get rid of the log from our own eye; then, perhaps we will see well enough to deal with the speck in our friend's eye (Matthew 7:5 NLT). If there is any cause on your part, ask God to forgive you for it and remove the burdens you are carrying so you are free to move forward in healthy living.

Examine yourself and be certain to attack the problem without attacking the person. The Bible instructs us that *A gentle response defuses any anger, but a sharp tongue kindles a temper-fire* (Proverbs 15:1 MSG). God's Word instructs us to manage ourselves and our emotions even if we are wronged and that we should be ready to forgive someone who has wounded us. No matter what another person does, you have the ability from God to forgive them and move on. You can do this with God's help by cooperating as much as possible with the other person. The Bible tells us we should do everything possible on our part to live in peace with everybody (Romans 12:18).

When you try to be a peacemaker, you are acting as a child of God. Jesus did not indulge in His own feelings; He followed God, and He instructed us to do the same. The Bible tells us if we forgive men their trespasses, our heavenly Father will also forgive us. But if we do not forgive men their trespasses, neither will our Father forgive us our trespasses (Matthew 6:14-15). Ask God to strengthen you and wait for Him to avenge you. Wait for God to reach the other person in His time—this may take patience. Control your tongue. Wait on God. And thank Him in the waiting that He will make all wrongs right.

God is a God of hope. When you have done everything you can, surrender the relationship to Him and wait with the hope He gives you. Know in the waiting that He will never leave you to feel alone or rejected. You will have freedom in your heart to hold out with hope if you are obedient to what God's Word instructs.

> "I am the vine; you are the branches. If you remain in me and I in you, you will bear much fruit; apart from me you can do nothing" (John 15:5 NIV).

God is your heart-to-heart true companion. He loves you perfectly and tenderly and does not want you to hurt. Place your hope for any broken relationship in Him, knowing He is the One who knows us each best and will direct our healing. Give your relationship to God through prayer and trust Him as you seek the hope He will instill in you through His scripture and the power of His Holy Spirit. His truth will come to light to guide you with all the hope you need.

Love does not delight in evil but rejoices with the truth. It always protects, always trusts, always hopes, always perseveres. Love never fails (1 Corinthians 13:6-8 NIV).

God's love never fails! That truth brings hope for any relationship.

. . . .

Cindy Rosenthal

 Cindy Rosenthal grew up in southern New Jersey and lived in Albany, New York, for almost eighteen years before moving to Florida three years ago. She has two associate's degrees, one in applied science and one in health services administration. She holds a Bachelor of Science in Health Services Administration and currently works as an office and compliance manager in healthcare. Before going into healthcare, Cindy spent twenty-six years in banking finance as a mid-level manager.

Cindy's greatest joy is music and worshiping the Lord. She spent thirteen years singing with Kol Simcha, a ministry group whose name means "sound of joy" in Hebrew, ministering all over the world and seeing hundreds of people come to know Yeshua (Jesus) as their Lord and Savior.

Cindy was blessed to be interviewed by Kimberly Hobbs on Women World Leaders' Podcast on May 22, 2023, wrote an article published in the 13th edition *Voice of Truth* magazine, and is writing a book entitled *When Lighting Strikes Twice.* Cindy's heart is to help people; she hopes her story will inspire and give encouragement to whoever reads it.

To contact Cindy, feel free to email: cindalarose@yahoo.com

From Survivor to Thriver

By Cindy Rosenthal

Thinking back on my childhood and the painful things I endured often brings me to tears. I am grateful to God for getting me through many storms—I wouldn't be where I am today or be a woman of faith if it weren't for my loving God. When I was very young, I never imagined I would be a child of divorce or that our family would become dysfunctional, but my parents struggled to stay together my entire life. I recall my oldest sister, Jackie, talking about how her friend's parents were getting divorced and me saying, "That will never happen to our parents." I hope my story will help others experiencing similar situations.

I was born in New York City. My parents moved to the southern part of New Jersey when I was just five years of age. We moved into a big house for a short time and then into an apartment. My middle sister, Rhonda, and I shared a bedroom adjacent to our parents' room. We would often wake up in tears to the loud sounds of our parents fighting—screaming at each other. Sometimes, I cried myself to sleep, fearful they would hurt each other.

There were also times when my parents would argue during the day. One day, an argument turned into physical violence. I watched my father put his hands around my mother's throat and almost strangle her. They didn't know I was there. I felt helpless. I watched in terror as the tears streamed down my face. My mother was crying and screaming in fear. Finally, my father let her go. He left that night and didn't return until the next day.

My father was also physically abusive to me. He often hit me and yelled at me. He would pick me up and scream so loudly that his face would turn red. He occasionally punched me in the face—calling it "discipline."

When I cried, my father would tell me to stop crying and then blame me for the physical abuse, saying things like, "You did this." I felt scared most of the time—like I could never do anything right. No matter how good I tried to be, I knew he was going to hit and scream at me. I remember getting up early for school just to get away from him. The weekends were hard when he was home because I never knew what he was capable of doing. There were rare occasions when he was nice, and I was happy, but those were very few and far between. Some weekends, Jackie and Rhonda would go out, leaving me home alone. My older sisters were always together, just the two of them. I was younger and not included much. To this day, I don't get included.

My parents' final separation happened around the time I was eight years old. I remember feeling relieved that my father would no longer be around to abuse me. Their divorce took two years to finalize. It was very bitter; they used us children to fight against each other. After a few years, the dust finally settled. Jackie went off to college, and Rhonda went to live with my father. I stayed with my mother. Both Jackie and Rhonda had grown very close to my father, and then they distanced themselves from my mother. They eventually stopped talking to her altogether. My mother struggled to be a mother to me. She couldn't deal with her other two daughters not speaking to her or having any contact with her at all. I found myself an only child with two sisters.

The next few years were very lonely and painful. My mother took the mantle of abuse from my father and began taking her frustrations and anger out on me. At one point, she punched me in the face and almost broke my nose. She hit the back of my legs and left me with large welts that took over a week to heal. Shockingly, I was used to this abuse from my father, so I didn't cry much at all. I would ask her to stop hitting me, and she would blame me for the abuse. After a while, It became so routine that I just became numb to it.

Still, I experienced pure joy on the weekends. My grandparents would pick me up on Fridays after school to spend the weekend with them. My grandfather would sleep on the sofa bed, while I slept in the bedroom with my grandmother. My grandmother and I were very close and had the best times together. We would talk for hours. She had a way of making me smile and feel like my whole world was perfect. My grandmother had diabetes and had to have extensive leg surgery. I remember the day she got home from the hospital; while my mother and grandfather were getting her belongings from the car, I found her lying on the couch, crying. I asked her what was wrong. She told me things and made me promise never to repeat them to anyone. We held each other and cried. To this day, I have never repeated what she told me.

My grandmother got sick continually; when she was at her weakest, I was the only person she would listen to. I would visit her as many weekends as I could, but eventually, my weekends with her had to end. I missed our time together so much. My grandmother passed away when I was fifteen years old. I remember the day she died like it was yesterday. She took a little piece of me with her. I still have her wedding band; I wear it every day. When I look at her ring, I remember all the times we had together and all we shared. Some were very sad, but most were wonderful. Sometimes, looking at her ring makes me smile and feel less alone.

As I reflect on those years and think about what sustained me through each day, music was the one thing that brought me joy. I was always thankful for music, which I began using as an escape at a very early age. My mother took me to audition for a Broadway vocal coach at the age of eight to see if I had the ability to take professional vocal training. The vocal coach told my mother I had a natural ability to sing and to get me training—I have been singing ever since. When I was a little older than a toddler, we would take trips to visit extended family. As we traveled, my sisters always told me to "shut up" because I would be singing too loudly. I sang in choirs and performed in small groups all through high school. I loved every minute of it. It was my escape from all the madness I was going through.

I continued to sing after high school. I studied with a new vocal coach who helped me develop skills to sing in bars, at weddings, and for other events. That lasted a couple of years. I received opportunities to go to California and be on different television shows, but I knew that was not what I was supposed to do. So, I separated from that coach and continued singing only for my own enjoyment for the following year.

In September 1989, my mother asked me if I would attend a "religious concert" with her that some friends had invited us to. I said absolutely no. I didn't want to sit in a synagogue, bored to tears watching a concert. For the next three weeks, she hounded me about the concert until I finally agreed to go. I walked into my first Messianic Jewish synagogue and was floored. All I could think was, *What is this place?* I met several people that night and was given a cassette tape as a gift. (It's amazing to me that cassette tapes were still sold at that time.) I listened to the cassette tape often; the message spoke to me. I learned of the Lord and accepted Him into my heart on October 13, 1989.

I knew my life had drastically changed. I studied and learned scripture verses about salvation.

For by grace you have been saved through faith, and that not of yourselves, it is the gift of God, not of works, lest anyone should boast (Ephesians 2:8-9 NKJV).

One of the first verses that I learned was in John.

> *For God so loved the world that He gave His only begotten Son, that whoever believes in Him should not perish but have everlasting life* (John 3:16 NKJV).

My life had changed significantly. I joined a music ministry called Kol Simcha, which means "Sound of Joy," and began singing for the Lord.

It was shocking to me that even at the age of twenty-four, my mother could still be so abusive. The first year after I accepted the Lord into my heart, she made my life so miserable. She was angry at me and would say hateful things. She felt that I had betrayed her and betrayed the Jewish faith. She was bitter that I had something she didn't. She would come to a Shabbat service with me occasionally, but she always came home crying, though she did not understand why. On Yom Kippur that year, I gave her an ultimatum. I said she could stay home alone or come to service with me. She came with me, and that night, she accepted Yeshua Jesus into her heart. I was so excited and happy for my mother. We both knew her life had changed forever.

About a year later, I moved to a house near the congregation with two friends. I loved sharing the house. I went on my first overseas ministry trip with Kol Simcha in 1993. When returning home, I spent a couple of days at my mother's house. One night, while at my mother's house, I was talking on the phone with my sister Rhonda. We talked about how she had been writing letters to our mother but couldn't continue to write. I told her she should talk to her on the phone. Rhonda went a little crazy; she was scared to talk to our mother; she said she did not know what to say or how to start a conversation. I told her to begin just by saying hello. Then I offered to put our mother on the phone and assured my sister I would stay on with her. She agreed. So, I went to my mother and told her to pick up the phone and say hello to her daughter. My mother was in shock, but she did it. I stayed on the phone with them while they spoke for over an hour. Then, my other sister, Jackie, and my mother spoke a couple of days later.

Approximately one week later, we all met for brunch at my mother's house for an in-person reconciliation of both my sisters, their husbands, and my mother. I made sure to show up late so they could reconcile without me present. When I arrived, I walked into the house and saw all five of them standing together, waiting for me. I remember thinking what a beautiful picture it was. I cherish that happy memory, especially as my world was about to get rocked again.

In the following two months, I lost two aunts with whom I was close. My Aunt Rita passed away from cancer on August 14, 1993, and then my Aunt Edith passed away on October 15, 1993. Their deaths brought up painful memories of my grandmother passing as Aunt Edith and I were just as close. We would talk all the time, and I even spent my vacations with her. When I had a few days off, she was the only person I wanted to be with.

I moved back in with my mother for about five years before moving into my own apartment. I cashed in every retirement account I had and spent every penny to furnish my new apartment. I loved it. Three months later, my apartment building was struck by lightning and burnt down. I was completely devastated. I came home from a prayer meeting to find almost everything I owned destroyed. I lost everything except what my mother and I were able to get out after the fire. And I had no insurance.

On April 1, 2004, I needed a fresh start, so I relocated to Albany, New York. My mother was not happy I was moving so far from her, but she understood. This was a new beginning, separate from my family. My life was mine, and I was finally making decisions without family interference. I was happy with my congregation and the people I had known for over ten years. I had an apartment and a good job; I felt like I was finally home. I settled in and worked in banking for eight years until I realized it was time for a major career change.

In September of 2012, I left the world of banking for good after twenty-six years working in New Jersey and New York. I went back to school to get my degree in healthcare. While in school, I got a job in the emergency department of a level-one trauma center. I worked hard. In April 2015, I earned my associate degree in applied science and became a National Certified Medical Assistant. Realizing my giftings were in administration, I returned to school and achieved my associate degree. In 2021, I received my bachelor's degree in health services administration. I was so excited when I found out I graduated Summa Cum Laude with my bachelor's degree.

After living in Albany for almost eighteen years, it was time to move. In January 2021, I moved to St. Johns, Florida, to be near my sister, Rhonda. I lived there for a year and a half while I finished school. Then, realizing I was unhappy and St. Johns wasn't where I wanted to be, I moved to Boca Raton. There were many challenges in my move to Boca Raton. I reserved an apartment but then realized it was not livable, so I didn't know where I was going to live. Then, there were issues with the movers. But the greatest challenge had to be as I was preparing to move—I was sitting at a red light a block away from my apartment in St. Johns when the car was struck by lightning. I heard it, I felt it, and I saw it. That had to be one of the most frightening experiences I ever had. I couldn't wait to get out of North Florida.

I finally made the move, and after staying for two months in a hotel and staying in a small cottage on a horse farm for a month, I found an apartment. I moved into my new apartment, confident that life would start fresh in South Florida. I knew God had a great plan for my life. I also knew God had some work to do. I reconnected with Jane "Goldie" Winn and started assisting her with events for her book and movie, *Rainbow in the Night*. I was having so much fun. I felt like the scripture verse, Jeremiah 29:11, *For I know the thoughts that I think toward you, says the Lord, thoughts of peace and not of evil, to give you a future and a hope* (NKJV) were finally coming true. The Lord was working in my life, giving me a purpose.

After moving to South Florida, it is difficult to express the amazing ways God moved in my life over the next year. I am now a different person; I am filled with HOPE. I have joy in my life that I didn't have prior to moving to Boca Raton. I have been released from so much hurt and pain from the past and now can look to the future. I am serving in several ministries; the Lord has blessed me beyond words. And I love sharing what the Lord has done in my life as an encouragement. This is my HOPE. God has the perfect plan for my life, as He promised.

> *You will show me the path of life; In Your presence is fullness of joy; At Your right hand are pleasures forevermore* (Psalm 16:11 NKJV).

Your trials and tribulations may be different than mine, but I want to assure you that God is in total control and is walking with you. He has a plan for you just like He had a plan for me. Hold close to Him. Ask His wisdom for your next steps. Trust Him through the twists, turns, and even turmoil. And, like me, you can go from being a Survivor to being a Thriver—in the presence of Yeshua Jesus.

Hope in Trials

By Kimberly Ann Hobbs

We can rejoice, too, when we run into problems and trials, for we know that they help us develop endurance. And endurance develops strength of character, and character strengthens our confident hope of salvation. And this hope will not lead to disappointment. For we know how dearly God loves us, because he has given us the Holy Spirit to fill our hearts with his love (Romans 5:3-5 NLT).

Are you going through a trial in your life right now or watching someone else you love endure heaviness or pain? Then there is no coincidence you are reading this encouragement. Perhaps you are dealing with a job loss, financial troubles, or difficulties at home or within your marriage. No matter what trial you are dealing with, it is safe to say that "you are not alone."

The difficulties the seasons of life bring can leave us excruciatingly lonely and in a fight mode just to survive! It is hard to hold on to the one thing we need when we face a trial—a positive attitude. But we can! Keeping a Christ-centered faith will produce and ensure the miracle you long for.

God's Word is filled with hope and comfort when it comes to the trials that we face. God promises us that what we are going through will never be wasted. He promises to work everything together for good, even through our trials, if we love Him and cling to Him.

All praise to God, the Father of our Lord Jesus Christ. It is by his great mercy that we have been born again because God raised Jesus Christ from the dead. Now, we live with great expectation, and we have a priceless inheritance—an inheritance that is kept in heaven for you, pure and undefiled, beyond the reach of change and decay. And through your faith, God is protecting you by his power until you receive this salvation, which is ready to be revealed on the last day for all to see. So be truly glad. There is wonderful joy ahead, even though you must endure many trials for a little while. These trials will show that your faith is genuine. It is being tested as fire tests and purifies gold—though your faith is far more precious than mere gold. So, when your faith remains strong through many trials, it will bring you much praise and glory and honor on the day when Jesus Christ is revealed to the whole world (1 Peter 1:3-7 NLT).

God always gives us the endurance to go through challenging times. When we are in the worst of our situations, in the darkest moments of our trials, It can be hard to believe that holding to Him will bring us strength and comfort. Can He truly equip us through our own suffering? Will He really empower us to be able to help or assist someone else facing the same darkness we have experienced? Oh yes, He can, He does, and He will. Through our suffering, God not only strengthens us, but He miraculously allows us to be transformed—giving us the ability to provide help for others yet to come.

God loves you so much, and the beautiful thing about His love is that He does not expect you to understand it. God knows His love is greater than anything you could ever hope for or imagine. He wants you to have faith enough to believe that He can do the impossible through your trial. God is faithful and desires to help you in your time of need. Pray to Him and watch

Him answer you through His Word, His Holy Spirit, and through other people. Pray and ask Him to speak to you, and then listen for His answer, which may come in an unexpected or unusual way.

> *I prayed to the Lord, and he answered me. He freed me from all my fears. Those who look to him for help will be radiant with joy; no shadow of shame will darken their faces. In my desperation I prayed, and the Lord listened; he saved me from all my troubles. For the angel of the Lord is a guard; he surrounds and defends all who fear him (Psalm 34:4-7 NLT).*

In the darkest of nights, God's light shines the brightest. God brings hope even in our trials, which are never easy but are an opportunity to trust in the name of Jesus. Your trial can be the very thing God uses to give you a tremendous testimony of what happens when we call out to Him and watch Him work in our midst.

God gives us beautiful hope even in the midst of our most difficult trials.

. . . .

Janet Carlton

 Janet Carlton grew up in two lovely suburbs of Cleveland, Ohio. She studied Elementary Education in college; after marrying John, she stayed home to birth and nurture their subsequent nine children—six boys and three girls. In the middle of her 3rd pregnancy, she and John moved to a small town in Minnesota near his family's cabin. There, they helped his father start a K-12 Christian school, from which most of their children graduated. When the school terminated after 30 years, Janet taught her last child at home. She and John are currently blessed with 39 grandkids and counting. She homeschools one of her grandsons full-time and teaches piano to six sweet girls, four of whom are her granddaughters.

Janet writes poetry and finds satisfaction in crafting letters and essays. Along with physical fitness and outdoor activity, she enjoys reading, studying, praying, and developing musical skills. She loves to play guitar with her church worship team and is privileged to sit under the preaching of her firstborn son, who fervently digs treasure from the Word of God. One of Janet's greatest delights is memorizing long passages of Scripture, which opens her understanding to the wonder of her salvation in Jesus.

Delivered From Death

By Janet Carlton

As a young child, I did not experience any significant trauma. My parents loved one another and each one of their four children. Dad held a prestigious job at a university, Mom had meaningful interests, and our lives were basically ordered with school, regular meals, holidays, trips, camping, etc. Barring some normal sibling spats, my three sisters and I shared common affection. However, one evening in 1965, when I was 13, a shock wave of darkness blasted the foundation of my presumed security. My family was watching TV in the den just off the living room of our large brick house, and I was standing casually beside the couch. Suddenly, completely unexpectant, a weird aura, as from a foreign realm, enclosed me in an abrupt and horrifying self-awareness. My mind shifted away from its comfortable surroundings, and I was momentarily paralyzed with a private terror. Dreadful thoughts upheaved my emotions: *Someday, I will die and be nowhere; I will helplessly disappear and vanish from this world into absolute nothingness; I will be gone.*

You see, beneath the relative stability of our home lay a huge fault line—my family denied the existence of God. The result was that I grew up without the testimony of a transcendent Creator or personal Savior—no prayer, no Bible study, no comfort of the Holy Spirit, no world view offering enduring safety. I was taught (and believed) that the universe was self-made by evolutionary processes and that human life was the highest form of intelligence. In spite of my sincere and caring parents, this shaky foundation left me open to great deception, and on that pivotal evening, I embraced the lie of annihilation.

> *At that time you were without Christ... having no hope and without God in the world* (Ephesians 2:12 NKJV).

My first reaction was to run from the den and take refuge under a curtained table in our downstairs bathroom. But even in that favorite little nook, inaudible voices told me I could never escape this frightening destiny. No one or nothing, I concluded, would be able to change the finality of ultimate death. I felt utterly alone and devastated.

Following this 'revelation,' the distraction of activities somewhat assuaged my raw and hidden fears. I was popular at school and stayed busy with sports and music. Every summer, our family relocated to our Michigan cottage, where we enjoyed recreation on a gorgeous lake. I was blessed with many privileges and opportunities. Yet, something was never the same after that experience in the den. In the midst of the duties and pleasures of teenage life, I increasingly pondered the absurdity of death. *Why does everyone die? Why can't we live endlessly?* I could not reconcile myself with that seeming reality. Disillusionment and hopelessness threatened my future outlook.

Later that year, another fear entered my life. Unreasonably, I began to be overly cautious about staying thin. Obviously, at 13, I was developing physically, but when the scale read 100 pounds, I determined to diet and unwisely reduced my food quantity to 800 calories/day. My parents probably considered this a harmless experiment, yet after three weeks, and at 84 pounds, I was panting my way up my school steps to second-floor classes. Though this weight loss wasn't terribly alarming since I was still under five feet; nevertheless, I broke the diet with excess, thus initiating a bent toward overeating. Although the problem wasn't acute at that point, it was about to compound.

That summer, a girl at our cottage explained that by sticking her finger down her throat, she could induce self-vomiting and avoid gaining weight after a binge. Foolishly intrigued by this idea (the word *bulimia* wasn't coined until 1979), I tried the method a few times with success and figured it was a convenient trick for emergencies. But rationalization for using this trick snowballed. Gradually, my stomach conditioned itself to regurgitate easily without the finger technique, and by sophomore year of high school, I was whirling in a cycle of gorging and vomiting several times a day. In between commitments and social desires, I was secretly driven by some inner monster toward voracious gluttony, enslaved not only to food but to the necessary toilet bowl. I was screaming inside, longing for health.

Each night, I vowed to conquer the insanity; each day, I failed, often running to the store and wasting money on my 'narcotic' food supply. This bizarre behavior continued for about three more years, while my parents, though slightly aware, never discovered the extremity of my addiction. We were financially comfortable and enjoyed many visitors, so evidently, the depleted groceries didn't affect them enough to investigate.

Throughout high school, I lived a double life, privately feeling frenzied and anxious, publicly appearing happy and attractive. I deceptively shoved my mountainous problems into a separate part of my personality when engaged in regular events. When I left the familiarity of home base, my defenses drastically weakened, making my freshman year at college nearly unmanageable. The incessant haunt of death, the emotional scarring of promiscuity, the crazy bulimia, and a newly acquired dependence on marijuana left my concentration for studies seriously depleted. I began to skip classes and lose ambition, deeming my formal education pointless. Campus life provided an opportunity for valuable friendships, but I was unable to focus on advancing them. Depression was a millstone around my neck, and my mental stability was disintegrating.

> *I know that good itself does not dwell in me, that is, in my sinful nature. For I have the desire to do what is good, but I cannot carry it out* (Romans 7:18 NIV).

In retrospect, I know God was stripping me of my rebellious pride against Him. While pondering the worldwide prevalence of corruption, I realized progressively that underneath the outward restraints of social morality, I harbored in my own nature the potential for much evil. A deep conviction of my human depravity disturbed me, though I didn't define it in biblical terms.

> *For the word of God is living and powerful, and sharper than any two-edged sword, piercing even to the division of soul and spirit, and of joints and marrow, and is a discerner of the thoughts and intents of the heart. And there is no creature hidden from His sight, but all things are naked and open to the eyes of Him to whom we must give account* (Hebrews 4:12-13 NKJV).

Near the end of that erratic academic year, by the Lord's grace, God-ward questions and thoughts began to filter through my mind. One classmate mentioned the idea of a Messiah. *What is a Messiah?* I silently probed. My roommate discussed praying to God... *How do I pray?* Research into forms of mysticism and astrology left me confused and empty. Some other power was pulling me into fresh avenues of thought.

One day, while dozing on a college library couch, I had a short, vivid dream in which I saw the face of my dear deceased grandpa. His countenance was ethereal, suspended in the clouds like the face of the moon, and he was gazing at me with his warm, cheerful grin. Upon awakening, an infant hope fluttered in my heart: *Is Grandpa still alive somewhere?*

As a young child, while my mother was gone for a few hours, I stayed with my great uncle and aunt, who were evangelical Christians. As I played on the floor of their cozy living room, they began to talk to me about heaven. I looked up and asked innocently, "Can I ice skate in heaven?"

"Oh, sure you can."

"Can I climb trees?"

"Of course, you can do everything you want in heaven."

At age 18, I revisited that conversation and wondered: *What is heaven? A place? A state of mind?*

After my freshman year, I quit college and began a relationship with a former high school acquaintance. He was Jewish, and in the midst of our conversation, he said he believed Jesus was the prophesied Messiah who would return someday to earth. I rolled my eyes, yet his words disturbed me. *What does he mean? Is Jesus a person I could really know?*

In June, when a girlfriend and I took a trip out west, I periodically discerned a tender spiritual presence watching over me. For example, while traveling through New Mexico, we inadvisably picked up two hitchhikers and accepted their offer to stay overnight in a cabin in the mountains. Come morning, our car and traveler's checks were gone! A written note stated that our money would buy guns to 'break' their friend out of jail and that our car would be returned. True to their word, the car was returned, yet amazingly, in those few days of abandonment, instead of panic, I experienced a special (almost angelic) peace, an energetic joy, even daring to imagine: *Is God here with me?* I was being drawn toward the One who is the Way, the Truth, and the Life.

Meanwhile, on the same trip, devilish influences opposed my leanings toward salvation. One night, when I smoked some enhanced marijuana on the couch of a California apartment, I was lured by whispers of diabolical enticements: *Kill yourself now. Get it over with. Be done at last with the dread of death.* In my drugged condition, those suicidal darts sounded logical, but by morning, mercifully, their poignancy had largely evaporated.

Back home in August, I decided to resume the conversation my aunt and uncle had initiated 14 years earlier. They assured me that my grandpa WAS in heaven, and after briefly sharing the gospel, they offered to pray with me to receive Jesus as my Savior. I declined, yet I left with my aunt's profound words tilling the soil of my conscience: *The Bible is the mind of God.*

Soon after, a street preacher at the Cleveland Art Museum confronted me about being born-again. This was new vocabulary! "How do you know if you're born again?" I inquired.

He smiled smugly, "Oh, believe me, when you are born-again, you will know."

I pondered the term *born-again*. Resistance was waning as my ears were being opened to the sovereign call of my Creator.

> *For by grace you have been saved through faith, and that not of yourselves; it is the gift of God, not of works, lest anyone should boast* (Ephesians 2:8-9 NKJV).

Once, as a preteen, I attended an event with my neighbor's church youth group. Before our rowdy fun of football in the snow, all the kids had recited the Lord's prayer. All the kids, that is, except me. I did not know the words. Now, much later, that living vernacular began ringing in my spirit like distant bells.

On August 31, 1971, my boyfriend stopped over while I was outside working on a refinishing project with sandpaper and rags. Unpredictably, he invited me to a prayer meeting at a local church that night. My reply was an impulsive "No!"

His dark brown eyes stared me down, "Why, what else would you be doing?"

Angrily relenting, I tossed my rag onto the patio. "Alright, I'll go."

That evening, I walked with him into that small church as a lost hippie, barefoot, in old corduroy jeans, and naive to the depth of my blindness. Everyone was friendly; the atmosphere was exuberant. Smiling people were praising the Lord out loud and singing songs with gusto. Following group prayer time, when the altar was opened for individual needs, a kind man approached me, asking if I would like to know Jesus. I told him I wasn't ready. In spite of my desperation, there I was, sluffing off an appeal from the Living God!

> *And this is the condemnation, that the light has come into the world, and men loved darkness rather than light because their deeds were evil* (John 3:19 NKJV).

Yet, these dedicated saints were insistent. A tall, hefty woman sat me down on the altar and began weeping extravagantly, begging me to call on Christ for salvation. "This is what you want," she sobbed, "I see it in your eyes. You can have eternal life; your sins will be forgiven; do not leave without accepting Jesus." She carried on profusely, and I was somehow enabled to listen to the gospel without counterarguments in my head. I sensed God's unparalleled love and comfort flowing from this woman's urgings, and miraculously, the last boulder of unbelief was hurled abroad.

I simply said, "Okay, I'll pray."

She led me in straightforward words of repentance while I was transferred from darkness and doom into The Kingdom of Light. Hallelujah! The Lord God Almighty reigns!

Following her basic instructions on how to nourish my nascent faith, I jumped up to join a circle of rejoicing believers who were dancing, singing, and clapping their hands. Peace poured into my soul along with astounding true revelation: See? You CAN live forever! This is the way.

As the children are partakers of flesh and blood, he also himself likewise took part of the same; that through death he might destroy him that had the power of death, that is the devil; And deliver them who through fear of death were all their lifetime subject to bondage (Hebrews 2:14-15 KJV).

The air was balmy when I arrived home after that awesome meeting. Before going inside, I crossed our street to the school soccer field and ran the length of it ecstatically. This joy was no fantasy or pretense. Through Jesus' atonement on the cross, I had entered another world—a world that my sinful nature had defied, but my newborn spirit now craved. I saw eternity stretched out in wonder. The shackling horror of extinction was displaced by elated worship, and, for the first time, I spoke intimately to the mighty, blessed, beautiful Triune God.

The next day, I tossed my marijuana, became chaste, and shunned drug and drinking parties. Untethered from gloomy burdens, I just wanted to get back to that church! Along with other new converts, I began attending services four times a week. Jesus was enthroned as the love of my life, and I was starving for the Word of God.

Your words were found, and I ate them, and Your word was to me the joy and rejoicing of my heart; for I am called by Your name, O Lord God of Hosts (Jeremiah 15:16 NKJV).

Along with behavioral changes, my empty well of melancholy and torturous longings began to brim with eternal springs of effervescent joy. The indwelling Holy Spirit was infinitely sweeter than any previous vice or experience. An anticipation of heavenly bliss overturned the despair of evolutionary ideology. I was certain I would live endlessly in the presence of God's perfect love. His kingdom would have no end!

> *There is no fear in love; but perfect love casts out fear, because fear involves torment* (1 John 4:18 NKJV).

Of course, on the heels of euphoria, I also encountered spiritual warfare. Jesus warned that entering His kingdom would include tribulation and trials of our faith. One initial test accompanied a job in the backroom of a candy store where I packed luscious boxes of chocolates. They were made on-site, and I was allowed to eat the mistakes. My resolve to submit to the Holy Spirit and resist the urge to binge was strengthened.

In 1972, God led me to a Christian university where I completed a degree in Elementary Education. Those were significant, healing years as I pursued Christ in close relationships with other young disciples.

While my struggle with bulimia continually diminished, total victory over its every tentacle finally manifested after about seven years of intermittent counsel, aggressive prayer, and scriptural confession. The reign of that cruel taskmaster crumbled, and I was amazingly set free.

> *Therefore if the Son makes you free, you shall be free indeed* (John 8:36 NKJV).

Jesus trains us to conquer our sins and fears, walk by faith, and fight for joy. In Him are hidden all the treasures of wisdom and knowledge. Underneath are His everlasting arms, so never is there a reason to despair. In valleys or on mountaintops, we can have fellowship with the Father, Son, and Holy Spirit and be adorned with bold assurance to believe the Word of Truth.

Like an inexhaustible gold mine, the Bible enriches us, multiplying our awareness and our application of spiritual riches. We need to keep asking, keep seeking, and keep knocking—God's ways are higher than ours, and He promises in Romans 8:28 that *all things work together for good to those who love God, to those who are the called according to His purpose* (NKJV).

Sisters and brothers, let us feast on and delight in the greatness of our salvation, reveling in its abounding provisions and its glorious end that will culminate in the new heavens and new earth. Someday, all true believers will live in a perfect, harmonious community overflowing with unimaginable light, love, and exalted worship. We will be faultless in the purposes and pleasures of our Lord, actively serving in His kingdom and expressing infinite creativity with beautiful bodies and sinless souls. No suffering in this life can overshadow the blessedness that is to come. This hope is worth all our devotion and patience until we see the wondrous image of our glorious God in the face of Jesus Christ, Yeshua Ha Mashiach, our Savior and Lord.

Saved!
By Janet Carlton

You hovered over my disordered soul
my polluted stream of consciousness
with crooked question marks
and run-on sentences
draining into holes.

Quit!
I used to yell to it
when on and on it went,

and I would dream....

beyond the haunt of hell
and guilty torment,
of meadows green,

deliverance from death,
while coiled in addictions.

Then finally!
By divine decree we met.

You spoke
of Living Waters from a well.
Could I resist?

Your pure, consoling voice
told everything
I'd ever said and done
and thought or wished.

In absolute relief
I raised my arms,
I leapt!
I sped!

Away with old beleaguering griefs.

You are The Fountainhead.

Hope in Living

By Kimberly Ann Hobbs

I shall not die, but live, and declare the works of the LORD (Psalm 118:17 KJV).

Our lives and how we live them are important to God. The word "life" appears so many times throughout God's Word—if it were unimportant to God, He would not have written about it so generously. On earth, our lives are filled with ups and downs, but there is a key to living with the right mindset despite the terrain we walk. What is the key to living well? The key is hope. Hope gives us the strength to traverse the peaks and valleys of this earth with joy.

Living the life God gave you is not optional, but how you live is your choice. Walking in the hope of God allows us to live abundantly, which is the "icing on the cake." Jesus said, *"I came that they may have life and may have it abundantly"* (John 10:10 ESV). God wants us to thrive, not just merely survive. He provided a way for you to know there is hope in living. He knows the life He created in you was meant to go on for eternity.

By our physical birth, we possess only physical life. No one has divine life when they are born. When we believe in the Lord Jesus Christ as our Savior, we receive Christ into us. In His Word, God told us He would help us have a better life. Only through Jesus and our acceptance of Him as Lord and Savior can we become born again, and then by becoming obedient to His commands, does God enrich and improve our lives. He gives us hope in living.

God's Word became flesh in His only begotten Son; God's Word is life.

"Martha," Jesus said, "You don't have to wait until then. I am the Resurrection, and I am Life Eternal. Anyone who clings to me in faith, even though he dies, will live forever. And the one who lives by believing in me will never die. Do you believe this?" (John 11:25-26 TPT).

Jesus explained, "I am the Way, I am the Truth, and I am the Life. No one comes next to the Father except through union with me. To know me is to know my Father too. And from now on you will realize that you have seen him and experienced him" (John 14:6-7 TPT).

Jesus came into the world so we could have a divine life. He gave us His Word so we could live knowing our lives can be fully involved with God forever. All His riches and the promise of living eternally with Him will come alive when we place our trust in Jesus Christ as our personal Lord and Savior. When this happens, we can then experience the fullness of God's attributes of love, justice, and holiness within our lives, giving us as human beings a chance to glorify our God, who is in the highest place, heaven. We can honor God, whose image we were created in, by living fully and abundantly. There is no greater hope than to live knowing Christ and exalting God.

The world has been tricked into believing that living is mere survival and that the fullness of living comes from harnessing the entitlement of human rights. But when we become selfish and think that the world revolves around us, our thoughts can easily turn destructive. When we begin to believe that how we think and feel on any given day determines the quality and worth of our life, we live without hope, joy, or purpose. We may even give up, thinking things will never get better.

But when we look beyond ourselves and trust God's plan and purpose for our lives, we begin to live in abundance. Our hope of living becomes based on glorifying our Lord and Savior with a heart of gratitude for living as we live out the purpose He has planned for our lives.

We each have been custom-fit to live in the hope and joy of the Lord. That hope in living flourishes as we begin to understand that whether we live here on earth or are taken home to heaven to be with Jesus, we will live in Christ for eternity. As Christians, our hope is in the living—our eternal and abundant living with our Lord and Savior in heaven.

. . . .

Anna Marie Valentine

Texas native Anna Marie Valentine lives in Hattiesburg, Mississippi. She is a licensed professional counselor, registered drama therapist, registered yoga teacher, and is pursuing her PhD in Mind/Body Medicine. She practices at March Christian Counseling.

Anna received her master's degree in Drama Therapy from New York University, where she worked as the expressive arts liaison, facilitating the integration of the dance, music, art, and drama therapy departments.

She has worked in both inpatient and outpatient settings, practicing counseling and creative arts therapy in New York City, Houston, and southern Mississippi. She hosts Christian-based wellness retreats for women and helping professionals annually.

Anna's podcast, *Moved By Grace Counseling Radio,* is on Spotify or Apple Podcast. Follow her journey at www.movedbygracecounseling.com

Anna's first book, *Simply Begin: Create, Meditate & Find Purpose* was published in 2023 and is available wherever you purchase books online.

She would like to thank her husband, Matthew, for his never-ending support and grace and her puppy-kids, Wilson and Cooper. She would also like to extend appreciation to her mother for always teaching her to shoot for the stars.

Freed by Faith

By Anna Marie Valentine

Have you ever felt so trapped in your suffering that you find it hard to think about anything else in the world? Have you ever felt so consumed in your mind that you cannot be present in the world around you? Have you ever experienced the feeling that you will never be able to heal from your pain? I have often heard that suffering is simply our inability to accept our circumstances. I would argue that suffering stems from a conscious or unconscious decision not to trust God with the reality of our lives. My decision to "white knuckle" my way through life ultimately led to my downfall. It led me to a life-and-death experience that forced me to examine my rigid idea of who Jesus is and who He is not. Through this response, I experienced the depth of Jesus' love when I finally surrendered to Him.

I am a stubborn woman, and it's not necessarily a quality I'm proud of. However, this quality has helped me to survive and figure things out on my own. This approach to life can be effective, but my strong, stubborn personality, culture, and drive to succeed did not coexist well with my desire to have a relationship with Jesus.

Psalms 50:15 *urges us to call on me in the day of trouble; I will deliver you, and you will honor me* (NIV).

I often wonder how life would have unfolded had I been able to bring my suffering to God first. It can be enticing to think, *What if?* However, I have chosen to use my experiences as monumental learning opportunities to approach life differently as I grow and mature. The story I want to share with you is a pure depiction of God's redemptive power and His ability to heal physically. My stubbornness drove me to the brink of death, and still, He fully restored my heart, mind, body, and soul.

I will always remember the day I realized this would be the fight for my life, and Jesus was the only way for me to be victorious. For many years, I was enslaved by the bondage of my body and the voice of anorexia. There are many layers to the story that led me to find myself on this path, but it was not until I was on the brink of death that Jesus Christ was able to pull me out of the depths of destruction and into His healing arms of compassion.

No one can serve two masters (Matthew 6:24 NIV).

If you are unfamiliar with eating disorders, this lethal condition can be difficult to understand. As a mental health counselor, I thought I understood symptomatology, yet I found myself living in a corpse. My body organs were shutting down, my mind was under daily captivity, and I had begun to believe that I would eventually pass on from this life with the direction my health was headed.

I grew up in a small town just south of Dallas, Texas. I attended a Christian school, and my mother attended church with my brother and me most Sundays when we were young. My dad was a pharmacist and business owner. We lived an extremely comfortable life. My brother and I never went without what we needed. At the age of 16, I was at a movie theater at an upscale Dallas shopping mall, celebrating a friend's birthday. My mom had come to pick me up, and when I left the mall, I was faced with a scene that completely turned my world upside down. My sense of security would be forever shaken.

While the movie was ending, a man approached my mother's truck in an attempt to rob her. When my mom responded by backing the truck away from the parking space, the man shot her in the face. I remember feeling as if I was floating outside my body as I started to process the horror that I had just witnessed. This was the first true disconnection from my body that I can remember. From that day forward, my journey was poisoned with crippling fear, angsty cries for a sense of security, and more confusion in my walk with Jesus than I could ever have imagined or anticipated.

My mother spent months in the hospital recovering and undergoing one surgery after another. While the community within my high school responded with compassion, support, and grace' the love I needed was just not available from these individuals. I didn't realize it at the time, or for years to come, that my only hope for healing was within Jesus Christ Himself.

I chased security and identity in every avenue I could possibly pursue.

My life dramatically shifted when I entered graduate school at New York University to study drama therapy. The one constant in my life after my mother was shot was my theater rehearsals. When the weight of the world began to press against my heart, there was a refreshing escape to go to rehearsal. That is where I felt a sense of belonging— with the artsy, unique members of the school. There, I could also "put on the role" of someone else entirely and step into another world. My graduate program allowed me to blend my love of theater with the healing and relief that it provided for me. This was a beautiful experience, but the main source of continued healing was missing my relationship with Jesus.

I had grown up in the church but never grasped the idea that Jesus (the Trinity) is a relational God. My Bible classes felt like fantastic history classes. Prayer never felt personal, and the verses were just phrases to be memorized.

Flash forward to my graduate school experience. One of the exercises for our class was to tell a story about our lives to another classmate. Amid this experience, one of my classmates shared her Christianity. Another classmate pushed back, explaining that Christians had been harmful to her in the past and that she did not feel emotionally safe. This was my first experience with severe interpersonal conflict regarding faith and religion. Although my faith was weak, I could still feel the deep-down whispers from Jesus, "This is not a depiction of who I am."

I lived in New York City for three years following my dreams of using theater to promote healing. I had many life-changing experiences working at my internship. I was engaging in therapeutic theater performances and living in a city that provided more opportunities than I could fathom. As life got busier, my income as a creative arts therapist was barely keeping me afloat. Again, without employing the power of Jesus Christ, I tried to find a way to control my unbearable fear. I took a deep dive into fitness and bodybuilding. At first, it all felt good. I was manipulating my temple to reflect the desired look for worldly approval and was sharing my journey online.

For most of my life, I felt as if every trauma I endured was random and completely out of my control, which was true to an extent. What I did not realize was that these experiences had damaged my nervous system and left me feeling overwhelmed and anxious at all times. I responded by keeping busy as a plight to "not feel my body." In my free time, I spent every moment I had pouring my energy into the gym and meticulously controlling my calorie intake. While I would attend church here and there, my relationship with God was absent. I could hear the slivers of His voice. At this point, I was not reading my Bible daily, so being able to discern God's voice from my thoughts and emotions was not possible.

This led me down a path to meet the biggest demon I would ever fight. The voice of anorexia was not logical in any sense, but it was overpowering, and it was real. I imagine my mind felt much like someone with an addiction as I willfully obeyed the demands to manipulate and restrict my body. Years went by, and my deepest passions were suppressed under the weight of my enslavement.

There is an outdated belief within the eating disorder community that an individual may never "fully recover" from an eating disorder. Additionally, I had a specialist tell me I would never lift weights again due to the brittleness of my bones. These rigid ideas consumed my thoughts, and the shame of my circumstances was beginning to feel unbearable. I remember thinking, *How on earth have I let myself get to the point where I will never be the same?* The deeper truth was that without the love of Jesus Christ, a part of me did not care whether I lived or died.

Then, a Christmas service changed my entire mindset. God revealed to me that I would perish unless I took charge and began to get comfortable with the uncomfortable. I will never forget that night because I made a covenant with Jesus that I would do everything in my power to fight the voice of the enemy.

From that moment, I made faith and recovery my number one priority. I fought hard with support from my therapist and an eating disorder recovery group. I would force myself to get uncomfortable almost daily. I know this might sound bizarre, but I remember crying one day as I ate a pop tart. It was sheer torture to force myself to rest in bed rather than go to the gym. I gained 30 pounds in a month. I have a petite frame, so this made me incredibly uncomfortable. As time went by, I allowed myself to begin to love and care for my body. The body that led me through all of my life experiences up until that point. Every time I felt like throwing in the towel, the Holy Spirit would meet me in my struggle, and I was able to press on.

God heals in non-conventional ways. As I was navigating my recovery, I was constantly in prayer. I was also volunteering and engaged with the local animal shelters. I had a busy work life, and the next blessing from the Lord came from Him directly. I received an email with available adoptable dogs, and I saw a picture that immediately changed my entire life. A sweet Golden-mix stared at me with big brown eyes, and I felt the Lord move me to go meet him. I have confidence that I would have been able to continue my healing journey, but my rescue dog played a crucial role in my ability to find peace in rest. I was not remotely in the market to adopt a dog, but I can honestly say I can't imagine my life without this sweet spirit that taught me how to calm my heart and mind. To this day, Wilson has walked with me through my life phases and chapters. Every day I have with him is a gift and a reminder of God's redemptive character.

A year later, my body regained bone density, and I was able to exercise in a compassionate, empowering way. I am a living testimony that you can fully recover from an eating disorder. Against all odds, I am the healthiest, happiest version of Anna I ever could have imagined. More importantly, I believe God allowed me to reach a place where He was my only way out of the darkness. I realize now that He was available and with me every step of the way. While I attempted to figure life out on my own, He patiently waited with his arms stretched wide open. He is a relational, loving Father. His power surpasses any resource we can try to create here on earth. He is eternal. He is kind. He is compassionate, and most importantly, He is the great physician—not just for our human bodies but for our hearts, souls, and minds.

If I have learned anything, I have been struck by the reality that the condition of our hearts and minds toward Jesus is often reflected in how we live our lives. I do not believe that I randomly "caught" an eating disorder or that I was genetically predisposed to it. Maybe those facts are somewhat true, but I believe with my full heart and mind that my condition was a result of the human-based fear that I had to figure out life on my own, which is so far from the truth that is available to every one of us. The world can feel unbearable without the promises of Jesus. I had a friend who once shared with me, "Anna, I'm so glad I don't have to orchestrate my own life. I'm so glad Jesus has done that for me." What a sigh of relief every time I remember this truth. It's natural to feel afraid. It's normal to experience uncertainty. The key is that we cannot allow ourselves to stay in these places.

Hebrews 11:1 states, *Now faith is confidence in what we hope for and assurance about what we do not see* (NIV). A universal truth is that we cannot ever fully plan for what our future will hold. But it would be a waste to live our lives in constant fear. Our job is to hold steady to the task at hand and engage faith to remember that our God has already written our stories for us. Regardless of what we experience in this life, we are never alone. He is pursuing us to live life in relationship with Him. If we can tap into this faith, He can truly start moving through us. The message I hope you take from my story is that even in our darkest moments, God is there. In our shame-ridden culture, He is our compassion. You have been designed for such a time as this. Never forget that you are never alone and deeply loved. Be free with faith.

> *It is for freedom that Christ has set us free. Stand firm, then, and do not let yourselves be burdened again by a yoke of slavery (Galatians 5:1 NIV).*

Hope in the Worry

By Connie A. VanHorn

Often throughout my life, I have been weighed down by worry. I became accustomed to worrying very early in childhood and carried the practice into adulthood. I found a little secret place inside myself to put my worry, and over time, that weight gradually became heavier and heavier.

But God offers us hope; He extends His hands to carry the weight of worry for us.

Before I embraced Jesus, I perceived Christians as carefree individuals without any problems. I believed Christians were flawless, and God had removed all their problems. However, I quickly discovered this was not reality. Christians are filled with the Holy Spirit and have faith in God, which allows them to be at peace *even though* they carry circumstances that warrant worry. I wanted that same peace.

It takes time to develop trust in God after committing our hearts to Jesus. I recall a moment in a park when I was anxious about having enough money to go to the store that day. I sat there in the grass, and I cried and prayed. I remembered a card in my wallet that I hadn't checked in a long time, but I didn't expect to have money on it. To my surprise, when I called the number on the back, there was exactly $150 on the card. I was overjoyed and grateful to God for His blessing and protection. These small instances gave me hope and gradually built my trust in God. Not every request I made was granted in the same way, but God often provided just enough to test my faith and keep me relying on Him, even when His answers were different from my expectations.

Do not be anxious about anything, but in every situation, by prayer and petition, with thanksgiving, present your requests to God. And the peace of God, which transcends all understanding, will guard your hearts and your minds in Christ Jesus (Philippians 4:6-7 NIV).

God's Word repeatedly tells us not to be anxious about anything but to bring our concerns and fears before Him in prayer. When we surrender our worries to God, we open ourselves to receive His peace, which surpasses all human understanding. Even when we are full of worry, His peace becomes a shield that guards our hearts and minds, giving us hope.

Whenever I am working my way through a difficult season, people ask me how I maintain a sense of calm and peace. The answer is simple—God! Attaining peace in Him took time to build as I trusted God. God has already prepared us for whatever is bringing us worry. He knows everything about tomorrow and the next moment. He wants us to take our cares to Him and TRUST. We can have confidence and peace knowing that God is by our side. His presence will bring us peace so we don't have to carry fear. I have peace knowing that He is here with me through everything.

Finding hope in the worry requires a shift in perspective from focusing on our problems to trusting in God's promises. Instead of allowing fear to consume our thoughts and emotions, we can choose to place our faith in God. As we give our worries to Him, He invites us to swap our anxieties for His peace, our doubts for His assurance, and our worries for His hope.

Therefore do not worry about tomorrow, for tomorrow will worry about itself. Each day has enough trouble of its own (Matthew 6:34 NIV).

Here are three things that have helped me when worry sets in and I need to find hope in the worry:

1. Pray and Surrender: When worry sets in, turn to prayer and surrender your concerns to God. Trust in His faithfulness and sovereignty, knowing He cares for you and controls all situations.

2. Focus on Gratitude: Shift your focus from worry to gratitude by counting your blessings and expressing thankfulness for the good things in your life. Gratitude helps us have a positive mindset and reminds us of God's faithfulness. Remember what He has already done!

3. Seek Support and Encouragement: Reach out to a friend, family member, or mentor for support and encouragement when worry is heavy on you. This can provide perspective, comfort, and reassurance. Finding hope in the worry involves placing your faith in God, trusting in His love and protection, and seeking His peace that surpasses all understanding. *Cast all your anxiety on Him because He cares for you* (1 Peter 5:7 NIV).

We can pray this prayer together right now as you are reading this. Let go of the worry and the weight that God never wanted you to carry.

Heavenly Father,

Thank You for all the blessings You have sent and the love You shower on your children daily. When worry consumes us, help us find hope in You. Teach us to cast our cares upon You and trust in Your will for our lives—even if that means going through hard things. Give us Your peace that surpasses all understanding and guards our hearts and minds. I pray that our worries are transformed into opportunities to grow closer to You and experience the hope that only You can provide.

Amen.

Shawna V. Sun

Shawna V. Sun is an evangelist, entrepreneur, and lover of the Lord. She was adopted as a baby from South Korea and grew up in a Christian family with two older brothers in the Midwest. She was raised in Nebraska and grew up in the Lord before her long journey of looking for God in all the wrong places. For nearly 20 years, she dabbled in nearly every spiritual path and got lost in deception and the New Age.

In 2020, Shawna had an encounter with Jesus that changed her life forever, returning to her faith as a prodigal. Since then, she's been on fire for Jesus. Her passions include film, business, worship, and traveling. She has a degree in Psychology and a background in personal training, marketing, and online business. In 2020, the Lord gave her a vision for a global film project, which is, aside from the Lord and family, her biggest passion.

Shawna is the mother of a beautiful 10-year-old girl. She and her husband and daughter live in Santa Cruz, California. She is currently working on her film projects for the Lord and helping Christian entrepreneurs bring their gifts to the world through online business.

The Lord Is With Us Always

By Shawna V. Sun

When reflecting on my life, I can see the hand of God from the very beginning, even when I didn't know Him yet. My journey began in South Korea. I was born of two people who came together in a secret affair. In the throes of passion, I was conceived by "accident." Although, with God, nothing is an accident. At that time, it was taboo for unwed mothers to get pregnant, so I was given up for adoption.

I stayed in an orphanage for nearly four and a half months before I was adopted into a beautiful Christian family in the Midwest of the United States. The enemy wasted no time as he came after me during my journey to the US. I got very ill while traveling and nearly died, but God is greater, and I survived. After I landed in Chicago, my new parents came to greet me. Finally, after they had worked their way through the adoption process and prepared for years, I landed in their loving arms. I was also greeted by my two brothers and foster sister.

Growing up in Midwest suburbia was lovely, and having a Christian family was a great blessing. My dad worked for a big trucking company, and my mom left her job as a paralegal to stay home with the children. Our family lived in a safe neighborhood and enjoyed the simple beauty of life with all the fun of the changing seasons. We enjoyed riding bikes, eating rhubarb pie, going to neighborhood barbeques, and swimming in the pool during the summers. In the fall, we enjoyed jumping in piles of leaves, eating pumpkin pie, playing football, and relaxing in the hot tub. Winter brought more excitement with piles of snow and snowman building. Then came the melting snow, spring flowers, Easter egg hunts, and angel food cake in the spring. Life seemed beautiful and almost perfect.

But when I was four years old, I was molested. The enemy struck hard and brought trauma on a core level. I remember going to tell my parents about what happened. They did not believe me. So from that moment on, I shut my mouth and lived with the lie that people wouldn't ever believe me when I told the truth. The wound impacted me deeply through my younger years and as I grew into womanhood. I suppressed the pain and trauma until it manifested in negative ways in my teen years. Like many young girls, I felt trapped in the jail of low self-worth and insecurity that manifested itself into eating disorders and deep depression.

When I was 16 years old, I met my first love. It was an amazing experience. We related to each other very well, as he was adopted, too. We got lost in love and relied on our romantic whirlwind to carry us through our high school years. Our relationship was beautiful, but I had difficulty trusting that love could last. After all, I had been abandoned and orphaned. I often thought to myself, *Who could possibly stay with me?*

Although I was raised a Christian, I was very much in love, and it wasn't hard to fall into fornication. It didn't take long for affliction to make itself known in my life. It got to the point where I was so depressed that I wanted to end my life. The deep, buried pain of being abandoned and molested had me believing the lie that my life didn't matter anyway.

I spiraled down into the pits of depression and tried to take my life. I managed to survive; the doctors claimed it was a miracle. I should have died due to organ failure from the overdose of iron pills I had taken. It was my mother's prayers that carried me through.

Life carried on, and I recovered from the depression. I went on to study psychology to try to understand everything I had been through. In college, I took my first yoga class and world religions class, which helped lead me away from the Christian faith. By the time I finished college and was living on my own, I had lost any connection to Christianity and Jesus. I was becoming more drawn to mythology rather than worshiping the true Savior of the world.

Around this time, I married my first husband, and we moved to California together. He joined the Air Force and was stationed in Monterey. I was excited to be living out my dream in California. Seeing the ocean as we would drive into Monterey gave me an overwhelming sense of being "home." That was it—I had finally arrived. My husband studied at the Defense Language Institute. Ironically, he was assigned to the Korean language. After a couple of years, he was commissioned to go to Korea. I did not have the maturity, nor was I walking with the Lord; I chose not to go. The marriage dissolved.

After that, I began to seek God in more of the wrong places. I was still looking for love and fulfillment in the world. I numbed the pain of the divorce with things of the world. I got involved in another relationship and began to explore the world of psychedelics and other exploratory paths. This only led to more affliction and depression. I found myself back in the cycle of suicidal depression. But God protected me yet again.

My deep search for true love, healing, and peace continued. I searched every spiritual path you can imagine. I went from one relationship to the next, seeking satisfaction, pleasure, and true love. In my desperate search, I was disappointed and completely distraught that I hadn't found my true calling or true love. I became so entrenched in the New Age that I thought I found true "enlightenment." I was being my own god (or goddess) and did whatever I wanted in the name of personal "empowerment." By this time, I had entrenched myself in the occult and sought after personal satisfaction, only to be left with disappointment and unfulfillment. One of the main paths I tried was Esther and Jerry Hick's Law of Attraction methodology to attain what I thought would be the "perfect" life for myself. I put into practice all the methods to "attract and create my dream life."

I wanted it all: the husband, the big house, a nice car, lots of money, and other material things I thought would define success in my life. I applied the methods, and sure enough, within weeks, I met someone I had "attracted" into my life. We met at a dance, and shortly after, I found myself living with him in a house in the hills. Six months later, we were married and were pregnant with our first daughter. During the first seven years, more and more doors opened spiritually. Sadly, the marriage began to disintegrate. We were chasing after the things of the world and the lust that never brought any lasting satisfaction. The enemy took hold. We grew more and more apart. At one point, we were so spiritually lost that we decided to have an open marriage. This only led to disaster. He began to date other women, and I opened the door to connect with other men.

At some point, we separated, and the marriage came to an end. I was seeing and dating other men; it was one of the most devastating times of my life. My life had fallen apart, all in the name of personal "satisfaction." I was only chasing after my own selfish dreams and desires. I began to cry out to the Lord, and for the first time in years, I stepped into a church. As I entered the church, I began to hear the worship music I hadn't heard since I was a girl. I began to cry. As the tears streamed down my face, I felt the power of the Holy Spirit hit me. But this was not enough to fully change me. I was lost and soon returned to dating the man I was with after my marriage. I thought I was in love with him while attached only to the lust of the flesh, pleasure, and sexual fulfillment. This kind of love was limited without the Lord as a solid foundation.

One day, while at the beach with my daughter and a friend, we noticed a man in the water with his children. He had two kids and was holding one in each arm. As we looked on, we noticed one child fly out of his arms and into the riptide. My friend and I dropped everything and ran into the water.

She grabbed one child, and I grabbed the other. The riptide grabbed my body and began to pull me down. Over and over, I was plundered under the water; it took all I could do to keep the child's head and mine above the water. At some point, someone came and grabbed the boy from my arms, and then I went under. I was losing strength as the cold water engulfed me. My body started going numb; I felt like a wet and soggy noodle. I looked up at the sky, barely keeping afloat. All I could notice was the vast sky.

I knew I had no strength to keep me afloat. I called out to God, "I have no more strength. I know it is up to you, God, if I live or die. I surrender." I continued to cry out silently to Jesus.

I saw the vast blue sky and the softness of the white billowing clouds. A peace came over me, and the world felt as if it stood still. I felt the calmness of the Lord's presence wash over me—the peace that surpasses all understanding. With no strength left in my body, I let go. Then, out of nowhere, someone grabbed my arm and proceeded to drag me out of the ocean and to the shore. My body was limp. After recovering, I was able to gather my strength and return to my feet. There were three men standing on the shore. I asked each of them if he was the one who had pulled me out of the ocean. They each said no. Then I asked the group of people standing on the shore if they saw who had saved me; they all said no.

At that moment, I knew God had sent an angel.

Although that experience brought me a glimpse of God's peace, I still did not follow His ways or give my life to Him. I did, however, become more and more curious about Him and the truth I had been so desperately seeking.

I began to research people who had direct encounters with the Lord. I watched countless videos on YouTube seeking the truth. I began to pray for a direct encounter of my own. Soon after, a woman messaged me on Facebook, asking if she could pray for me. She sent me a link to a video for a book about people who had direct encounters with the Lord. I immediately ordered the book and read it within days. A couple of months later, I received a call from the ministry telling me that the Lord would visit me in the night. I took communion and sat up till midnight waiting. I fell asleep, not knowing what to expect.

The following morning, I woke up on the couch wondering if anything had happened in the night. I got up to move, and the peace of the Lord hit me again. I felt His presence and knew He had touched me in the night. I knew my life would never be the same. After this encounter with the Lord, a fire ignited in me. I began to read the Bible and countless other books. I would endlessly watch sermons online. I found a local church and attended all the weekly services. I could not get enough. I wanted more and more and more of Him. I laid myself down on the floor in the living room and gave my life to Jesus, saying, "I only want to serve you, Lord, and will do whatever you ask me to do." The Holy Spirit entered my body, and I received a vision. The Lord showed me the vision of a show to work on. I began this work, and soon, massive doors began to open, putting people in place who would be a part of it. Things were happening supernaturally.

Then the enemy began to set traps, bringing men who were counterfeits into my life. The enemy knew my deep desire for a godly marriage and also the unhealed parts of my soul. I heard whispers in my ear that the Lord was bringing someone into my life on a specific date. I joined different online dating sites because no eligible men my age attended my church. The lying spirit told me this person would come into my life in three months. After a week on the sites, I had enough. I was going to close all my accounts. As I was about to close the last one, I saw a picture of a man who caught my eye. He sent me a message, and I responded. It didn't take long to set up our first date to meet. We decided to meet at one of my favorite restaurants in town.

We began to date three months to the day the spirit had predicted. Shortly after, we were married. In my naivety, I thought I was being obedient by marrying him, but then the abuse started. It came in every form—mental, emotional, verbal, financial, and sexual. I didn't want to break my vows, so I stayed with him for months. Then I started to receive death threats, and I found out he had been sleeping with my friend. When I filed a restraining order against him, I discovered he had a record of seven offenses.

After that, the enemy set yet another trap. A man from the church suddenly appeared in my life and wanted to be my "knight in shining armor." He stepped in to help me, and we quickly found ourselves in a relationship and love affair. We rushed into a marriage even though I knew the Lord told me to wait. Once again, things blew up in my face. My new husband ended up relapsing into alcoholism and had a psychotic break. After he left, I was devastated. I had only wanted to create a beautiful life and have a family for my daughter. I wanted to show her how a godly marriage and family could be. I was crying in pain on my living room floor, crushed by yet another disappointment. The wound of abandonment was crushing me, and I had experienced my greatest fear. I needed a turning point.

The Holy Spirit began to minister to me. He showed me all the strongholds that were running in my life. He led me to tear them down one by one and replace them with the truth. I started to feel free. Over the course of four days, I felt more liberation and healing. In my 20 years of being lost and searching for healing, I had never experienced anything like this with the Lord and the Holy Spirit.

The Holy Spirit guided me in every area of life. I broke the stronghold of all of the experiences of trauma I had in my life. I could see how the enemy had been afflicting me through his lies. As all the lies came down, I began to feel a breakthrough in my life on a level I had never experienced. More and more changes started happening in my life. The places where the enemy had come in to steal, kill, and destroy began to be restored. I began to experience restoration in every area of my life. With peace and joy now in my relationships, finances, and health, I felt truly confident and comfortable in my skin for the first time. I tore down the strongholds I had from being abandoned, molested, struggling financially, and from every affliction. Everything in my life was shifting. I felt at peace more than I'd ever felt before. I came to a place of peace and contentment with being.

I felt satisfied in the Lord.

> *You make known to me the path of life; in your presence there is fullness of joy; at your right hand are pleasures forevermore (Psalm 16:11 ESV).*

As I clung to the Lord, He unexpectedly brought an amazing man into my life. We were married on November 24, 2023; I know this marriage is a gift of heaven.

> *I will restore to you the years that the swarming locust has eaten, the hopper, the destroyer, and the cutter, my great army, which I sent among you. "You shall eat in plenty and be satisfied, and praise the name of the Lord your God, who has dealt wondrously with you. And my people shall never again be put to shame. You shall know that I am in the midst of Israel, and that I am the Lord your God and there is none else. And my people shall never again be put to shame" (Joel 2:25-27 ESV).*

The Lord has shown me that no matter what is broken in my life, He can use the break for a breakthrough. No matter what the enemy means for evil, God will turn around for good. No matter how dark and intense life can be, God's victory will always be greater. The Lord is with us always.

Hope in God's Word

By Connie A. VanHorn

For the word of God is living and active, sharper than any two-edged sword, piercing to the division of soul and of spirit, of joints and of marrow, and discerning the thoughts and intentions of the heart (Hebrews 4:12 ESV).

When life gets hard, we can find ourselves searching for a glimmer of hope to hold onto. In these moments, turning to God's Word can give us the comfort and reassurance we desperately need. The Bible is filled with promises for those who seek out hope in its pages.

One of the most powerful verses that speaks to the hope found in God's Word is found in Romans 15:4, which states, *For everything that was written in the past was written to teach us, so that through the endurance taught in the Scriptures and the encouragement they provide we might have hope* (NIV). This verse reminds us that all we read in the Bible is not just words on a page but living and breathing truths that have the power to bring us hope and encouragement in our darkest moments.

When I first became a Christian, I would easily get confused when reading the Bible. Some of the teachings were difficult to understand, and my connection with the Holy Spirit, which is key to drawing us into His Word, was still in its infancy. It wasn't until I connected with our triune God on a deeper level that I was able to grasp what He was speaking to me through Scripture. My journey of seeking, praying, and ASKING Him to help me understand ultimately led me to a deeper relationship with Him.

Through daily devotions, attending church regularly, and seeking guidance from other believers, I began to see the Bible in a new light. This transformative experience has brought me closer to God and helped me to understand His love and purpose for my life. The Bible became alive! I found hope and peace nestled in its pages. It changed me, and if you open the Bible and ask the Holy Spirit to open your heart, it can change you, too. We can turn to God's Word as a source of hope, protection, and security in times of trouble, and we can place our trust and hope in the promises it contains.

> *You are my refuge and my shield; I have put my hope in your word* (Psalm 119:114 NIV).

As we submerge ourselves in Scripture, we are reminded of God's faithfulness, love, and purpose for His people. The amazing stories serve as a testament to God's commitment to His children. When we read HIS words, the Holy Spirit reminds us that the same God who was faithful to His children from the beginning of time is also faithful to us. He will never leave us nor forsake us. His words remind us that we are never alone and that He has a plan for each of us. Let's hold onto the hope that comes from knowing God's love is unwavering. Keep faith, keep praying, and keep believing in the power of His Word. Stay strong and trust in God's perfect timing.

As you navigate the struggles and difficult storms of life, cling to the hope found in God's Word. Draw strength from its promises, find comfort in its truths, and rest in the confidence that our hope is secure in the hands of our loving Heavenly Father.

. . . .

Darlene Eldred

Darlene Eldred is a friend to chaos and excitement and continues to thrive despite what life may present. Her greatest achievements call her Mom (Mommy when they need something), and hearing Nana is music to her ears.

Darlene lives in West Palm Beach, Florida, just a few miles from her oldest daughter, Jessica, with her husband, Dwight, and daughter, Rachel. She takes every opportunity to visit her home state of Maryland to get regular hugs from her youngest daughter Rebekah.

You might run into Darlene cleaning an Airbnb, sewing, crafting, driving friends here or there for appointments, participating in a small group at church, teaching English to kids in China, or one-on-one tutoring in the area. In season, she answers to Mrs. Claus with her husband, the jolly old elf himself! Her favorite times are spent with family, and everyone who knows her can attest she's got more energy than the average bear! Life has thrown a few curve balls, but God has blessed her with the energy to weave and dodge through, creating a legacy of Faith and Hope, living one day at a time!

Choose Peace

By Darlene Eldred

Life is about choices, and one thing I've learned is to choose to fight for my peace each day. I look back and realize life would have been so much easier had I learned to listen to the "still small voice" early on in life.

Growing up in a large, fractured family was anything but secure. Mom was married four times, and each marriage brought more children. Likewise, each divorce ripped them away. I observed a lot of what was going on in our home. Always curious and an avid reader, I knew there was more to experience away from the chaos in my home. Happiness, fun, and survival meant being anywhere but home. And to go places, I needed to be cute and quiet and do what was asked. What no one ever taught me was to choose wisely.

By the age of four, I learned that wearing a dress around men made for easy and painful experiences. By six, I was being groomed by my mom's third husband, a supposedly staunch Catholic who eventually deserted the family. By 12, I learned to carry my soda in my hands at all times because siblings might think it funny to put something in my drink that would knock me out. Once, a spiked drink left me prey to my sick brother-in-law. Hence, by middle school, my virginity was a thing of the past, and the search for a safe place was my goal.

Because my voice was stifled at a young age, I promised myself never to get married as many times as my mother and never leave my children alone with strangers. The struggle to control my world was real! I preferred to work alone rather than in groups because I never believed others could be invested in shared accolades. I truly thought it was easier to accept failure if I had no one to share the blame. Accepting the consequences of my own poor choices was, and still is, one thing, but when someone else's poor choice adversely affects me, it's a whole different matter.

In 2006, a poor choice cost my beautiful, talented, and very active 14-year-old daughter everything but her life. Plans of early graduation, vet school, jockey training, and modeling all evaporated because of a silly car chase. While I was sound asleep with my husband of just five years, my daughter snuck out to help a friend find her boyfriend. The car she was a passenger in spun out of control and rolled into a ditch. With no airbag, she hit her head so hard it caused a traumatic brain injury, rendering her quadriplegic and mute. From that Thanksgiving night to the 4th of July the following year, my life revolved around work, hospital visits, house renovations necessary for the change in my daughter's medical status, fundraising efforts to help us manage the bills, and meetings with lawyers who were working to keep a terrible situation from becoming even worse.

Please don't ever assume a tragic accident automatically warrants a big payout. In our case, the car insurance company paid out $150,000. After lawyer fees and medical grabs, a mere $60,000 remained. At the time, I had no idea what our future needs would be, but I soon learned that equipping a van for wheelchair transport was $60,000. There were no big payouts that even touched our financial loss.

That first year was tough, filled with my full-time teaching job, church ministry, adjusting to caregivers coming and going, doctor appointments, and the typical schedule demands. But life finally seemed to settle, and the routines were in place.

Then, one day, what looked like a home invasion turned out to be my husband clearing us out. Honestly, that was a worse blow than Rachel's accident. Total rejection! I remember the pastor and another elder sitting at our kitchen table, suggesting I needed to do more, give more, and be more. The church I adored and where I had diligently served alongside my husband supported only him, compounding my rejection. Thank God for my village! I was sustained by the people and things God seemed to put in my path, even when I didn't know I needed them.

One friend encouraged me to sit alone for a few minutes each morning with no Bible, journal, or music—just sit in complete silence. During one of those times, as I was thanking God for saving Rachel, I clearly heard Him guide my realization: *Her accident had saved me. Her sacrifice had saved me.*

I clung to Philippians 4:13—*I can do all things through Christ who strengthens me* (NKJV). I repeated the verse multiple times each day, often smiling through the tears.

Once again, I established my new routine and completed my master's degree in time to renew my teaching certificate. At least, that was the plan. Man plans, and God laughs. Two days before Christmas break, I learned I was four-tenths of a credit shy of the hours needed for renewal due to the fact my master's was in business, not education. There were ways the county could have helped; after all, I'd been a teacher for 32 years. Rejection again!

I often wonder if my choice to push for Rachel to receive the special education services she deserved, a huge cost to the county, had any influence on the lack of support I received. Or perhaps it was my challenging behavior. I witnessed a lot of questionable conduct in the school system. I watched teachers move up without regard for their lack of "fruits from their behaviors." And too often, politics and personal connections, sometimes intimate personal connections, became the impetus for advancement. I had a reputation for speaking out in support of the underserved; I was a whistleblower for sure!

So, when I was told there was no evidence of classes I took within the county to support my certificate renewal, again, rejection. But what about the Master of Business Administration with an emphasis on non-profits that I had just finished in record time? Apparently, my classes were ¼ credit classes, and since it wasn't a Master of Education, only a few courses were applicable, rendering me .4 credits shy of the needed requirements. This was an easy way to terminate my contract. I was beaten, and at that point, I gave up! I later learned my county coursework was in my previous name (now changed from my divorce), and I had way more credits than needed.

The stronghold of pride took over; this rejection was just too much, and I walked away from my career, my safety net of 32 years. Approaching homelessness, I tried sharing a home for Rachel with her birth father, but that bridge had been destroyed, and old patterns eventually reappeared. With no job, no home, and few prospects, Rachel and I moved to Florida, where my oldest daughter and grandchildren lived. I joined a church, and my new village began developing in such a big way.

It would take two years to fully establish Rachel's home health care and nursing, which meant full-time caregiving on my part. It was a long two years; I reached my breaking point. I wheeled Rachel into the Social Security Administration office and cried from exhaustion and frustration. At the SSA office, I waited our turn. Then, when called, I wheeled her to the little cubicle and laid the file on the desk, fully prepared to let the state assume care of Rachel. Oh, the stir in that office. Once my financials were fully uncovered, disclosing there was no huge financial payoff I had squandered, the services started pouring in. Rachel received nursing and home health care within 24 hours. I was tired. Very tired. And at that moment, God moved, and "the system" heard me.

In a nutshell, I grew up and became my mother. My first marriage had ended due to boredom when my high school sweetheart lured me away with flashy promises. Number 2 was the resurfaced teenage love that turned into both physical and emotional abuse; I spent the next 13 years struggling to hide my mistake of marrying him. Then, my third marriage was to a man who I thought was a strong Christian, but he rejected me at the lowest point in my life and was supported by many of my fellow church members in the process.

It wasn't until I realized my choices were rooted in my abuse and rejection from childhood that I found true peace. My greatest breakthrough came from joining a survivors of sexual abuse group. There, I was able to come to terms with my own childhood molestation, teenage rape, and physical and psychological abuse.

As a child, I had been taught to respect my abusers. I learned that the quieter I was, the faster the pain would go away, and the more treats would surface. As an adult, I became easily triggered. I seemed to see predatory behavior everywhere. And as a teacher of students in middle and high school, I was on high alert. Sometimes, I became so disrespectful to people who I saw as potential predators that my lashing out overshadowed the real villain. Often, the very students I was seeking to protect became the safety net for the perpetrators.

Joining a group of sexual abuse survivors helped me come to terms with how childhood abuse impacted my choices and my behavior into adulthood. Suddenly, the reasons behind my poor choices came into view; I was able to shed so much trauma and forgive the perpetrators. Most importantly, I was able to forgive myself. I learned that I was inadvertently living a life as a victim, sometimes forcing that role into existence rather than running from it. With the help of a Christian therapist and EMDR (eye movement desensitization and reprocessing therapy—a method of healing from past trauma), I learned about personal triggers. I'm still a work in progress. However, I've learned to stop blaming the past and recognize I am a survivor!

Once home health care was in place, I began to search for employment. I was able to purchase a dilapidated mobile home, and with the help of my church, I was slowly but surely renovating it. Then I met a wonderful woman in one of my Bible studies who renovates homes into Airbnbs; she was asking for help, so I obliged by cleaning the homes between clients. We became good friends, sharing experiences of God showing up for us again and again. Suddenly, my life was falling into place again.

Low points tried to seep in, such as when I get carried away thinking about the goals I once had. "Oops" is all I can say. I have regrets, but now I consider my missteps my proverbial stepping stones. I look at my life and see how God lifted me from the curve in the road and put me back on His path multiple times. I have learned to avoid statements like "I'll never do that" or "I just don't get why so-and-so does that," knowing that God, in His infinite wisdom, helps me learn through some very uncomfortable events.

The really tricky low points come when I see a picture of Rachel before the accident. She loved her horse, Klowy, and was all about showing her off, running as fast as she could. She played soccer and was a force to be reckoned with on the field. School was never difficult academically, but oh, how she challenged teachers to be the best source of information they could be. She loved to challenge everyone.

I look at the wedding party pictures from Rachel's sister's wedding, thinking that she would have gushed all over Rebekah. But instead, she sat on the side, her wheelchair too cumbersome to squeeze in. And since it was not "her" day, I certainly couldn't force inclusion.

I can get lost in the what-ifs so easily. Facebook has a way of helping me remember the great losses as her friends get married, become parents, and achieve life goals as expected. The hardest pill to swallow is the silence. It's not just the realization that I'll never hear her voice again but that without vocal ability, she can't engage well enough or fast enough to sustain a conversation necessary to develop friendships. She was such a presence when she walked into a room. Full of excitement in such a loving way.

But God. He always picks me up again, and reassurance rushes in. I remember Christian recording artist Jeremy Camp taking time to shake Rachel's hand and give her an eye-to-eye hello and Avril Lavigne looking straight at her, saying hello. I think about being on a cruise when strangers came and pushed her wheelchair as if dancing. And then there is the divine protection when total strangers walk up to us asking if they could bless us just as the rent is due or the gas tank needs filling. One man approached us when I was loading Rachel into the van after church, saying, "Miss, please go immediately to Walmart around the corner; I will meet you there. Your tires need replacing, and God has led me to help you." I did as he asked. The serviceman at Walmart was amazed I was even able to drive the van.

Time and time again, God has met me where I was and solved a problem I didn't even realize I had.

I can choose to focus on Rachel's missed goals, or I can focus on the blessings God continues to pour out on us! The way Satan works is in scripture in John 10:10, Jesus says, *"The thief comes only to steal and kill and destroy; I have come that they may have life and have it to the full"* (NIV). He didn't say living life to its fullest would include walking, talking, and being in good health.

People ask me, "How do you do it?" It is so easy to explain. When someone saves you, aren't you naturally inclined to be at their beck and call?

God used Rachel's accident to save me.

Do I get tired? Yes! Changing an adult's diapers in the middle of the night is not fun, but God gives me strength!

Do I get frustrated? Most definitely. How many times have I said, "God, come on, this is ridiculous"? But then I choose to rest in His arms and dry my daughter's tears, knowing she suffers so I can be free.

It's so hard, but consider the cost Jesus paid, making our hope in salvation possible.

It's frustrating to miss activities because they are not wheelchair accessible, but then I remember the strangers who lifted Rachel's wheelchair up steps so she could attend an art show in her honor. And the time the crowd parted to give her a better view at an event. And the front-row seats that just "happened" to be available in a sold-out venue. We are blessed indeed.

I now hold on to Galatians 6:9—*Let us not become weary in doing good, for at the proper time we will reap a harvest if we do not give up* (NIV). Being a full-time caregiver is difficult, but where her accident has led me is a blessing.

Jesus never gave up on me, and believe me, I am a force to be reckoned with. As I look back on my darkest times—childhood rape, physical abuse, the loss of three marriages, rejection at church, rejection in the workplace, and then my daughter's accident—never ever was I alone.

As for today, I met and married (yep, # 4—just like my Mama) my best friend. He is a man who has seen his own share of loss; his wife of 45 years died shortly after they lost their second son to muscular dystrophy at age 42. My husband looks for opportunities in our limitations and, alongside me, helps us reach for the stars. Together, we have hope and truly understand the importance of listening as we walk with God.

I've also been blessed to pay it forward, sharing my past marital struggles as we lead in the Re-Engage Ministry at our church. Shame and embarrassment are gone. And every day, it gets easier to be still and know that He is God (from Psalm 46:10)!

Whether you turn to the right or to the left, your ears will hear a voice behind you, saying, "This is the way; walk in it" (Isaiah 30:21 NIV).

The promises I made to myself as a little girl have been replaced with determination to be all that I can be—right where I am! I'm still learning to slow down, but God is working with me. He is with me every step of the way!

Hope in Peace Through Salvation

By Connie A. VanHorn

We often find ourselves searching for hope, especially in the difficult moments. The world can be an incredibly challenging place, filled with darkness and trials that test our faith and resilience. However, in the middle of these hard times, there is always light that can shine so brightly—the hope we have that comes from finding peace through salvation in God.

When we accept Jesus Christ as our savior and experience the transformative power of salvation, we are met with an unexplainable sense of peace. This deep inner peace and sense of calm does not come as a result of the absence of life's challenges or conflicts but in spite of them. It is a peace that fills the void in our hearts and calms our noisy souls, bringing serenity and assurance that can only come from our Heavenly Father.

One of my favorite scriptures that I memorized early in my Christian walk and has guided me in my peace is Philippians 4:7 (NIV). It states, *And the peace of God, which transcends all understanding, will guard your hearts and your minds in Christ Jesus.* This verse reminds me that the peace I receive from God is not temporary, but it is a safe shield that continually guards my heart and mind, allowing me to navigate life's challenges with bold faith, courage, and confidence. With this kind of peace, we can travel through all the tough moments and be assured that God is there, too.

You will keep in perfect peace those whose minds are steadfast because they trust in you (Isaiah 26:3 NIV).

God wants us to trust Him and make Him the foundation for experiencing perfect peace. When we place our faith in God and trust in His promises, we are granted a peace that surpasses all earthly understanding, anchoring us in hope and assurance.

For me personally, the experience of getting saved and establishing a relationship with God nearly ten years ago was a turning point that filled me with a peace I had never known before. It was a peace that circled within my circumstances and brought a sense of wholeness and completeness I had longed for. In fact, the gift of God's peace and patience were my first noticeable changes after He rescued me and changed my heart. Through salvation, God not only forgave my sins, but He also wrapped me in His peace, transforming my heart and mind in ways I could never have imagined. It was a radical change that I'll be grateful for all my life!

God loved me enough to send His son to die for me, so I will love Him enough to give my life back to Him.

Finding hope in peace through salvation is a journey of surrender, trust, and transformation. He wants us all to come to Him. He calls to us repeatedly until we finally surrender and set our hearts on Him, and then He claims us as His own. The majestic God of the universe, the King of kings and Lord of lords is after *your* heart!

Although my transformation to peace was instantaneous, for most, letting go of fear and doubt and embracing the peace that only God can provide takes time, growth, and perseverance as you turn to Him again and again. Keep turning—God will always be there! As you build a deeper relationship with Him, your heart will be filled with a peace that anchors you in hope and sustains you through life's trials. He will always guide you! Remember—in God's presence, there is a peace that surpasses all understanding, offering you hope and comfort in every season of life.

He's got you!

Keep going!

Shine bright!

. . . .

Dawn Vazquez

 Dawn Vazquez is a former model with over 13 years of experience in development construction finance. She is also the owner of a photography business and the founder of Women Empowering in Real Time, through which she speaks to and encourages women to revisit their faith, walk in God's Word, and prove that through God, all things are possible and everything is fixable. Dawn is a proud author, having written in Women World Leaders' magazine, *Voice of Truth,* and the best-selling and international best-selling book, *Miracle Mindset: Finding Hope in the Chaos.*

Dawn consults and speaks with women from multiple countries and continents regarding health and business. She's appeared on podcasts, briefly hosted her own Facebook Live show—*Real Talk with Dawn,* is sponsored by The Naked Warrior Recovery (Former Navy Seals fighting PTSD by way of a CBD line and Green Drinks), and does ministry work within her own community.

Dawn's hope for you in reading her story is that she can give you the courage to rewrite your own!

A Journey of Resilience and Faith

By Dawn Vazquez

In the midst of darkness and uncertainty, a glimmer of hope can ignite the spirit and guide one through even the darkest storms. This is my journey, marked by challenges, heartbreaks, and unexpected turns, but also by the unwavering strength found in my faith. My journey with God has not been easy, and I hope that by sharing my story, I will be able to give hope that God is alive and moving in our lives even when we can't understand or see it. God wants us to let go and trust Him!

My world seemed to crumble and fall all at once. I was unaware that God was purposely stripping me so that He could build me back up in His image. As the weight of my failing marriage and shattered dreams began to bear down on me, I sought out rest and protection in the arms of my loved ones. In conversations with my mother, I shared the struggles that plagued my household, seeking guidance and understanding. On a December day, as the anticipation of Christmas filled the air, I discovered the wires of the meticulously placed Christmas lights had been cut. It was an odd occurrence, yet I chose to put it aside and focus on my thriving photography business, Dawn's Photography.

While capturing precious moments for my clients, I received an unexpected visit from my father and a group of supportive relatives. They arrived in large trucks, determined to protect and uplift me. With a deep sense of intuition, my father declared that my marriage was over. Despite the pain and confusion, I trusted my father's wisdom and retreated to my mother's house.

Sitting in my mother's driveway at the age of thirty-nine, I faced the daunting reality of having no place to call home. I had to completely start over and surrender whatever plans I thought I had for my life. I had to let go; this meant letting go of everything. God was going to strip me completely but build me back up to something strong and beautiful. I couldn't see it at the time, but He was reshaping my life to look like His masterpiece—not the one I was creating for myself.

During my marriage, I achieved great success in my career in construction finance. I worked hard to pass the state boards of Florida, allowing me to own two homes and build a stable future for myself. However, even in the midst of this accomplishment, I faced pressure from my spouse to conform to societal expectations.

One such expectation was regarding my BMW 528, a car I owned outright with no financial burden. My spouse believed that bringing this car into our neighborhood would be considered pretentious and insisted that I sell it. By this point, he had already convinced me to sell both my homes. I struggled to let go of these material things, but I knew God was doing something different. As hard as it was, I LET GO!

Proverbs 16:3 became my anchor, reminding me to commit my plans to the Lord and trust in Him. It says, *Commit to the LORD whatever you do, and he will establish your plans* (NIV). This verse encouraged me to let go and trust that God had a plan for my life and would guide me in making decisions that aligned with His will.

As I faced the pressures, I also found comfort in Psalm 118:8, which declares,

It is better to take refuge in the LORD than to trust in humans (NIV). This verse reminded me that my ultimate trust should be in God, not in the opinions or expectations of others. It gave me the courage to stand firm in my convictions and not compromise my true self.

In the end, I made the decision to surrender and trust God fully, and while I reluctantly sold my BMW 528 and my homes, I chose to keep a tiny plot of land set in the majestic landscape of Citrus Springs, Florida. I still hold it presently. It is a reminder to me that material possessions do not define my worth or value. Psalm 37:4-5 guided me in this decision. *Take delight in the LORD, and he will give you the desires of your heart. Commit your way to the LORD; trust in him, and he will do this* (NIV). This verse reminds me that when I align my desires with God's will and trust in Him, He will act on my behalf.

I found the strength to navigate the pressures and expectations of my marriage. I learned to prioritize my relationship with God and trust in His plans for my life. Even in the face of societal pressures, I held onto my faith and embraced the truth that God's opinion of me is what truly matters.

Looking back, my journey through marriage and career taught me the importance of staying true to myself and seeking guidance from God's Word. By reading scripture, praying, and trusting in God's plan, I found the strength to resist societal pressures and embrace my true identity. I had to learn that it wasn't my BMW that defined me, nor was it my marriage or social status. Only God defines my true worth, and sometimes, we have to lose everything, so all we have left is God.

As it says in Proverbs 3:5-6, *Trust in the LORD with all your heart and lean not on your own understanding; in all your ways submit to him, and he will make your paths straight* (NIV). I am grateful for the lessons learned and the faith that carried me through.

When I embarked on this new chapter as a photographer, I had no formal training or education in the craft. It was a leap of faith driven by a desire to create a new identity for myself. Little did I know that God had a bigger plan in store for me. As I ventured into wedding photography, I realized that my background as a former model and my passion for empowering women could be combined to offer a unique experience. I started offering makeup services alongside photography, helping brides feel beautiful and confident on their special day. It was a way of using my own experiences to uplift others.

There were definitely moments of uncertainty, but I again turned to scripture for guidance, being reminded to trust in God's plan, even when it seemed unconventional or uncertain, and gaining the courage to step out of my comfort zone and embrace the unknown.

As time went on, I learned the art of photography. I taught myself how to capture moments, evoke emotions, and tell stories through my lens. It was a journey of self-discovery and growth, one that was fueled by a passion for creating lasting memories for others. As I look back on those early days of my photography career, I am humbled by the opportunities and successes that came my way. I can see how God used these experiences to help shape me into the woman He created me to be.

The world of photography taught me the importance of trusting in God's plan and stepping out in faith. I found the strength to pursue a new career path, even without formal training. Through God's guidance and my willingness to embrace the unknown, I found success and fulfillment in wedding photography.

But now, even my photography career, once thriving, seemed uncertain as my clients were left behind in Connecticut. To add to my distress, now residing in Pennsylvania, I had no choice but to commute back and forth, seeing through my commitments to weddings booked months in advance. I questioned God's plan but continued to move forward in complete trust!

I braved the elements; my hands were freezing while photographing an outdoor wedding, but I dismissed the discomfort as a simple cold. However, as time passed, I began experiencing a myriad of symptoms, leading me to seek medical advice. Visiting multiple specialists, six in total, I found myself waiting anxiously for the results of my bloodwork. July 28, 2011, the day etched in my memory, as it was exactly one month and one day past my birthday, arrived with a devastating diagnosis: I had diffuse systemic scleroderma, a terminal illness. The doctor's words echoed in my mind, urging me to make peace with my mortality and prepare for the end.

As I lay in that magic bed, an adopted name given to it by my mother, battling my illness, I turned to scripture for hope and healing. These words remind me that God is not only the ultimate healer of our souls but also the one who can bring healing to our physical bodies.

In the face of my despair, I found strength in my faith. Turning to the timeless wisdom of the Psalms, I sought comfort in the words of King David, who himself endured trials and tribulations.

The Lord is my shepherd; I lack nothing.
He makes me lie down in green pastures,
he leads me beside quiet waters,
he refreshes my soul.
He guides me along the right paths
for his name's sake.

Even though I walk
through the darkest valley,
I will fear no evil,
for you are with me;
your rod and your staff,
they comfort me.

You prepare a table before me
in the presence of my enemies;
You anoint my head with oil;

my cup overflows.
Surely your goodness and love will follow me
all the days of my life,
and I will dwell in the house of the LORD
forever.
(Psalm 23 NIV)

Psalm 23 is often interpreted as a reflection on the relationship between God (portrayed as a shepherd) and the believer (portrayed as a sheep). It expresses trust in God's guidance, provision, and protection. The imagery of green pastures, still waters, and paths of righteousness paints a picture of God's care and leading.

The psalmist acknowledges that even in challenging times, such as walking through the valley of the shadow of death, we have no reason to fear because God is with us. The mention of a table prepared in the presence of enemies signifies God's provision and blessings, even in the face of adversity.

Though the outcome of my diagnosis seemed bleak, my faith became a stream of hope, illuminating the path ahead. Through my deep trust in God's plan, I discovered a newfound resilience within myself. Despite the uncertainty and the limitations imposed by my illness, I embraced each day with gratitude, cherishing the moments of joy and connection. In fact, God was using this hard thing to continue my growth and complete dependence on Him.

Overcoming the challenges and struggles, I triumphantly participated in a 5K walk for diabetes, defying the expectations of my terminal illness. Of course, my mother was completely against this idea, but I was fiercely determined. My father comforted her, assuring her that no matter what, he wouldn't leave my side, and he didn't. And while I can't tell you we broke any kind of time record that day, God showed us that with Him, all things are truly possible.

Through this experience, I shattered the stigma surrounding my condition. Psalm 118:17 became my anthem: *I will not die but live, and will proclaim what the Lord has done* (NIV).

Then came another blow. My father went home to heaven. After my father's passing, I felt a calling to return home to Florida. It was a decision met with resistance and anger from my mother, who had tirelessly cared for me during my illness. She reminded me of times that she had to call on my brother at two o'clock in the morning to literally pick up my nearly lifeless body, the hours of destruction I ruthlessly imposed on the en suite bathroom, and the fact that my aunt and cousin would have to hold me upright in the shower just to wash my hair.

However, with time, she came to understand that my desire to spread my wings and live again was a testament to God's grace and restoration in my life.

Even in the face of uncertainty and fear when COVID-19 hit the world in 2020, I refused to turn back or allow my illness to define me. The world seemed to be falling apart, but I was still rising. I was rising in the presence of the Lord and willing to accept whatever He had for me. I decided to use the hard things I endured to help others. I took the focus off of myself and shifted it onto others.

Standing strong in my faith, I became a speaker and author, working with women around the world to inspire them with the message that through Christ, all things are possible. Proverbs 31:25 encapsulates this empowering journey: *She is clothed with strength and dignity; she can laugh at days to come* (NIV).

I have found strength in my struggles and clung to my Christian faith. The Psalms have been a constant source of comfort and encouragement, reminding me of God's unfailing faithfulness. Psalm 23, in particular, has been a guiding light for me during the hardest moments in my life. It reminds me that even in the valley of the shadow of death, I can find peace and restoration in the presence of the Lord.

During my research on health and happiness, I explored various modalities, always keeping my strong faith as the foundation of my journey. I delved into the practice of meditation, seeking a deeper connection with God and a greater awareness of His presence in my life. Psalm 46:10 guided me in this pursuit. *"Be still, and know that I am God. I will be exalted among the nations, I will be exalted in the earth"* (NIV). Through intentional breathing and conscious awareness of my surroundings, I found a sense of peace and renewed strength.

God's plan became evident as I encountered remarkable individuals who supported and pushed me to my limits. These souls became instruments of God's love and grace, helping me discover my purpose and potential. Their guidance, coupled with my unwavering trust in God, propelled me forward, even when the pain seemed unbearable—even when I didn't see God's plan.

I made the decision to explore alternative, organic methods of healing, moving away from the multitude of medications prescribed by doctors. I realized that God's natural remedies are found all around us, on the very earth we walk upon.

Meditation became a discipline, even on the days when I felt weak and lost. Through these moments of stillness and connection with God, I found the strength to persevere. Isaiah 40:31 assured me, *But those who hope in the Lord will renew their strength. They will soar on wings like eagles; they will run and not grow weary, they will walk and not be faint* (NIV).

My story is a testimony to the power of faith to secure and anchor one's soul in the stormiest of seas. Let go and let God! That is a reminder that hope can arise, guiding us through the hardest struggles and leading us to a place of healing and restoration.

As I continue this journey, I remain steadfast in my faith, believing that with

God by my side, I can get through anything. I know that whatever He takes away or gives to me is for my own good. I had to endure a lot of hard things, but in return, God took me from debilitated to exhilarated. I wouldn't trade this journey for any material thing this world has to offer.

I am grateful for the opportunities and blessings that have come my way, and I will continue to rely on God's guidance as I navigate the path ahead. As it says in Jeremiah 29:11, *"For I know the plans I have for you,"* declares the Lord, *"plans to prosper you and not to harm you, plans to give you hope and a future"* (NIV).

God has a plan for me, and God has a plan to give you a hope and a future, too. It doesn't matter what you are going through. God is with you. God wants us to let go and let Him take the wheel. One of the hardest things I had to learn was letting go, but as I'm writing this, I am full of hope, knowing that God has me and His plans are great. Our hope is alive; our hope is alive in Him! Trust Him.

Hope in Meditation

By Kimberly Ann Hobbs

Meditation is often thought of as a way to bring peace and calmness. It is a practice of focusing the mind on a particular object, thought, or activity to train oneself to be stable. In the Bible, however, "meditation" refers to various practices involving God and His Word—spending time contemplating and praying with Him. The ultimate effect of biblical meditation is to draw closer to God, transforming your life so you can be more effective as a believer.

When our minds are freed from distractions that pound at us every day, we are able to empty ourselves of thoughts of ourselves and our imperfections and instead be filled with the greatness that only God can give. When we meditate properly as Christians or Christ-centered followers, our bodies become mentally and physically calm, and our spiritual health improves— our belief system becomes strengthened as our faith builds our trust in God.

When we practice meditation in the right form—biblical meditation— we focus on God and His Word, which fills us with mounting hope and allows us to experience the peace of God that passes all understanding.

Philippians 4:6 says *Don't be pulled in different directions or worried about a thing. Be saturated in prayer throughout each day, offering your faith-filled requests before God with overflowing gratitude* (TPT).

Scripture shows us that even Jesus Himself meditated. God the Father and God the Son had such a strong connection because Jesus engaged in heavy prayer. He even modeled meditation for us by teaching us how to pray (Matthew 6:9-13). Abraham meditated with God when he pled to the Lord to spare the city of Sodom for the sake of ten righteous people who might live there (Genesis 18:23-33). In the Old Testament, we also have an example of Joshua's meditation: he kept God's law in his mouth and meditated on it, becoming strengthened to lead his people faithfully.

> *Study this Book of Instruction continually. Meditate on it day and night so you will be sure to obey everything written in it. Only then will you prosper and succeed in all you do* (Joshua 1:8 NLT).

When we meditate on God and His Word, our obedience to Him is strengthened, and our ability to hope for greater things to come is expanded. Biblical meditation also helps us understand how loved we are by the God of the universe and reminds us that He alone can bring us hope by strengthening us in our weak areas. As we meditate and reflect on scripture, we open ourselves more fully to God. In response, He pours out His truth, strength, and love into our souls; He fills us to overflowing.

As God reveals things to us through His Holy Word, our souls begin to calm in His presence. We become filled with His perfect peace. This practice offers such outstanding benefits that bring us hope. We can experience it all by meditating on God and His Word.

> *You will keep in perfect peace all who trust in you, all whose thoughts are fixed on you!* (Isaiah 26:3 NLT).

There are many different kinds of meditation in this world today, but can we agree that the meditation between you and your heavenly Father, God, yields the ultimate result of this time-invested practice?

God offers us the greatest form of meditation—pondering His scriptures and interacting with Him in prayer. This is the only form of mediation that can lead us to perfect peace, because our heavenly Father is the God of peace.

May our God of peace bring hope to your soul as you sit in His presence, meditating on Him and His Word..

. . . .

Pamela Frontz Saieg

Pamela Frontz Saieg, an educator with a heart for Jesus, began her journey in Pennsylvania, teaching in the high school and impacting students through Bible Studies. She also advocated for the elderly, opening new horizons for them in their later years.

Pam moved to Florida and taught elementary school art for 31 years in public schools. She witnessed students' extraordinary artwork and prophetic drawings depicting the Bible as they developed a prophetic ability they didn't even know they had. Their prophetic aptitude was astounding. As the children continued "seeing" Biblical pictures and drawing them, she realized, "If the kids can see, so can we."

Pam's faith-filled career inspired the birth of "VisionWriter," a vessel for individuals, families, churches, and cities to unite and manifest their visions, echoing the unity heralded in John 17:23. "VisionWriter" hosts conferences and workshops. Her multiple books can be found on Amazon. Pamela can be contacted at VisionWriter12@gmail.com

Pam's true passion is to glorify God and help bring unity and vision to the body of Christ as we journey to the Secret Place of the Most High. "If the kids can see, so can we!"

Finding Hope in the Night

By Pamela Frontz Saieg

Do you believe in the impossible? I enjoy looking at the heroes in the Bible and being reminded that God can do the impossible; He can even do the impossible through me. I would like to take you on a journey that completely changed my life, starting with my favorite people in the Bible. This is my story and where I found hope in the night.

In the Bible, we read about God's chosen people doing the impossible. Through these stories, I started to believe I could do the same. I could change the course for generations to come. It was in these stories that I found hope.

In the Bible, Esther took her stand. Noah built. Nehemiah gathered families. Daniel opened the window. David danced, inquired of the Lord, and fought. Rahab believed. Moses climbed the mountain of the Lord and went toward the burning bush. Joshua waited and then took the Promised Land. Abraham made a covenant. Isaac believed. Jacob laid his head. Joseph came out of the pit. Elijah built an altar. Anna prayed. And it all began with belief.

The Bible records many men and women who stood for the righteousness of God. Taking a stand can begin with us today. Now is the time to take the stand, sit, build, and gather your family, even though you may take some heat. Open the window and see the future. Dance, inquire, and fight with guidance from the Lord. Believe God, ascend the mountain of the Lord, and move with a burning desire for Him.

We can lay our heads on our pillow at night and expect dreams, visions, and an open heaven. We don't need to stay in the pit. You can build a prayer altar in your home or community, pray there, and leave a rich legacy.

> Let each generation tell its children of your mighty acts; let them proclaim your power (Psalm 145:4 NLT).

With all the amazing women and men in the Bible, you may wonder, *Where do I fit?* I asked myself that so many times, and I still do. I wonder where I am when my life is falling apart, and I don't see God moving. I ask how I can believe when so much is happening to me that is not right. *Where do I fit in God's plan? Do I even fit at all?*

After a very difficult marriage, divorce, and abandonment, my children and I were left reeling with fear, doubt, unbelief, and exhaustion. How could I provide for my children when left with all these problems? The most difficult time was when my children were taken, and I didn't know where they were! I DIDN'T KNOW WHERE MY CHILDREN WERE! *What should I do? Where do I go? How do I figure this out? Who do I call?*

That night, my life changed forever. But hope met me in the darkness. I went out to the front yard of my home, the home on which the bank had begun foreclosure proceedings. That night was dark, spiritually and literally. With no moon and no stars, the darkness surrounded me. I closed my eyes, raised my hands, and said, "God, if I ever needed You, I need You now!" As tears were coming down my face, something that I can't even describe came over me. I opened my eyes, and the entire front yard of our one-acre lot and surrounding area was engulfed in light. I felt a presence behind me, and I SLOWLY turned around and saw two huge angels at the front door of my home. THEY were providing the glow! Their swords were stretched out, not towards me, but arching over as if to provide protection.

For a moment, I stared in shock, looking through the tears at what I was seeing. I blinked several times, thinking, *Is this real?* Peace came over me, and then they were gone. I fell to my knees, crying and thanking God, and I slowly rose and walked through the very same door where the angels were posted. I went to bed and slept peacefully. My children were returned the next morning.

I learned so much that night, though I could not process it at the moment. This happened over 35 years ago, but it feels like it was just yesterday. I experienced hope in the night. God in the night. Peace in the night. Surrender in the night. Resting on God's promises in the night. Only God....hope in the dark of night!

> *For He shall give His angels charge over you, to keep you in all your ways* (Psalm 91:11 NKJV).

Is it possible that of all the faith heroes in the Bible, I could be one of them? If the Bible were to include people in this generation, might I be one? Did I pray with expectation that night? I don't know! But I prayed, and God showed up. I was changed forever; I am changed forever. I know there are angels; I saw two of them. My eyes were opened to the spiritual realm. I know that realm is just as real as the physical one!

After that, I began reading the Bible more, realizing the triune God is so amazing. I had known God was the God of the universe, but that night, I knew He was the God of me and that He loved me just as I was, and He loves me today just as I am now.

I knew my life had changed forever, and from that point on, I would always seek God. Did things change right away? No. But I trusted God more, and my faith grew. He showed me many miracles to grow my faith in Him. When I needed the lawn mower to work and didn't have money to get it fixed, I cleaned the spark plug each week, but it still didn't work. So I laid hands on it and commanded it to work. It did! Every week, I followed the same regimen: clean the spark plug, lay hands on it, and command it to work. That really happened.

When I needed a new pool pump to keep the pool from getting green while trying to sell the house to prevent foreclosure, I removed the pump and put it on the counter, forgetting that a potential buyer was coming to see the house with the realtor. The people asked, "Why is the pool pump on the counter?" The realtor explained. The people did not want the house, but they left a check with the realtor to give to me to get the pump fixed. Hope came when I found the check on the counter that night.

My life has been filled with many exceptional stories; I was learning to be a faith-filled woman. And my strong, blossoming faith was not just for me but also for my children and grandchildren. At that time, my children were in elementary school. Now, my grandchildren are in elementary school. My hope-in-the-dark journey prepared me to be a faithful mom and grandma ("Mimi," I am way too cool to be called grandma).

Getting excited about a generational journey is a God-given gift, even when we may not have those generations yet. How I handle my life, being faith-filled and telling it to the next generation, will speak volumes to my children and grandchildren.

As I continued my journey and read my Bible more, I began reading the Old Testament and was amazed by Esther. The Bible doesn't tell much about Esther's younger years or older years, and that's okay. But we do know that her growth and strength changed her life and the lives of her family and nation.

We may have many dark nights and think we can't get through it. At those times, God wants us to cry out to Him. Esther didn't see angels, and you may not see angels, or maybe you will. But our hope is always alive in the dark, even in the darkest moments of life, and if we let Him, God will build our faith through those times.

Esther went through various stages that led to her destiny, which undoubtedly left a legacy. That is something we all likely want to do. I want to pave the path as best I can for the generations coming after me. I want to fulfill the purpose God predestined for me.

> In him we were also chosen, having been predestined according to the plan of him who works out everything in conformity with the purpose of his will (Ephesians 1:11 NIV).

We can learn from and exhibit the same courage and faith that Esther showed as we move forward toward our destiny—a destiny that will undoubtedly leave a legacy. Many may experience trauma that can block forward movement. I experienced heartache from a broken relationship, betrayal, and abandonment. Those three words don't even register the trauma I endured. But by trusting God and crying out for healing, reading my Bible, going to church, and developing a relationship with the Holy Spirit, the trauma ceased, the residue calmed, and deliverance came. Amazingly, I began giving Esther Conferences. Only God could take a broken woman and give her a testimony to help others!

Years ago, I was presenting an Esther Conference using artwork to present visuals of what God can do for His people. This is a precious testimony from one attendee that will bless you.

"I knew I needed to attend the Esther Conference, and I was right. I had issues from a recent divorce. When you spoke about broken hearts, I saw something red coming toward me. It was the same hand that was in the artwork that was in the foyer. In the hand was a red heart. I heard God tell me, 'Beauty is in the eye of the beholder, and I am your beholder.' That day,

I knew my heart was healed." ~ Conference Attendee.

When we soak in His presence, God will break off trauma and heal our hearts; that is why spending time with God is so important! The Holy Spirit will instruct our hearts as we rest, read our Bibles, worship, and remain still in His presence.

> *"Be still, and know that I am God"* (Psalm 46:10 NIV).

Do we spend time just soaking in God's presence? When our intimacy with God develops, He begins to unfold the destiny He has planned for us. We begin to learn about our destiny as we take hold of the grace and favor God offers us as He creates the path before us. When we submit to His will, He continually offers and provides far more than we can think or imagine. Even on our darkest nights, God will show up for us. There is always hope in the night!

We know God has plans and purposes for us.

> *"For I know the plans I have for you," declares the Lord, "plans to prosper you and not to harm you, plans to give you hope and a future"* (Jeremiah 29:11 NIV).

Destiny was awakened in Esther when her cousin Mordecai wailed at the king's gate, bringing attention to the upcoming ordered destruction of the Jewish people. His willingness to alert Esther led her to her "for such a time as this" moment! Esther was positioned to run interference and save God's people. We often hear of having a "for such a time as this moment," but do we understand that we, too, may be called to such a moment? As we walk the path God has for us, we must be aware that we have a destiny and purpose. God wants each of us to fulfill the destiny He has purposed for each of us.

Your eyes saw my unformed body; all the days ordained for me were written in your book before one of them came to be. How precious to me are your thoughts, God! How vast is the sum of them! (Psalm 139:16-17 NIV).

God knew our footsteps before time began. That is eye-opening. Just like the woman at the conference whose eyes were opened!

The enemy will come against our destiny; this is where we need warfare. The enemy came against Mordecai, who was the one instructing Esther. Mordecai would not bow to enemy tactics. We need to learn this too. We need to learn strategies, insights, and tactics that the enemy uses to war against our destiny. We need to have a strong community around us to support and counsel us at all times.

I have forgiven in the sight of Christ for your sake, in order that Satan might not outwit us. For we are not unaware of his schemes (2 Corinthians 2:10-11 NIV).

Mordecai counseled Esther. She learned to be aware of what was really going on in the kingdom outside the palace. The enemy was trying to destroy the Jewish people. Esther's "for such a time as this" moment was on the horizon. Esther heard her call but was afraid. She knew she was in a position to speak to the king, but she also knew that by speaking to him, she would be risking her own death. Mordecai continued to work to persuade her.

"For if you remain silent at this time, relief and deliverance for the Jews will arise from another place, but you and your father's family will perish. And who knows but that you have come to your royal position for such a time as this?" Then Esther sent this reply to Mordecai: "Go, gather together all the Jews who are in Susa, and fast for me. Do not eat or drink for three days, night

or day. I and my servants will fast as you do. When this is done, I will go to the king, even though it is against the law. And if I perish, I perish" (Esther 4:14-16 NIV).

What changed for Esther? Perhaps Esther gained strength as she more clearly understood her calling. Surely God gave her the strength to stand up for her people. Esther heard her call and went forward courageously. And so can we. Esther had dealt with the trauma of being orphaned and fears from being taken to a foreign land and held as a prisoner-wife. But Esther changed from being afraid and courageously stood up for herself, her family, and the Jewish people.

God will show us. The triune God will instruct us.

> *I will praise the Lord, who counsels me; even at night my heart instructs me. I keep my eyes always on the Lord. With him at my right hand, I will not be shaken* (Psalm 16:7-8. NIV).

We have to fight for our destiny. The enemy doesn't want us fulfilling our purpose on this earth, but God paves the way.

In the years since seeing those angels, I can look back and realize I was courageously making my way through as Esther did. I kept moving forward, even though there were many dark nights. Along the way, breakthroughs came, and I began to understand that there was more for me to do. God always brought me hope in the night during those times. I now know that courage and strength are crucial as we fulfill our destiny and reign in our lives as God intended.

We may go to church and pray and think that is enough. But although going to church and praying are necessary, Jesus also has given us each a mission in this world.

Speak up for those who cannot speak for themselves; ensure justice for those being crushed. Yes, speak up for the poor and helpless, and see that they get justice (Proverbs 31:8-9 NLT).

> Be on your guard; stand firm in the faith; be courageous; be strong (1 Corinthians 6:13 NIV).

> Go and make disciples of all nations, baptizing them in the name of the Father and of the Son and of the Holy Spirit (Matthew 28:19 NIV).

We are a chosen people, a royal priesthood. We are God's special people. And we are called to declare the hope and salvation that God offers to those in darkness, those in despair who are enduring their darkest nights. Esther was amazing, but YOU are amazing! Esther had a calling, and you also have a calling! Let's learn from Esther. Will we take the time to trust? Will we shift our thinking to align with God's thinking? Following God's call and relying on His strength to fulfill that call are the best things we can do for ourselves, our families, our church, and our region. God has called the Esthers and Mordecais, and He has called YOU!

God is calling everyone from every generation.

After all, Mordecai sat at the king's gate and spoke strategies to the younger generation—his niece, Esther. And Esther saved herself, her family, and future generations throughout the entire Jewish nation. Let's do the same! We can break off the orphan spirit. We can break through any opposition that is coming against us. We can break the chains that hold us down and be a generation that rises up to say, "For such a time as this." Change starts today. We will break open into destiny and leave a powerful and hope-filled legacy for the next generation—for our HOPE IS ALIVE!

Hope in Breaking Strongholds

By Connie A. VanHorn

When we refer to strongholds, we are talking about deeply ingrained patterns or beliefs that have a hold on our lives, often passed down through generations. Strongholds can be addictions, destructive behaviors, or negative thought patterns that seem impossible for us to escape. However, with hope in Jesus, we can trust in God's power to break these strongholds and bring about transformation in our lives. Our hope and trust should be in God's power to break any stronghold that holds us captive.

> The weapons we fight with are not the weapons of the world. On the contrary, they have divine power to demolish strongholds. We demolish arguments and every pretension that sets itself up against the knowledge of God, and we take captive every thought to make it obedient to Christ (2 Corinthians 10:4-5 NIV).

Something must be broken to demolish a stronghold. You can be the curse breaker. Overcoming generational curses is a powerful way to create change and leave a positive legacy for future generations. In Exodus 20:5-6, God says, *"You shall not bow down to them or serve them, for I the Lord your God am a jealous God, visiting the iniquity of the fathers on the children to the third and the fourth generation of those who hate me, but showing steadfast love to thousands of those who love me and keep my commandments"* (ESV). Through our love for God and obedience to His commandments, we can break free from the cycle of generational curses and pave the way for a better future for our children and their children. This can be our legacy, but we must be willing to stand up and fight for it!

For you have been my hope, Sovereign Lord, my confidence since my youth (Psalm 71:5 NIV).

Putting our hope and trust in God is essential to releasing the grip of a stronghold and finding freedom. When we place our hope in God, we can rest assured that He will guide us, protect us, and empower us to overcome the strongholds in our lives.

Ultimately, our hope in Jesus gives us the courage to live in freedom and leave a lasting legacy. In John 8:36, Jesus declares, *"So if the Son sets you free, you will be free indeed"* (NIV). It is through our faith in Jesus that we can break free from the chains of sin, shame, and bondage and walk in the freedom He has promised us.

As we go through life and face difficult and even scary things, let's walk with courage, knowing we can demolish strongholds and generational curses by remembering to put our hope and trust in God. Only He has the power to break every chain and set us free. By leaning on Jesus, we can find hope, freedom, and the ability to leave a legacy that honors Him.

. . . .

Toni Lee

Toni Lee, a Boston native, attended L'Escuela Diplomatica in Havana. She subsequently returned to New York City to graduate from Chapin Private School and to study languages at Barnard College. A former nationally-ranked equestrian in the hunter-jumper circuit, Lee placed 16th Nationally in her division. Lee raced IOR sailboats in the Southern Ocean Racing Circuit, crewed on the Key West to Havana Sailboat Race, sailed transatlantic, and explored the Amazon River by canoe.

Toni Lee considers her most important introduction was to the Man Who Saved her life. Nothing in her life has ever been the same since June 10, 2000.

Toni Lee's personal passion for motivating and helping empower women is based on her strong faith in God, which resulted in her volunteering to teach micro-enterprise to women in the hard-to-reach places in the world, traveling to China, Indonesia, Cambodia, West Africa, and into the jungles of Panama. She is a founding member of the Planned Giving Council for Place of Hope, a foster care agency in the Palm Beaches.

Lee especially loves helping women connect with God in a way that brings hope and positive life transformation through knowing the Lord in a personal way.

The Silent Scream

By Toni Lee

Can you imagine arriving at the age of 52 years old and coming to the realization your entire value system has been a lie?

I came from a privileged New England family, where perfection was a very high priority. I was taught if I were pretty enough, smart enough, and married within the right social standing, my LIFE would be perfect. The fairy tale would come true.

I felt like the Avis car commercial, "You are only #2, so you have to try harder." I became driven and focused on external symbols of satisfaction. I wore the "looking good, larger-than-life" act on the outside. I repeatedly suffered the inevitable disappointments, as each flash-in-the-pan "new best answer" would fail.

I used drugs, alcohol, and powerful career trophies to fill the voids within me. I would pride myself on titles such as "International Marketing Director," "a ranked rider in the United States equestrian jumper circuit," or even the "trophy wife of the founder of a multi-billion-dollar computer corporation." At night, when the masks were laid at the bedside, I would have what I called "the worm" walking around my heart. The worm would whisper, "This is not the way life is supposed to be. Something isn't right!"

An indescribable hollowness would rush back. The silent cry of desperation would rise up in my throat. No hope again.

Today, I am convinced that God did plant a homing beacon in my heart. The urgency and yearning never diminished as I looked for the answer everywhere except in Jesus.

What if some were unfaithful? Will their unfaithfulness nullify God's faithfulness? Not at all! Let God be true, and every man a liar!" (Romans 3:3-4 NIV).

The Evidence

Let me tell you about this faithful God and the faithless woman He loved! Years ago, I stood in the rooms of Alcoholics Anonymous (AA) and begged, "Dear God, IF there is a God, please help me!"

I prayed to a God I did NOT believe in about an addiction I couldn't beat.

He answered me immediately that day! Since March 6, 1982, I have been free of cocaine and alcohol. AND...I went on about my life, never noticing the miracle. *That was lucky,* I thought.

Soon after, I stood in a New York hospital beside a gurney. My only son, Shannon, had suffered a severe brain aneurysm. Once again, I begged a God I did NOT believe in, "Please God, oh please don't take my baby."

My son survived. Not one remnant of the brain injury remained.

Once again, I went about my business and ignored my recent cry of desperation. Once again, I did not notice that God had answered me! My son and I had beaten this crisis, too.

Subsequently, while fox hunting in Virginia, I had a violent horse accident.

I awoke from the crash to find the entire left side of my body numb and not responding. The right side of my face was ripped open, my mouth smashed, and my teeth loosened in the jaw.

As I lay there on the ground, I prayed, once again, to a God I did NOT believe in. I begged Him to let me walk. Within months, I was walking and riding again. AND...I went about my life, forgetting my foxhole petition to a God who still answered prayer. I gave Him no credit for all the miracles raining down in my life.

Turning Point

As I look back, I can see that all these seemingly unrelated answers to the prayers of an unbeliever would one day be strung together. Each answered prayer, a single pearl, threaded next to another into a necklace of evidence, showing me that God had always been there, even when I didn't believe in Him.

In January 2000, I was invited to a Bible study breakfast in Palm Beach. Still on the hunt for something "new and different," I shrugged indifferently and accepted the invite. The speaker said the answer to end my emptiness was through a man named Jesus. I had been exposed to religion growing up, but no one had ever talked about having a RELATIONSHIP.

This was the first time I had ever heard someone say, "God loves you and has a plan for your life." How could anyone love me knowing the act I kept behind the looking-good mask? I was such a sham and burdened by shame for my past drug and alcohol actions.

The speaker went on to tell how I was separated from a relationship with this loving God by the choices and priorities I had been chasing. Jesus chose to die, offering me a new life totally forgiven and set free from my past in exchange for His life! Jesus was the bridge back across to a deliberate personal relationship with God! It didn't matter where I had been; it mattered where I was going!

> For God so loved the world that he gave his one and only Son, that whoever believes in him shall not perish but have eternal life. For God did not send his Son into the world to condemn the world, but to save the world through him (John 3:16-17 NIV).

I sat there, overwhelmed with a familiar sadness. My heart whispered, *Maybe this message really is different.* But again, I went rushing out the door, chasing my powerful career and ignoring the message of hope and forgiveness offered that morning!

The Dam Breaks

By Spring 2000, my whole world came crashing down—I had been divorced for 18 months, and three houses were distributed to my ex-husband. I had to sell my string of competition jumpers (horses). My Olympic trainer disappeared. Not ONE friend from my old social circle remained.

During this time, I had been an investor in a private placement with a dot-com company. I proudly watched my thousands of shares balloon from ten cents to nine dollars, which represented a gain of millions of dollars. I felt invincible, puffed up, exhilarated, and in a shop-til-you-drop mode! *You're in the money now!* I felt powerful. I could rule the world! Suddenly, the price per share went back from nine dollars to five cents, deflating like a soufflé! This was financial Houdini at its best!

I went from riding the crest of self-sufficiency to standing among the piles of ashes that represented everything I believed would bring me happiness: money, power, prestige, marriages, children, significance, career accolades, social status, and intellect. I was numb. And I had no answers. Everything I had been taught to believe in had failed me.

> *"Do not store up for yourselves treasures on earth, where moths and vermin destroy, and where thieves break in and steal. But store up for yourselves treasures in heaven, where moths and vermin do not destroy, and where thieves do not break in and steal"* (Matthew 6:19-20 NIV).

During this chaotic time, a woman I had met in January at a Palm Beach Bible study kept telephoning me. I would run into her at the Palm Beach galas. She would look straight into my eyes and ask me, "How are you?"

I would retort, "FINE," air kiss her, wish her well, and run in the opposite direction.

I now call this woman my beloved tree frog. In South America, there are tiny, exquisite, iridescent green tree frogs. They have giant eyes, smooth skin, chiseled long limbs, and enormously long fingers. Their overriding assignment in life is to STICK almost inseparably to whatever they put their little digits on. And boy, do they stick. And so did this woman.

Repeatedly, this woman would invite me to church. Finally, on June 10, 2000, capitulating to her persistence, I agreed to accompany her. I truly don't remember what the pastor said in the service, but I felt a wash of understanding just crack me open.

Knees will Bend

All my posturing and bravado evaporated as I again heard the message of love and hope in Jesus. I stood there in the middle of the church service, begging Jesus to come into my life. "Please forgive me, change me. Help me! I will do it your way. Thank you for giving me another chance to be free of my past and start life over again! Thank you for being the GREAT God of second chances!"

> Lord, you are the God who saves me; day and night I cry out to you. May my prayer come before you; turn your ear to my cry. I am overwhelmed with troubles and my life draws near to death (Psalm 88:1-3 NIV).

Instantly, I realized I had been stripped of everything I had believed in. I FINALLY heard God calling me to Him. My self-sufficiency and value system had failed, and I could now see this patient, loving God who had always been there protecting me answer me. I never noticed before WHO had been pursuing me!

> The Lord appeared to us in the past, saying: "I have loved you with an everlasting love; I have drawn you with unfailing kindness" (Jeremiah 31:3 NIV).

That service was a turning point in my life. I felt the promise of being A New Person. I hadn't come to Jesus at my best and full of good works. I had come disillusioned, bitter, and shattered. I deliberately asked God to take control of my life. That night, I went to bed; as I turned over on my left side with my pillow, it felt as if Jesus had wrapped His arms around me. The shameful memories of being liked "a bit too much" by friends of the family were washed away. I slept the sleep of an innocent child for the first time since I was a teenager.

> I will give them an undivided heart and put a new spirit in them; I will remove from them their heart of stone and give them a heart of flesh (Ezekiel 11:19 NIV).

I had a complete heart transplant! The rough edges of my personality were gone! I can't even bother with mascara—it's bound to come running off at any moment when I burst into tears of gratitude and wonder!

Now, I have a totally different value system. Someone has changed the prescription in my glasses. I don't wear a heavy coat of armor to go out and do battle with the world. Rather, I am filled with a peace and joy I never felt before asking Jesus into my life. I belong with new friends who love me unconditionally, just as I am. All the raw, jagged pieces on my insides finally fell into place. At last, my insides and my outside match. Life flows with a balance, calmness, and purpose.

I'm currently back in the real estate business after promising I would never return to that career. But I perform differently because I am now a Broker with a "Servant's Heart." I work for my REAL EMPLOYER and have a new rule book—the Bible.

Everything I have belongs to God. I'm His account executive! It's not about Toni Lee anymore. I remind myself that all the success in my life is a gift from God. I never want my success to turn into my god again!

> But remember the Lord your God, for it is he who gives you the ability to produce wealth, and so confirms his covenant, which he swore to your ancestors, as it is today (Deuteronomy 8:18 NIV).

Reconciliation

One of the results of my radically transformed life includes the healing of the ruptured relationship with my mother. This story is a perfect example of my God of the Impossible! Our relationship was very bitter and seemingly irreconcilable. The years would pass without communication except for the obligatory happy birthdays or season's greetings. I had distanced myself completely.

Years before, I tried to make amends, but it was dictated merely by obligation, not heart. The bitterness stayed no matter how hard I ignored it or pretended it didn't matter anymore.

During my first year in Bible study, I read Matthew 5:23. *Therefore, if you are offering your gift at the altar and there remember that your brother or sister has something against you, leave your gift there in front of the altar. First go and be reconciled to them; then come and offer your gift* (NIV).

OH NO! I actually UNDERSTOOD those verses!!! They spoke to me so clearly! I needed to clean up any outstanding resentments in my life. Then, after I mopped up the wreckage of the blood bath with Mother, I could come back to the altar and leave the gift of a clean heart before God! I had to straighten things out with Mother.

By that time, I knew very well from watching others in Bible study that God's marching orders were to be obeyed. Obedience brought blessings. And partial obedience is *DIS-obedience!*

By sheer will, I picked up the phone and invited her for Thanksgiving. I started praying over the ensuing months about having a change of heart. I figured that since it was June, I had plenty of time to change my attitude. But NOTHING shifted my resentments, and it was getting closer to November. On Thanksgiving Day, I heard Mom being wheeled up the driveway by her nurse.

I distinctly remember hanging onto the edge of the door jamb saying, "Oh, God, what do I do? Please change me?"

Then, as loudly as a silent thought could land in my head, the idea came: *Toni—you can love your mother for nothing else but that she gave birth to you so you could be here on earth to serve ME!*

I can truly tell you that when I opened my front door and saw my mother for the first time in ten years, I saw her with transformed eyes. What was so impossible in my resentments that could have caused such a loss of time in our relationship? I was actually overjoyed to see my mother. I had missed her!

A few weeks later, at the age of 84, my mother had a total hip replacement. Just before she went into surgery, as she lay on the gurney, it was my turn to hold her in my arms. It was my turn to offer comfort and tell her how much I LOVED HER. My tiny, frail mother had become a friend.

Jesus looked at them and said, "With man this is impossible, but with God all things are possible" (Matthew 19:26 NIV).

Before Mom died, my God of the impossible healed the resentments that had kept us separated. I explained to Mom that I wanted her to be in heaven when she died. Then, we prayed to have Christ come into her life and make peace for all the mistakes she made. We prayed for her to understand she was completely forgiven. She became a child of God! When she died, I was at her bedside, ushering my mom into the arms of Jesus.

I don't want to paint a rosy picture of my life during the years I've been a "believer." I didn't float off exempt from life's daily problems. But I've really learned to see life through God's plan and promises.

I've had five major breast surgeries, with a potential 6th on the horizon. I've had two back procedures to try and relieve constant debilitating pain so that I can keep walking. My step-sister in Boston had a cerebral hemorrhage, battled paralysis, and died. My older half-sister died of cancer. My full brother overdosed on Oxycodone because he couldn't bear to live with no hope and was in bondage to drugs and alcohol.

"I have told you these things, so that in me you may have peace. In this world you will have trouble. But take heart! I have overcome the world" (John 16: 33 NIV).

But during all of this insanity and sadness, I NEVER questioned, "Where is GOD in all this?" But instead, I said, "WHAT would I have done without YOU, LORD?"

> God has said: "Never will I leave you; never will I forsake you" (Hebrews 13:5 NIV).

I now carry a power pack of confidence—like internal ballast. I stand on the promises of God. I know that God, with His constant, unconditional love, will always be near me as I inch my way closer to Him. I have Someone Who is Faithful, Mighty, and Forever Mine. I am the daughter of the KING!

So, from drug addiction to sobriety, from my son's cerebral hemorrhage to his complete recovery, from my paralysis to walking again, from broken relationships to restoration, I stand here now with a heart full of joy instead of hunger.

Life before Jesus was all about questions with no answers. Now, at night, instead of the worm whispering, "Life isn't turning out the way it was supposed to be," I go to sleep knowing that I found the Answer of all Answers in Jesus.

Jesus is truly victorious.

> For I am convinced that neither death nor life, neither angels nor demons, neither the present nor the future, nor any powers, neither height nor depth, nor anything else in all creation, will be able to separate us from the love of God that is in Christ Jesus our Lord (Romans 8:38-39 NIV).

Hope in Breaking Free

By Connie A. VanHorn

It is for freedom that Christ has set us free. Stand firm, then, and do not let yourselves be burdened again by a yoke of slavery (Galatians 5:1 NIV).

The concept of hope in breaking free from the strongholds of this world and living a life of surrender to Jesus is a powerful idea that speaks to the core of our experience with God. The essence of hope centers around letting go of the past and the things that keep us chained up and embracing a life of freedom and hope in Jesus Christ. This freedom is rooted in our faith and the gospel message of salvation and redemption through Christ.

Hope is an essential part of our Christian faith; it is often described as being the anchor of the soul. Hope is the belief that no matter how difficult the circumstances, there is always a reason to believe and trust in God's plan. As part of breaking free and living a life of surrender to Jesus, hope is the driving force that motivates us to let go of the past and the things that hold us back. It is the assurance that through Christ, we can find freedom from our chains and live a life of purpose and fulfillment.

We have this hope as an anchor for the soul, firm and secure. It enters the inner sanctuary behind the curtain (Hebrews 6:19 NIV).

Breaking free and living a life of surrender to Jesus is a process that often requires courage, faith, and trust. It means letting go of our own desires and goals and submitting ourselves fully to God's will. This act of surrender is not a sign of weakness but a demonstration of strength and humility. It is realizing that we can't free ourselves from the chains of sin and bondage on our own, but we can be free through the power of Christ working in us.

Letting go of the past is often one of the most difficult aspects of living a life of surrender to Jesus. The past can be a heavy burden that weighs us down and prevents us from moving forward—it may be filled with regrets, mistakes, hurts, addictions, deaths, and other things that keep us chained to our old life. But through Christ, we can find forgiveness, healing, and redemption. He offers us a new life and a fresh start, free from the guilt and shame of our past. We get to start again. He files off the old and paints a beautiful canvas of the new.

Living free indeed in Jesus is a life that brings joy, peace, and fulfillment. Living free offers us a life of purpose and meaning, where we are no longer slaves to sin and self-doubt but children of God who are loved, valued, and cherished. Living free offers us a life filled with hope, faith, and love, where we can experience the fullness of God's grace and mercy.

Hope in breaking free and living a life of surrender to Jesus invites us to let go of the past and learn to trust. You can trust the One who holds the universe—the One who holds YOU! That is where we begin again. In Jesus, we find healing, redemption, and a new life. May we all embrace the strength He offers and exhibit the courage necessary to break free from the chains that bind us as we choose to live a life of freedom in Jesus.

May the God of hope fill you with all joy and peace as you trust in him, so that you may overflow with hope by the power of the Holy Spirit (Romans 15:13 NIV).

. . . .

Kat Quinn

Kat Quinn's unwavering success is a testament to her ambition, self-acceptance, and altruism—a potent combination that has been the bedrock of her journey.

Her deep-rooted faith has been an anchor, guiding her through every endeavor. The principles ingrained by her spiritual beliefs have seamlessly woven into her personal and professional pursuits, shaping her as a beacon of positivity and compassion.

As a multifaceted individual, Kat Quinn wears many hats—lifestyle guru, web designer, digital marketer, operations expert, program manager, avid writer, and public speaker. Her operations and program management skills allow her to excel in organizing and leading complex initiatives efficiently and precisely.

Kat's true calling, however, lies in offering consulting and coaching services to empower others to uncover their life's purpose and courageously chase their aspirations.

With a heart overflowing with empathy and a mind brimming with wisdom, Kat Quinn is a force to be reckoned with. Her ability to inspire and uplift those around her is unparalleled, leaving an indelible mark on all who cross her path.

Hope Arise

By Kat Quinn

At times, life can throw the most unimaginable darts that hit us when we least expect it, leaving us hurt, crushed, and surrounded by darkness. We have a choice to make in those moments—we can either remain debilitated and stuck in the darkness, or we can choose to stand firm in our belief that God is in control and works all things for good. Even in those dark moments, hope can arise. As you read my story, I pray you find a sense of hope and comfort, knowing that God is always by your side and willing to take every dart thrown at you.

Have you ever felt like life was spinning out of control, like everything you once knew was slipping away? I know that feeling all too well. I was an ordinary girl trying to make it in high school, just starting to think about my future. Then, my life changed in an instant. In a sea of students, I was the one who was pregnant. Walking the halls with a pregnant belly, I felt the weight of stares and whispers. Suddenly, I was the most popular girl in school, but not for good reasons.

One night, while I was attending a party, something unimaginable happened. I was being pursued for sex by someone who disregarded my refusal. I heard the chilling words, "I am going to do it anyway." That moment left an indelible mark on my life. There is nothing like having your power taken from you to make you feel shameful, humiliated, fearful, anxious, confused, and rattled to the core. The level of emotion that comes with knowing someone could harm you in that way is overwhelming. It caused me to pull inward and withdraw from the world around me. However, against all odds, hope found its way to me.

Shortly after the party, my mom managed to get the truth out of me, and before I knew it, I found myself sitting in a doctor's office. As I shared my situation with the doctor, she inquired about the date of my last period. After I provided the information, she surprised me by saying, "Well, that would put you at about eight weeks, and we can hear the heartbeat." I was puzzled as to why she opted for a Doppler ultrasound instead of a simple urine test. While lying there, feeling the device move around my belly, I found myself silently praying to God, desperately seeking answers.

When the doctor finally announced, "There it is," I was taken aback by the unexpected revelation. We would later realize that we had miscalculated the time of conception; I was only four weeks pregnant at the time of the ultrasound. It should have been impossible to find a heartbeat at this stage of pregnancy, but God knew exactly what I needed that day. He continually revealed Himself to me throughout the entire journey. Even though I was scared and hurt and didn't know what to do or feel, He guided me. He showed me the way and gave me the exact amount of strength I would need for every moment going forward.

> *Trust in the Lord with all your heart and lean not on your own understanding; in all your ways submit to him, and he will make your paths straight* (Proverbs 3:5-6 NIV).

As the doctor started discussing my options, hinting at abortion, a surge of strength coursed through me. I met her gaze with determination and firmly stated that I was going to have this baby. I was resolute in my decision, knowing deep down that I couldn't end the life growing inside me, no matter the challenges ahead. Leaving the office with prenatal vitamins, brochures, and uncertainties, I had no idea I was embarking on a journey already planned for me. Every step seemed to fall into place seamlessly, with my Father guiding me and tending to every detail along the way.

> I will instruct you and teach you in the way you should go; I will counsel you with my loving eye on you (Psalm 32:8 NIV).

I took the initial step of confiding in my school counselor about my situation. Her immediate suggestion was a school specifically for pregnant teenagers. The thought of attending a fourth high school, especially during my senior year, was overwhelming. Having already moved around due to my family's military background, the idea of starting anew once more was disheartening. Tearfully sharing my concerns with my mother, she advised me to speak to the principal instead. His response was a stark contrast to the counselor's. He assured me the school was there for me and pledged to do everything possible to help me graduate. True to his word, he stood by me every step of the way.

The completion of the first step on my journey marked a significant milestone. Gradually, I began sharing my situation with my close circle of friends. Their consistent support, love, and loyalty overwhelmed me. From helping satisfy my cravings by swapping breakfasts with me to carrying my backpack and helping me study, each friend shouldered a piece of my burden. They were my bright lights during a time of confusion and hardship. Whenever I felt discouraged, a comforting word or gesture from a friend or family member lifted my spirits. The truth of the verse, *Sweet friendships refresh the soul* (Proverbs 27:9 TPT), resonated deeply with me as I realized the invaluable role these friendships played in my life. God had placed these friends in my path for a reason. On the flip side, a small group of strangers, unaware of my circumstances, resorted to hurling vulgar insults, mocking me, and making already challenging days even more difficult to bear. The superficial allure of popularity in high school came with its own set of pitfalls and challenges.

A family friend suggested I reach out to a local nonprofit called Pregnancy Assist, which provided support for individuals facing decisions about keeping or placing a child for adoption. Through their workbooks, counseling sessions, classes, and resources, they aimed to help individuals make informed decisions and offered ongoing support. As I explored one of their workbooks, my certainty about keeping the baby grew stronger. When I attended an appointment with my closest friend, who was there to support me, the counselor outlined the various programs available to assist me in the next steps. However, amidst the discussion, I heard a voice questioning why I was overlooking something. I initially dismissed it, but the voice persisted, leading me to a profound realization: I was meant to give my child up for adoption. Interrupting the counselor, I expressed my decision, surprising both my friend and the counselor. Despite their disbelief, my friend respected and stood by my choice, guiding me through the adoption process. He provided constant support—to the extent that onlookers assumed he was the father, a misconception he never corrected. In his friendship, I found peace and a sense of love that helped heal past wounds.

As I began the adoption process, I poured over books compiled by potential parents, studying pictures and reading heartfelt letters detailing their desire to adopt. Despite numerous interviews, none of the prospective parents resonated with me on a spiritual level. Time continued to slip away as graduation approached, bringing the impending birth of my child closer.

Frustrated and feeling like I had exhausted all options, I cried out to the Lord once more, seeking guidance. In a moment of desperation, as I questioned the whereabouts of the right parents, my phone rang. It was the adoption agency, and the woman on the line was brimming with excitement. She believed they had found the perfect match. As I received the book showcasing the potential adoptive parents, one particular image stood out to me: the potential father cradling his daughter on his chest and reading a book. In that instant, gazing at the picture, I felt a deep sense of certainty that this couple was meant for my child. Without hesitation, I contacted the agency, and an interview was promptly arranged.

As I geared up for the interview with my parents, we meticulously outlined a set of questions to pose to the prospective adoptive parents. To our amazement, during the call, they preemptively answered each question before I could even ask. They not only possessed all the qualities I had fervently prayed for in potential parents but also had attributes I hadn't even thought to pray for, such as owning horses—a passion of mine since childhood. Although my son wouldn't experience this love for horses with me, I found hope in knowing he could with his new parents. It became evident that God not only understood my desires but also knew precisely what my son needed. His hand was evident in every detail, no matter how minute. Despite my concerns about having enough time to cultivate a relationship with the adoptive parents due to my advanced pregnancy stage, once again, God exceeded my expectations. Not only did we establish a profound connection, but this bond also proved to be healing for both parties involved.

> *Take delight in the Lord, and He will give you the desires of your heart* (Psalm 37:4 NIV).

It was revealed that the prospective adoptive parents had come close to adopting a child prior to our meeting. They had joyfully welcomed the child into their home, only to have the birth parent retract consent within the narrow seven-day window allowed for such decisions. The heart-wrenching experience left the couple shattered, prompting them to take a step back from adoption to heal. However, they eventually felt a divine nudge to try again. Despite facing obstacles with their paperwork repeatedly getting delayed, they persisted until, almost miraculously, everything fell into place. Meanwhile, as I encountered my own frustrations and considered giving up, unbeknownst to us, two separate parties were fervently praying. Through unseen yet undeniable divine intervention, God was intricately orchestrating every detail to bring us together at precisely the right moment in His perfect timing.

> And we know that in all things God works for the good of those who love him, who have been called according to his purpose (Romans 8:28 NIV).

Throughout the hard journey I traversed, God's presence was unmistakable. While He did not cause the rape or the trauma I suffered because of it, He certainly orchestrated moments of redemption and restoration. He provided me with a sweet friend who stood by my side, escorting me to prom without hesitation despite the inevitable rumors that followed. He placed dedicated teachers in my path who invested in my success, offering encouragement, tutoring, and constant support as I worked to graduate. He surrounded me with friends who showered me with love at a baby shower, gifted me with tokens to remember my son by, and celebrated both life and my resilience, even though I would not be raising my child. He guided me to parents who embraced me with genuine love, taking the time to listen to my wishes and allowing me to play a part in naming my son.

But God's grace extended even further. When I entered the hospital, initially scheduled for a brief stay, I was granted an additional day, affording me precious moments with my son and the chance to process my emotions. The compassionate nurses, understanding my story, delayed my discharge and ensured minimal disruptions, showing me immense care and empathy. Once all the necessary paperwork was completed, a small service led by my pastor was arranged in the hospital room. Each person present had the opportunity to share, pray, or offer blessings. A special moment occurred when my atheist friend, who had walked alongside me throughout this journey, expressed how he had come to understand the concept of faith through our shared experiences.

As I reflect on the seeds sown through faithfully walking this journey, I am aware of the lives touched and transformed by sharing my testimony, especially those who have been blessed to know my son. Your own story will echo this truth as you surrender and allow God to move boldly in your life. What may currently appear senseless or too destructive to bear fruit holds the potential for a divine opportunity. I could have chosen to sit and stay in the aftermath of a highly destructive moment, shutting out God and succumbing to the enemy's lies—consumed by bitterness and anger. While those emotions surfaced, I refused to stay in them. Instead, I faced each moment, worked through it, and then released it.

Whatever challenges you are facing—an unplanned pregnancy, loss, divorce, bullying, financial hardships—remember, we serve a God who always shows up. Despite the daunting circumstances, He manifests in ways beyond our imagination. The blessings I experienced in that particular incident alone are too numerous to list here in this short chapter. However, I hope I've been able to reveal that God's beauty and perfection are present even in our hardest moments.

> *See, I am doing a new thing! Now it springs up; do you not perceive it? I am making a way in the wilderness and streams in the wasteland* (Isaiah 43:19 NIV).

We can always find hope in our pain. We can always find hope in God, especially in the darkest moments and even in a traumatic experience like rape. It's truly amazing how God can bring beauty from ashes, turning something so painful and devastating into something beautiful.

If you or someone you know has been a victim of rape, please know that there is help and hope available. You don't have to carry the pain alone. Jesus is there to bear that burden for you, to bring healing and restoration to your life.

Let's stand together in prayer and faith, believing God can remove all the pain and darts, and He will give you a future filled with hope and promise. Our hope is alive in Him; He is the source of our strength and comfort. Reach out for support, seek help, and know that you are not alone on this journey toward healing and wholeness. God's love and grace are greater than any darkness or despair. You are so loved, and you are deserving of a beautiful future filled with hope.

Dear Heavenly Father,

I lift up the woman reading these words to you, Lord. I pray you will open her heart to your possibilities and grant her renewed strength. May your presence move so powerfully in her life that it is unmistakably clear that you are at work. Let your glory shine brightly; may she be consumed in the depth and vastness of your genuine love. Help her be firmly rooted in the truth that you work all things for her good; remove any doubts about your presence in her circumstances.

Father, make the impossible possible in her life. Open the doors that need to be opened and close those that need to be shut according to your plan for her life. We thank you that you go before us, leading the way, and that no earthly force can hinder your will. Shield her from any weapons formed against her and reveal the abundance of plans you have for her, surpassing even the number of hairs on her head.

Lord, I speak blessings over this woman and ask for an increase in every area of her life. May everything she lays her hands on prosper, guiding her into a deeper understanding of her identity in you. Holy Spirit, open her eyes and ears to hear you in ways she has never experienced before. We surrender every aspect of our lives to you, Lord, for your glory and declare all these prayers in the mighty name of Jesus.

Amen.

> "No weapon forged against you will prevail, and you will refute every tongue that accuses you. This is the heritage of the servants of the Lord, and this is their vindication from me," declares the Lord (Isaiah 54:17 NIV).

Hope in Forgiveness

By Connie A. VanHorn

And whenever you stand praying, forgive, if you have anything against anyone, so that your Father also who is in heaven may forgive you your trespasses (Mark 11:25 RSV).

We all get hurt by others. A wound inflicted on us by someone else can be painful and debilitating, even if, or maybe *especially* if, that wound was caused by a loved one. Why does it sometimes seem like those wounds caused by others never heal? I've personally traveled down this road, and I'm here to tell you that they can heal. Although the scars might last a lifetime, God has given us the power to speed along the process of healing, taking us from debilitated to exhilarated. It all begins with one of the greatest gifts we can give ourselves: forgiveness.

We all encounter moments of hurt, betrayal, and disappointment. These experiences can leave us feeling angry, broken, and bitter. Forgiveness requires us to let go of the anger and resentment we hold towards those who hurt us. It is not always easy. Forgiving someone is a conscious choice to release the burden of pain and choose compassion and understanding instead. When we forgive, we open the door to healing and restoration, allowing hope to enter our hearts once again. The power of forgiveness can truly transform our lives and bring a sense of hope and healing. Forgiveness is where our open wounds begin to close.

Jesus constantly taught us about forgiveness. In His Word, He reminds us of the importance of forgiveness. In Colossians 3:13, we are urged to *Bear with each other and forgive one another if any of you has a grievance against someone. Forgive as the Lord forgave you* (NIV). Just as God extends His forgiveness to us, we are called to extend that same forgiveness to others. In doing so, we free ourselves from the chains of bitterness that keep us from our purpose and closeness with God.

When we choose to forgive, we are not saying that the hurt wasn't real or excusing the actions of the person who caused our pain. Instead, we are FACING it head-on and choosing to release it, trusting in God's promise. God makes all things right! Forgiveness is a powerful act of faith that allows us to move forward with hope and purpose, knowing that God's love and grace are greater than any hurt we may endure. It takes courage to let go of past hurts and choose to forgive, but the rewards are extraordinary. Embracing forgiveness transforms our lives, filling our hearts with hope. You deserve to be free from the weight of unforgiveness.

Forgiveness is an act of hope because it assures us that all is not lost, even in the midst of painful memories and unresolved hurt. When we let go, we begin to let loose the bonds of those who caused us harm, perhaps even those who have died or moved on from our lives. The gift of forgiveness opens the possibility of life being different going forward.

Forgiveness is a gift to the other person, but it is also a gift to the forgiver. Forgiveness brings freedom. By forgiving another, you don't only free the one who has hurt you; you also free yourself. It doesn't matter what the circumstances are.

It is never too late to forgive. Whether you need to forgive others or yourself, take the first step towards healing by extending grace and mercy. Find hope in forgiveness and experience the power of God's love in your life as you boldly align yourself with His will.

Seek God in and through forgiveness and experience the MIRACLES that come from extending love and mercy to others.

> *Do not judge, and you will not be judged. Do not condemn, and you will not be condemned. Forgive, and you will be forgiven (Luke 6:37 NIV).*

This verse reminds us to be kind and forgiving towards others, just as we hope others will be toward us. Let's strive to approach every situation with love and understanding, remembering that we are all flawed and in need of grace.

Today is the day. We will release the burden of pain together. We can start right now by praying this prayer and moving forward as we choose to let go of resentment and embrace compassion.

Heavenly Father, thank you for the gift of forgiveness and the hope it brings. Please help us to release our hurts and grievances and extend grace to those who have wronged us. Give us the strength and courage to forgive, knowing that through your love, we can find healing and restoration. May forgiveness be a source of hope and renewal in our lives. In Jesus' name we pray. Amen.

Afterword

By Connie A. VanHorn

As you finish reading the final pages of *Hope Alive*, we pray you are filled with so much hope that despite whatever challenges you may face, you will go forward with courage and joy, knowing there is always hope in Jesus. Through the stories we have shared in this book, we are confident you can see how faith and trust in God can transform our struggles into victories, our tears into hope, and our lives into a living testimony of His goodness and faithfulness. May this book remind you that you are never alone; God is always with you, guiding you through this life and onto the next.

We can be confident that our hope in God is not just a fleeting emotion; hope is a steadfast anchor for our souls. It is a reminder that no matter how debilitated we may feel, we can be exhilarated by the power and presence of God in our lives. Hope does not come from our circumstances; hope comes from the unchanging love and faithfulness of our Savior. Our Hope is Alive!

Take these beautiful stories and carry them with you as you continue on your own journey of faith. Be encouraged to keep going, to never give up on hope, and to trust in God's plan for your life. We hope this book has inspired you to walk confidently, knowing that with God, all things are possible.

> *But I will hope continually and will praise You yet more and more (Psalm 71:14 NKJV).*

We pray that *Hope Alive* will be a book of light and encouragement for all women who are facing struggles and fears. Always remember that YOU are loved, valued, and cherished by a God who never gives up on you. We can cling to the hope we have in Jesus, knowing that, in Him, we can find true and lasting joy.

We extend our deepest gratitude to all the readers who have embarked on this Hope journey with us. Thank you for allowing us to share these stories with you and being a part of this community of hope-seekers and believers; we are grateful for the opportunity to walk this path of hope together.

> *May the God of hope fill you with all joy and peace in believing, so that by the power of the Holy Spirit you may abound in hope (Romans 15:13 RSV).*

Let us close in prayer:

Dear God,

We thank you for the sprinkles of hope and the assurance that you are always with us, guiding us through the storms and lifting us up in times of need. As we conclude this journey, we pray for your continued presence in our lives and for the strength to hold on to hope and trust in your plan. May the stories we have shared serve as reminders of your unfailing love and grace, filling our hearts with joy and peace. Bless each reader who has joined us on this journey; may they be filled with renewed hope and faith.

In your precious name, we pray. Amen.

We have this hope as an anchor for the soul, firm and secure. It enters the inner sanctuary behind the curtain (Hebrews 6:19 NIV).

More WPP Anthologies!

The authors of *Miracle Mindset: Finding Hope in the Chaos*, have experienced the wonders of God's provision, protection, and guidance. These stories and teachings will ignite a spark within you, propelling you to encounter the marvel of God's miracles, even in the chaos.

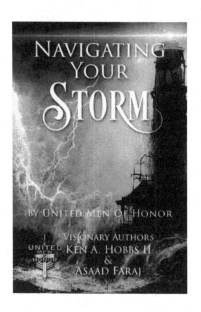

Life is full of storms and rough waters. The stories in *Navigating Your Storm: By United Men of Honor* will give you the ability to see the light of God and navigate your storm victoriously.

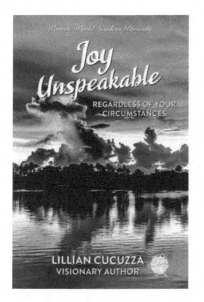

With *Joy Unspeakable: Regardless of Your Circumstances*, you will learn how joy and sorrow can dance together during adversity. The words in this book will encourage, inspire, motivate, and give you hope, joy, and peace.

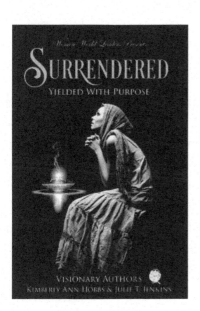

Surrendered: Yielded With Purpose will help you recognize with awe that surrendering to God is far more effective than striving alone. When we let go of our own attempts to earn God's favor and rely on Jesus Christ, we receive a deeper intimacy with Him and a greater power to serve Him.

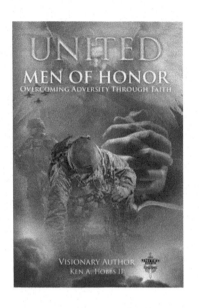

United Men of Honor: Overcoming Adversity Through Faith will help you armor up, become fit to fight, and move forward with what it takes to be an honorable leader. Over twenty authors in this book share their accounts of God's provision, care, and power as they proclaim His Word.

Embrace the Journey: Your Path to Spiritual Growth will strengthen and empower you to step boldly in faith. These stories, along with expertly placed expositional teachings will remind you that no matter what we encounter, we can always look to God, trusting HIS provision, strength, and direction.

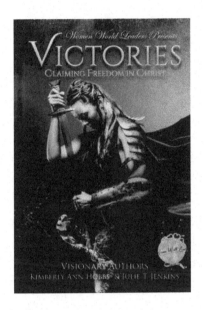

Victories: Claiming Freedom in Christ presents expository teaching coupled with individual stories that testify to battles conquered victoriously through the power of Jesus Christ. The words in this book will motivate and inspire you and give you hope as God awakens you to your victory!

WPP's Mission

World Publishing and Productions was birthed in obedience to God's call. Our mission is to empower writers to walk in their God-given purpose as they share their God story with the world. We offer one-on-one coaching and a complete publishing experience. To find out more about how we can help you become a published author or to purchase books written to share God's glory, please visit: **worldpublishingandproductions.com**

Heartbeat of a Survivor tells the story of Nita Tin, a Buddhist born and raised in an opulent lifestyle in Burma. As her country came under the control of a ruthless military dictator, Nita's whole life changed. Forced to flee her home, her soul was soon set free in a greater way than she ever dreamed possible.

At seventeen, Audrey Marie experienced a sudden and relentless excruciating firestorm of pain. *Chronically Unstoppable* tells of her true-life journey as she faced pain, developed strength, and battled forward with hope.

The world has become a place where we don't have a millisecond to think for ourselves, often leaving us feeling lost or overwhelmed. That is why Max Gold wrote *Planestorming!*—a straightforward guide to help you evaluate and change your life for the better. It's time to get to work and make the rest of your life the BEST of your life.